To my fri
best of luck fore
Bill Bailey
7/21/20

Son of the QUEEN CITIES

A Black Banker's Civil Rights Era

Memoir in Poetry, Prose and Play

William R. Bailey

AuthorHouse™
1663 Liberty Drive
Bloomington, IN 47403
www.authorhouse.com
Phone: 1-800-839-8640

Published by AuthorHouse 10/06/2014

ISBN: 978-1-4969-1726-3 (sc)
ISBN: 978-1-4969-1724-9 (hc)
ISBN: 978-1-4969-1725-6 (e)

Library of Congress Control Number: 2014910242

This book is dedicated to the courage and fortitude of JoAnn, my children, mother, father, brother, sister, relatives, friends and acquaintances, who tolerated my presence and contributed to the spirit, love and essence of my life.

W.R.B.

Contents

Preface

From as far back as I can remember, when I first learned to write, I wanted to write down and keep my thoughts. Why, I don't know. I guess it just seemed to be a way to keep from forgetting valuable life-moments. My early efforts, at a very early age, naturally, were primitive and quite forgettable. I have nothing left that I wrote before I was ten years old. Maybe what I have written since then deserves to be lost too. However, I did save some of my youthful and older scribbling, since age ten to come back to later, for whatever they were worth. Memorable poems? Stunning prose? No! They were just vivid memories in my own private treasure of many, many memories.

Some of what I wrote, at a very early age and even later, as you might expect, was passionate, simple verse, simple songs and rhymes. I share some of them here with you, for your own insight into my youthful feelings and early life. In some of my writings, describing early years, I tried to remember as best and as honestly as I could the way it actually happened. To tell a full and true story, beyond my own memory, sometimes I wrote from the memory and eyes of a much older and more discerning person. Always it was someone that I trusted for their honesty and integrity. With age, I hope that you will see that my writing grew in quality and thought. Rather than style my quest was always for truth and authenticity.

In aggregating this biographical collection, I was worried that some of what is here could be called "preachy," self-righteous-sounding, maybe even a little pretentious. I apologize if that is so and if it offends rather than entertains. My sole purpose in these writings was not to convert the reader, but to be illuminating, provocative; to bare what was in my soul at that moment. As I wrote I wanted to give my children or anyone else who knows or wants to know me, a true glimpse into my origins, life and professional careers, as I remembered them, and in some early instances as they were described to me. I never tried to be vulgar or apologetic. I tried in my own way to be an honest artist and I always tried to avoid unreadable, poetic fogs and obscurities, to win encomia from writing's elites.

I do not consider myself a poet, but I can write my kind of poetry that describes my feelings, memories, observations and hopes in my own way, even if I have to mix styles to do so. When writing I always wanted to be as human and as truthful as one can be, with simple American words, telling a simple American story, about my feelings and my life. I will be immensely rewarded, if just a single soul appreciates just one sentence, or phrase that I wrote. I hope that what follows will not bore you, and that you will enjoy reading these words as much as I enjoyed writing them …

……*William Reed Bailey*
(Eden Prairie, Minnesota- 2014)

The Big Bang

There was nothing. Can you imagine nothing?
Can you imagine not even imagination?

Then in less than a nano-instant, God blew herself up!
There were no heavens to rumble, no gawking witnesses,

to the creation of something, the beginning of imagination.
Instantly there was sound, time, then space and distance.

Light became an eternal traveler. The velocity of energy slowed.
to become atoms, gases, masses, then the solids we see today.

The road to creatures, ideas and abstraction was a long one:
a journey fraught with the vicissitudes of matter and energy.

Consciousness in creatures became a powerful gift, however
brief, it's wondrously bright and gloriously...flicking life.

The ultimate, most precious gift from God though,
is the presence of her in everything...even imperfect us.

As we all eventually disappear and return to nothing,
will it just be God reconstituting, reclaiming, herself...

just reversing the beginning...gradually...surely...
in her own planned...deliberate...and inevitable way?

Eternal Traveler

Studying the cosmos...it easily...becomes clear...
that time is distance...and distance is time...both
god-like to us... almost illusions... in their gross
superiority...to present...to now...The two cannot

exist…in a time and distance universe…that must always have an end…if it has a beginning…since it care-takes…all there ever was…to itself…

Light that is known …to have come to us…from the beginning…suggests that we live forever…as travelers…in moments of time…which never die… but exist somewhere…distant from here…from now …and that…if we could see…could go…where the light came from…or where it goes…we would see… all there ever was…or all there ever…could be….

My God

If it were I…back in that creative… human creature moment…who had created God… I think I would have made it (her) story instead of (his) story…It seems only right… If it is to be God…I would have wanted God to be bigger…stronger…greater than me…an "it"…a rival to great mountains… vast oceans…endless skies…rather than a "he"…like me…limited…vain…weak…unable to restrain… Since I believe I am as great as any man…and I know me well…I must know men…My God would not have been created in the image of such a lowly man…a tiny he… such as I… But if humanness…is the only choice I have…it would have been only reasonable…to me… that my God would be created in the image of that beautiful…yes powerful…darkly…lo…the mysterious creature …we call "woman"…a creature who was and remains…after all…the mother…birther… and nurturer…of every human being…there ever was…or hopefully… ever will be…

the stain

slavery...that ancient stain...on a
young nation with promise...
it touched and crippled everyone and left
on each...a scar...that won't
go away...right up to this very day...
can time heal us...we need it so...
i hope so...yes...i hope so...

Lula and Lewis

Lula...my grandmother...was out
of Vynnie and Ruben Barnes...almost

certainly descended from ancient
West Africans...and proud old tribes...

Grandpa Lewis was from Abe...and
Nancy Stewart....Like all of us since...

they were rooted in slavery...and mixed
with old...and new...black and other

blood... They were also plain...simple
folk...born free...but from human loins

...that bore memories of the cruel lash...
None ever escaped the soil...nor the

harshness of brutal...near-slavery...
Theirs was a bitter...woeful life...yet

they lived...loved and fought...until
it ended...first one...then the other...

a thousand miles...and 10 years apart...
Out of their 12 offspring...only 10...

survived.... William...Ann...Frank...
and Corine...Next came Janie...Lula..

Julius...and Ernest...who...in march
step... were followed by Ulysses...and

Ruth...I would come out of Corine...Like
originals...they also called her "Dimple"...

I often read...or wrote her name...but
I can't ever recall calling her Corine...

Eliza and Tom

Richard...my Dad...named after a handsome
black uncle...never knew much about Tom
...his sturdy daddy...my grandfather... Seems
Tom...flushed with anger...killed a man...
shot him to death...at a Sunday picnic...when
the man put his hand on Grandma Eliza's fried
chicken...before he was invited... My granddad went to prison...for a long time... He
died not long after he was freed...Richard...
was just a little fellow then...just a babe...

Before her living clan...fertile Eliza had already
had two babies...Ella and Martha...who
like far too many black babies...back then...
died before they were 7...when the thin farm
house...tenderly built with love...and
hope...caught on fire...from wind and lit
candles... Then came Estelle...who would
almost mimic Eliza...and have 12 of her own

...Next came...uncle "Cat"...his real name was
Tom too...then Jack...whom most people
didn't know...was christened...Lonnie...
Soon there was "Banks"...somehow
a proud nickname for John...

In order they followed...Lillie...Bernard
...Louis...Susie Mae...and Richard...the
middle kids...Then one died early...before
even a name...before Eliza had Sarah and
Evelyn...by a rich white man...after Granddad died...
Eliza kept right on living...working...remembering
and loving...every single one...and growing...
and still raising "chaps"...up there in Charlotte...
right on up to a 1955 end...at age 74...according to
Evelyn...the last one of them all...

William Reed

The pains started late Wednesday...a cool...but
bright day...They...convulsing rhythmically...

continued through the long night...on into
Thursday...Richard...nervous...impatient...said

little...Corine was brave...unlike the last time...
when...a frightened eighteen year-old...squeezed...

and gave birth to Joe...her first born...Her Mama
Lula... was there back then...but she hasn't come

yet...neither had Floree...a cherished neighbor...nor
Ann...her older sister...Last time...little Joe was

with them less than a month...She prayed...this
one...would make it...This one?...Oh, God...she

didn't have a name!...Why she thought...hadn't
they settled on a name...for this one!...She and

Richard had talked about it...still no name!...On
into the sweaty night...into Thursday...November

11, 1937...she labored...Early morning the white
doctor...is there...at Good Samaritan...the Third

Ward...hospital for Negroes...in Charlotte...Finally
that afternoon...*it* arrived..."What are you going

to call him?"...the doctor...smiling proudly...asked...
"I don't know"...she replied..."Well he's a fine one...

Call him...William...after me...That'll bring him luck
and you too"..."All right...if it's OK with...Richard...

Can I have him now?"..."Sure can...Here is little...
William Reed"..."Thank you...Doctor Reed...thank you"...

A Mother's Whisper

You were suppose to be a beautiful star,
a pale blue sky, a priceless diamond,
a soft, warm breeze, a calm river, a
malleable petal on a delicate bloom,
a fragrance to intoxicate, a first ray of
sunshine, the first leaf of Spring, a red
to rival ruby, a warmth to heat cold blood,
a taste sweeter than the sweetest...but you
are not a single one of these. No, my baby,
you are, to me, more precious, more dear
than twice the sum of each and every
one...of these...every single one....

Richard and Corine

Richard, the progeny of sufferers and fierce warriors.
Corine, was mixed: black, Irish and Cherokee.
They were victims of an American apartheid chorus,
and like many before them they yearned to be free.

Neither ever finished high school,
nor owned much in their life, not even a house.
Not unusual back then, it was almost a rule.
Dirt poor blacks were just happy to have a spouse.

Both were young, Corine just a mere teen.
Handsome Richard was unstable, dogged by illness.
Carolina blacks, 70 years from slavery's guillotine,
they were still hopeful, eager and dreamed of success.

Richard's Mama Eliza, was apprehensive when,
he announced that he'd found the woman for him.
Eliza, knew that the pain could begin all again,
that both their bright dreams could quickly dim.

Eliza also knew that it would take a special woman,
not usually found in someone so innocent, so young.
Eliza would pray and she swore, "I'll do all I can,
to keep this marriage from becoming unstrung."

It started off well and showed some promise.
In time there were four offspring, only three survived.
Like all young marriages there were moments of bliss,
times of happiness, when it was hard to feel deprived.

Richard was handy and willing, a strong worker.
Corine, like her mother, was tough, skilled, devoted.
Both delighted in each other, especially he in her.
She smiled most days but concerns remained unsaid.

Then it started, the tests, the personal trials, the reality.
The full force of his illness came crashing to the ground,
upon a young woman who never understood this destiny,
this disruption, and why her world was so upside down.

Nothing seemed to work, as she sought understanding.
He retreated into shame and the comfort of his mother.
She found the start of a long life of anxiety and longing,
that would never heal, no not quite…ever leave her.

They soon drifted off to find their own way.
He, a dependent, not able to fully assume,
the normal manhood he wished he could play.
His life would be a rose that would never bloom.

She sank into poverty and fought mightily for dignity.
Never once did she think of abandoning, of leaving,
three children, without which, she could surely be free.
She swore to do what she could with their upbringing.

From Corine I later learned a great deal.
Richard, well he was just not there.
Scores of years later I am still trying to heal,
to get over a kind of fatherless despair.

Theirs was a common story for most American blacks,
with a harsh, unforgiving, sometimes cruel existence.
I wish there was some way to bring them all back,
to thank them for the long fight and their tough resilience.

Their simple, unhappy lives were not unimportant,
to the growth and maturation of a very proud people.
For them we all have to do our very best…to plant,
seeds that can grow to the very top of their steeple.

Hey

Hey, I felt good yesterday.
But not so good this ole day.

Richard got sick again last night.
And Mama, she just can't find the light.

When Richard gets sick sometimes it's awful.
He becomes a demon fighting his skull.

He even broke the sink down one night.
But he found himself and put it all back right.

Sometimes he is very, very scary.
But I know he has a whole lot to carry.

So what! I'll never stop loving him dearly.
After all, he was the first I ever saw clearly.

But, hey! I'll feel good tomorrow!
I know how to shuck the sorrow.

How to shrug it off and just forget,
How to keep on smiling and not even fret.

I Love My Mama

Man, oh man...do I love my mama...
I don't know why...I never had
another to compare...Maybe it was
because she was always there...

Naw...that ain't it...Everybody's
mama is always there...ain't they?...

Maybe it was the fried chicken…or
the biscuits and syrup…or the
buttermilk…and RC Colas…
she shared with me…all the time…

Naw…that ain't it…Everybody's
mama does that …don't they?…

Could it have been that warm
firm breast you felt from a hug…
when things weren't right…
after you been in a fight…

Naw…that ain't it…All mama's
hug you after that…you agree?…

If you ask me…it's every one of
these…over and over again…
that makes that feeling…come…
Man, oh man…do I love my mama!…

Six-Year Old Man

Most days I was just eager to play with mud,
and worms and bees. I liked the worms best,

because they could not get away. Mud was also
fun. You could stir and pat and draw and sway,

and if you stayed out of water you could go home
with a nice clean shirt that day. Mama liked that.

Then there was the warm sun and bright blue
sky. I liked those hot, slow, lazy Carolina days.

I even liked it when it sprinkled rain, as long
as the sun also shone. For it was then that, a

peg in the ground would let you hear the devil
play, and beat up his wife, if you listen to Ole'

Jack Barnes. Ole' Jack, he always got his way.
He could out run you, beat you up, and scare

you to death, on Halloween. Yet he liked me,
I was his little buddy. If only he knew how

much I mocked him, how often I knocked him
down and beat him up when he wasn't there.

And when he wasn't there, I outran him fast.
I out jumped him, hid good and scared him too.

I always threw further than he did, that is, until he
came. Then I started losing all the games again.

I hated it, but you know, I just always had to see
him. I often wonder what ever happened to Ole' Jack.

Then it happened, the day my world changed. My
daddy, the tall one, the strong one, the tender one,

the frightening, but loving one, took me by the hand.
He said let's go walk. We need to talk, man to man.

Wow! That's something, he called me a man! I felt
real good, bigger, smarter, even taller. But where

would we go? What would we do? Throw the ball
again? Drink grape sodas? Watch the turtles? Laugh

with the other sweaty, black men? No, none of these.
We would just walk and talk. Then it hit me, you know,

like a surprise. He carried a suitcase; the one with the
broken lock. It was stuffed full and tied with a string.

I thought, why take the case just to go for a walk.
What could this mean? Were we going someplace?

Maybe to Grandma's? But she lives the other way.
Richard used to do that a lot, when he and Mama

yelled. Sometimes I thought he liked Grandma better
than us. We walked until we got to the baseball field.

Some big boys were laughing and playing ball. We,
my Daddy and me, had been there before. I always

looked forward to the happy day, when I could play
ball with the big, fast boys too. Bet Ole' Jack Barnes

wouldn't mess with me then. Then he looked at me
and said, "I have to go away. For me, you see, this is

not a good day. I feel bad. Your Mama and I don't see
eye to eye any more. It is best that I leave and try to

make a new life for us. When it comes, I'll be taking
the bus, and after that I'll be getting on a train. You go

on back to the house now. Take care of James, Gwen
and Corine. You are the man now, till I come back.

You are in charge. You have to be a man. Be a good
boy, go to school, keep the fire burning, and don't talk

back to your mother or grown people. "Hurry now, I see
the bus coming. I'll write you a letter." I turned and

walked slowly away, confused, not knowing. I stepped
on a black bug and glanced back at the big bus. Richard

peeked back at me, coughed and got on the bus. I skipped
at first, then I started to run, as fast as I could. I ran and

ran, all the way to Renner Street, to tell Mama. Through
the years I occasionally thought about that day. How it

started out so wonderfully, so full of joy. and ended so
flat and dull, with Mama so quiet. But I kept getting taller

and taller and feeling like a man. Eventually, I got over
the loneliness and hurt, that the letter never came. To this

very day it never came. But bitter, unforgiving, I could
never, ever be. I now understand the sorrow and the pain,

that a man suffered so, for an illness he didn't understand.
Today I love him for just giving me, me. He wasn't

there to give me lessons, but I got them anyway, through
his genes, his spirit and an undying, unspoken love.

Soft Sweet Persimmons

A searing hot sun…clear sky day…

an early morning meander down

a red-brown and dusty path…long…

skinny legs and small hands looked for the

Persimmon tree…Soft…sweet…orange-red

Persimmons…with just a hint of friendly

piquantness on eager lips…indeed…a prize

for a small Carolina boy…unmindful of most

life-things…but dead worms in a jar…muddy…

wet shoes…and a nagging curiosity about not

having seen Richard…his daddy…for weeks…

Oh well…he can bury the worms…clean and

let the shoes dry…run errands…for his mama…

but bringing Richard back…to play and eat with..

was something he didn't know if he could ever do…

Locusts, Red Clay and Caterpillars

It was not hard to get there; you had just one block to walk. Back then it seemed like a long block, but today not really. Sometimes the store was open when you went by, sometimes

not. The store was really just another house with a welcome front room. Funny how I always got thirsty when I went by that "store." I guess it was those RC Colas that Dimple, my

mother, loved so. Some days I went to get them twice, once three times. Other days I sat on the store's steps or meandered about. Across Freemont Street, behind a wire strung fence,

there was to my six-year old eyes, a huge locust tree. At
certain times that old tree would let fly its locusts, those long,
dark locusts with the sweet, chewy middle. Jack Barnes taught

me how to eat those locusts. I tried to teach Gwen to eat them,
but she spit it out. Sisters, what do they know, I thought they're
all dumb except some of them can fight, I learned later. Mine

could fight pretty good, if she had a little short stick or a finger
nail, a rock or something in her hand. After locusts, it was
across Renner street to Grandma Eliza's. Oh boy did I love that

lady. Even if she scared me sometimes. She was taller, blacker,
warmer, tougher than Dimple. She always wanted us there with
her, to feed us, touch us or just to play. We could run through her

house, step on caterpillars on the front porch, or wander off to
chase and play with Manuel or Beverly. Sometimes we stayed
overnight with Grandma Eliza. Dimple, sometimes frowned and

didn't always like that. She seemed to want us to always be with
her at home. I guess she needed us but I really didn't know why,
because sometimes in the dark night at home, I heard her cry,

about being all alone with, " all these kids." Dimple cried a lot
when we moved to Douglas Street. Douglas Street was just down
from the Water Works. We only had lights in just a part of the

Douglas house. It was next to and behind another, bigger house.
Most times we had to use the toilet in the back of the other house,
except at night when we peed in or used a slop jar. Yuck! But I loved

it when they made quilts in the house up front. You could hide
underneath the tight stretcher and watch fingers fly. The old ladies
sewed, sang songs, laughed and joked about men. You could hear

some pretty rough stuff, if they didn't know you were there. Sometimes they knew I was there and they picked on me. But I didn't get upset. After all, I was a man too. Douglas Street was fun most

of the time. Every day I could ride my toy fire truck and go dig for red clay. My Mother ate red clay and Argo starch too. It was some kind of chemical thing or anxiety I guess. I loved that little truck with

its seats and big pedals. It even had a ding-dong bell to let you know I was coming. Sometimes I took the fire truck, Gwen and James, over to Wilbert's house. He was my older cousin, bigger than me.

We had fun washing the truck and putting out fires all day. Once I made a big mistake when I stayed way too long. Rushing anxiously, I had to go find Gwen and wake up James, and pedal furiously to get

back home before Dimple came. When I got home she was already there pacing and worrying. She screamed at me about cars and danger and her babies, how I let the fire go out and how I let her down. She

wanted to hit me I know. I could see it in her eyes. I felt bad for a long time after that darkest of days. Even fried chicken, fish or potato salad, didn't taste good any more. Not long after that day, Papa Lewis

came to live with us in the back room, where there was no electric light. Papa was my Mama's Papa: tall, strong and quiet. He needed a safe place to stay since Grandma had gone away. He told us she had just "up and

left," to go somewhere up north. I wondered where that was, that up north, he talked about. Papa was a tough one, much tougher than Richard was. And he had big hands, a wrinkled face and a broken tooth. He loved bitter,

black coffee, and seemed sad most days. The only time he laughed was when he watched us fight or play. He called us "chaps" and got very annoyed when we mocked the way he sipped that hot coffee, and how he fell asleep in the big chair. Papa used to have his own house, in nearby Huntersville. We went there a lot. Dimple said it was a farm. He had dogs and cows and some kind of crops grew there. Grandma Lula used to feed us

syrup, cheese and biscuits, and let us pump the churn to make butter. We never quite did. Papa liked Grandma then. I even saw him kiss her once, on her lips. Then it happened; the day they cooked the possum. Yipes!

They had to trick me to eat some, called it chicken. Funny how Gwen and James ate and ate. It didn't bother them. But that day was also a happy day; a cool day, real cool. Dimple told me it was soon going

to be my first day in school. Me! Finally going to school...Biddleville School, I soon learn to say. Now maybe those big, light-skinned kids down Douglas Street, will let me shoot marbles and mock teachers and

talk school talk. Now maybe I can play ball with the big kids on the playground, and even work in Mr. Green's store for licorice and green peppermint sticks. Papa told me school was going to be my first big

step, my first really big step to be the man I always told him I was. We talked a lot about me being a big man, the head of the house. Funny how I always walked high up on my toes a lot, after talking to Papa.

Help Her Lord

It was late at night...real late..
I heard some talking...so
I put my ear to the wall...
It was my mama...Dimple...
She was talking...but no
one was there...I listened
real hard...

> *"Lord, forgive me for*
> *bothering you with*
> *this...but I can't*

take care of all
these kids by myself…

Can you help me…Lord
Can you please help me…
If you don't help me…Lord
I sure don't know what
I'm going to do"…

I felt bad when she started
to cry…and I fell asleep…with
a very small wish of my own…
hoping the Lord would help her…
I think he did…after a while…

Mama's Bedtime

Did you ever watch little children play?
Man, oh man, they can make your day
They can jumble and rumble, turn all around,
bat each other over and fall to the ground.
Then jump right back up and grab some hair;
Yell, wrestle and claw for skin and air.
They fight till they're tired with faces all red.
Then Mama speaks…Poof…they're off to bed!

Big Man

Mama used to tell me,
boy, I'm counting on you!
I'd stick out my chest,
put a swagger in my walk
and lower my voice to talk.

I'm glad she didn't know
that last night I struggled so,

to get free and run away,
from the bad ol' boogey man,
I'd seen that day.

I was watching a big green turtle,
caught by one trying to sell it,
when a piercing, siren sound
startled me! Not again! Gotta git!
I went flying across the ground.

This is it! Shucks! This is it!
Puffing and huffing I hit the door,
as the big red thing coming after me;
got closer and closer and then went on by.
I was so scared I couldn't even see.

So boogey man, boogey man,
go find another scared little boy.
Please disappear and stay away.
I'm a big man now, ain't scared no more.
My Mama's counting on me today.

Gwen and James

Gwen...my only sister...was all curiosity...
and as Dimple...strong of will...deferential
sometimes...but still persistent...determined...
and she can love you to death...James
Leon...my younger brother...was all mirth...
devilment...and challenge...mostly a free spirit...
He would challenge even Paul Bunyan...

From the day I first realized their presence...
not much has changed the basics...their
predictability...their attributes...When Richard...my

Dad left…they easily yielded…to my lead…which
I…the oldest…at six…gladly assumed…We loved
each other…without much question…at all…

We were almost…always there for each…
standing shoulder to shoulder…ready to
accept the challenge…We got this firstly…
from our surroundings…our circumstances…
but mostly we got it from Dimple…my Mom..
who would challenge a gorilla…then love it too…

Ol' John Lucky

I was just six and easily frightened.
Even a siren, from a fire truck would
make me run. We lived alone, the four
of us. I was the biggest male in the house,
and I brought the coal in for the fire.

Dimple, my mama, always told me
I was the man, and I always tried to
be just that, and then I met Ol' John
Lucky. Lucky was one Ol' scary man.
He looked old, but he really wasn't.

He was just a mite taller than me.
But he had long mixed hair and a scraggily
beard, and he shuffled and grinned a lot.
I had to watch him all the time, because
he always grabbed and pulled at, Dimple.

Lucky, had this old guitar. One string was
missing. He tried to sing and make us all dance.
But not me, I wouldn't stoop and prance. I
kept my eye on him and tried not to laugh at his

tricks, his wide eyes and his old rumpled clothes.

Everybody else seemed to love Ol' John.
Even Dimple, laughed with him and I didn't like that.
I didn't like a lot of people, Dimple liked, especially
Ol' John Lucky, with his foul breath and broken tooth,
broken guitar and "we's and youse," for we and you.

I even noticed that he had a hole in his shoe.
I guess his ol' foot gets wet ...when it rains.
Dimple, asked me one day why I didn't like Ol' Lucky.
I lied and said, "Oh, I like him! He's all right." But I'm
telling you now, I didn't like stinking, Ol' John Lucky.

The Big Switch

"Go get me a switch boy,
and don't you tarry.
You used up all your credits,
and you got no more to carry.

You run off on me for the last time,
leaving these little kids all alone.
When I say stay here and watch the fire,
you'll do what I say 'til you get all grown."

She's pretty mad, that's easy to see.
I was only gone a little short time.
But what she wants to do to tiny me,
the police would call a great big crime.

But I sure ain't going out and twitch,
to find a big switch for my own backside.
I'll walk real slow and find a little switch.
Maybe God will help let her madness subside.

My Aunt Floree

She was a very pretty lady, my Aunt Floree.
She lived next door and she really adored me.

In my very first picture, she's holding me up.
I'm told she was second to help me hold a cup.

When Floree and Dimple, my Mother, got together,
they would laugh and joke like two cats when they purr.

Floree, especially, liked to poke fun at men.
Against those two, no way a man could win.

They even laughed at me when I ran from a fire truck,
with that high wailing siren that made me run and duck.

Then on a day called Christmas, she made it all up to me,
with a little, riding fire truck under our Christmas tree.

When I got big, Dimple let me go to the store.
Yes, all by myself, I was just a little past four.

Even Mr. Green, the store man, thought I was something.
He told my Mama, Dimple, that boy can do anything.

One day Floree said to Dimple, why don't we do this.
Let's send Billy to the store with a very short list.

Old man, Lace Green, will get a Carolina kick,
out of a harmless, but neat little boy trick.

So they gave me a note for only Mr. Green to see.
They wanted *2 grape sodas, crackers and a can of pussy.*

I ran real fast to the store, cutting through the back yard.

When he saw the note Mr. Green smiled, then laughed real hard.

When I got back, Dimple and Floree were laughing too.
Of the three things they sent me for, I only had two.

Mr. Green said the sodas and crackers was all I could bring,
because there ain't no way that he had that other thing.

dirt

dirt where things grow....

out of blue...brown and black...

invite a taste...a challenge..

to all those...little green things...

that know more...than humans...

about starting...growing...becoming...

imagine a taste...of dirt...if you can...if

you are awake...today...or tomorrow...

if you want to grow...too...

and know the magic...

that can come...

from a taste of dirt....

dead flesh

they said you catch possums…
in graveyards where you bury the dead…
since possums eat dead flesh…

to snare them…follow the barking dogs
look up in trees…that's where you'll
find them…clinging to branches…
sometimes with little ones…clinging to them…

be sure to bring a croaker sack ..to put
them in …to take home…kill…then burn
the hair off…gut …and put them in the oven to roast
for dinner…for somebody else who eats…
dead flesh from a graveyard

Sharecropper's Granddaughter

Little Gwen…ran away and got lost…
I know she has peed by now…
Could Huntersville's white people…
have diapers…or…will…
Papa Lewis…have to grow them too…
before…she gets found?

early memory

stuff them in your shirt…
walk…to stairs…shadows…
behind the door…check…
smell them…sniff long…
funny…strange feelings…why?…it
could be just me…today…
might also be me forever…
i thought…why do only girls wear these?…

Biddleville School

My exposed left arm...held tightly to my body...ached with the worst pain...worse than the pain I felt...from a couple of twisted twigs... when Dimple... my mother... angry about something I'd done...stung my pitifully...spindly legs...A short time before...I had just received...a dreaded vaccination shot ...Now with the left sleeve...of my undershirt... tucked at my waist...my blue plaid shirt laid across my right arm...like a grim-faced waif...I walked home from my second day at Biddleville School ...in Charlotte...North Carolina... Six-years old...and unashamed of my near-nakedness in the August...Carolina sunshine...I remembered the admonition...from the Doctor...to not let anything... touch my wounded arm...for at least a few hours... I didn't... and I was anxious to get back home...to Douglas Street...to Dimple...to talk about that big needle...and what had happened to me...at school that day...

I don't remember much about my very first school...I do remember my teacher...a very firm...commanding...but friendly black lady...who liked to wear frilly white blouses ...and she smelled good too...I remember that I was one of the tallest kids...in my class...and I could run with the fastest...I remember recess...taking a half-nap on my desk...and of course reciting the A-B-C's...or writing them...in white chalk...on a blackboard...Oh...and I remember that gray-haired...blue-eyed...white man ...the doctor who gave me the vaccination...with that big...ugly needle...That needle would leave me...with a scar the rest of my life...A lot of the kids cried... when they just saw the needle...I don't remember crying ...but I do remember a queasiness...and almost fainting when I felt the sting...of that long... ugly... instrument of pain...

Still...I loved going to Biddleville School ...the only segregated ...all black school...I would ever attend...not that the words... "segregated"... or "integrated"...meant anything to me... or most Negroes...back then... in 1943...in segregated Charlotte...North Carolina... I liked going to Biddleville because it meant that...finally I was on my way to being...the "big man" ...that Dimple... my mother...Richard ...my father ...Papa... my grandfather...almost everybody...it seemed ...wanted me to be... Biddleville was my big man validation...For as far back as I could remember then...I wanted to be old enough...to go to school...Finally I was there... Now I was on my way...Here comes the "big man"...I strutted...

Just a few months …after that vaccination day at Biddleville …the only school I would ever attend…in North Carolina… Dimple…would take me…and my siblings away from Charlotte…and Biddleville…to a new home up north…in far-away Buffalo…New York …I was both sad and excited …when I heard the news that we were leaving… Some years later… as an older…but still young man…I again visited Biddleville and my old… very first neighborhood on Renner Street …While my grandmother's house…at the corner of Freemont …was gone by then…the little "shot gun" house where we had a fireplace and an indoor toilet…though empty…was still there… I was struck by…how much smaller …how tiny and quaint it looked then… compared to my long ago…six-year old eyes… Looking at it…and Biddleville school…I wondered if we ever leave a place…when it stays in our memory…I think not…I concluded…I think not….

Small Eyes

It's funny how small eyes…see big things…
wide open spaces…long…forever roads…

never ending days…weeks that seem like
months…and event times…that never come…

For small eyes…life moves…at a snail's pace…
Yet…they just have to keep looking…exploring

the spaces…journeying the long paths…living the
days…the months…the pause-times that always

come…Those eyes soon learn…that space…and
distance…time and days…are not really what

they seem…not really as big as they think they are…
when they see…when they live them…before they

reach a travel's end… It suggests that small eyes…
never cease to be…never become more than small…

before they stop traveling...before they grow...
large enough... to finally see it all...as it really is...

Going Up to Buffalo

It was magic...Two days before...my Mother Dimple had come to Biddleville School...to tell the teacher...I would not be back again... Now...today...we were in a taxi...with bags and boxes...wide eyes...and sad eyes...headed for adventure...on a long train ride to "up north" ... that mysterious...far-away place...Papa Lewis...said Grandma Lula...had run away to ...Papa Lewis...was sad when we all hugged goodbye...James... Gwen... Dimple...and me...I thought I saw a tear in Papa's eye...as I looked around to wave...so long... goodbye... to my fair-skin friends... next door...That day was a warm... hazy blue...lazy... Carolina day... with a faint smell of ...fried fish...as we left Douglas Street... We raced down Beatties Ford...past the Water Works...French Street...the Johnson C. Smith campus...lots of green trees...into Trade Street ...Then the taxi slowed and bounced across the old...no longer used...trolley tracks... to the Southern train station...in Uptown... Charlotte ... I tried to remember if I 'd put...that jar of worms back outside... before we left... so they could get some air...Oh well...too bad for them...Anyway too late...I was happy that day...I was going far away...I squeezed my fist...in expectation...

There was a flurry...a blur of things...the station...people buying tickets...from the "Colored" ticket counter...carrying boxes and bags... and coats we did not need...Then the great...big ...black train...but it was...nothing new for me...I had seen them before...smelled their smoke... heard their high...hoarse whistles...and their...choo...choo...choo... over in DeRider...where Papa and Grandma ...used to live...Why I even knew ...how wide the tracks were...how to run the rails and throw rocks at the beasts...as they flew by... and how to pick up coal...fallen from... the fast moving trains...to take home...for Grandma's cooking stove... But to actually...be inside the monster...the seats...the rows... the smells... the people ...that was real exciting...for a wide-eyed six-year old...me...

My heart pounded as Dimple...explained...we were going to stop and see Richard...in some place called... Washington...D.C...Richard was my Dad…who lived in… Washington …with his brother…Bernard… not with us…in Charlotte…like he used to… Seems like… many years… since Richard left…but…it really was just months ago… Funny how a year seems so long…when…you are little…and six or seven…Houses seemed bigger…and streets seemed longer…back then too …And…Oh yes… train rides took forever!…

The ride was magical…wondrous…filled with awe…Things outside… like birds… cows …and horses were eating as we whisked by…Things inside…like the big white man…in black …who took the tickets…and the soldiers…and sailors…some carrying big bags…Then there were the candy and sandwich boys…who came on the train…every time it stopped…We never bought anything …since we had a big bag of chicken and biscuits… Dimple was quiet… when I asked if she had ever rode…a train before… She quickly said… yes…but because she smiled…I wondered why then… hadn't she told us before…like other exciting things she'd done…and told us about…After awhile…James and Gwen… tried to cut up some… running the narrow aisle…and picking at the black lady…in front of us… but they were soon sprawled …sound asleep…I stayed up…with at least one eye open…watching everyone… watching everything…wide awake… all the way up to Washington…D.C…

We bounded from the train…struggling with bags…big boxes…other stuff…Then up walks Richard…my Dad…He seemed tired…but it was him…hugging us…and asking us everything …It was exciting to see him again… Soon we were in another taxi…that rushed us through a strange…but wondrous city…Richard had a room at his Brother Bernard's house …in Washington… Bernard…whom I just vaguely remembered seeing somewhere before… in Charlotte…at Grandma's house…maybe… He was friendly…and he liked to tickle us a lot… Richard's room was dark… somber…not bright…not happy…not welcoming… In the kitchen…we ate cheese…drank milk…and laid down… because Dimple said …we only had six hours…to stay…I slept deeply…The hours flew… then sleepily…again…we were in a taxi…going back to the train station… to catch another train…to take us to…that somewhere …up north place… called Buffalo…

When he put us on the train…and hugged us…I could feel the moisture…from Richard's eyes…Gwen asked…why he was not coming too...I forget what he said...I kept waiting to see...if he would hug... Dimple...like he used to in Charlotte... He did...but it was not the same... I didn't think they liked...each other...anymore... As we scrambled...to board the train...Richard...handed Dimple a few...balled up dollars... and waved goodbye... once again... Little did I know...that it would be nearly two decades...before I would see...or speak to ...my daddy Richard again... Later...riding the train...I pounded a knee... and regretted not reminding him about the letter...he had promised to send me...but hadn't...so far...

Relative of Romare

Growing up I always...wanted to be a relative...of Romare's
After all...he is from Charlotte too...Why he could have even

been my big brother...or better still...fallen in love with Dimple
...my mother...and been...my father...I wonder if she...ever knew

Romare...like she knew Doctor Blackman...and that Alexander
fellow...But neither of them are like...Romare...After all...

Romare and I have a lot in common...except for me...not being
famous or a genius and all...But he is a painter...so am I...His

family is large...so is mine...He knows what it is...to be hated...
and discriminated against...so do I...He went to...the March on

Washington...so did I...and he has raced down...Second Street...
and watched the trolley go by...He bought a ticket...at the Colored

counter...in the train station...and rode the train...north...past places
and Washington...D.C...to New York City...He too... fell in love with

Harlem...Best of all he loves Ellington and Jazz...just like I do...Yes...
I think it would have been nice...to be a relative of Romare's...real nice...

the queen cities

later...thinking back on the
moment...as i went from one
queen city to another...i thought
what makes a city a queen?...
could it be a charlotte can't
be a king...even though it is
the largest...why must it
be a queen?...buffalo says
it is a queen too...could
it be because it's too small to
be a king...given the big
sprawl...new york city...
it all makes you wonder
if there is a king...out there...
somewhere...looking for a mate
and two dowager queens are...
vying...strutting...for notice...
trying to be what they used
to be...or want to be...they
didn't ask me...but if they
had...i would have thrown
away...rusty crowns...and
tattered robes...and named
them both... "the good city"...
giving them both...a star
to reach for...a place to be...
something worth strutting for...

Buffalo

A young brawny Nation...not even 50...with a burning quest for the far west...for commerce...Untying a hunger for adventure and challenge... using mules... with Irish sweat...at a dollar a day...they dug the mighty Erie Canal...At first called Clinton's Ditch...with pulling mules on a path...and tanned Hoggies...steering the narrow barges... through...Cohoes...Rome...Oneida...Canastota...Onondaga... Syracuse...Rochester...Lockport and finally Buffalo...who out-dug Black Rock...to be the western end...They found their way...Soon mighty grain towers...stored flour...and Iron ore piles from Duluth... helped forge steel...build bridges...and something called Tesla's electricity...lit up and ensconced Erie's dowager...Queen of the Lakes...to her rightful place...Young and frisky...she helped to birth princess cities...in Ohio...and Indiana...and fueled the venue of big shoulders...Chicago...She would wear a proud crown...a star filled frock...and dance at the ball...a hundred years plus... from then...

Next Stop: Buffalo

I had never seen anything quite like it before...A long ramp up... then as we pushed through the big brass door... a great cavernous hall opened before our eyes...The long...energy sapping... train ride was over...We were a tired...twenty-seven year-old...single mother ...with three wide-eyed little guys...looking for a new way of life...Charlotte... North Carolina ...and Richard...my father...were behind us...It was the beginning of a new chapter for us..."Is Buffalo up north"...I had asked her..."Yes Billy...but don't you fret...you'll be happier than you were...in Charlotte... You'll like it here."...she said...

I was glad the man in the red hat was there...He helped us carry those heavy bags and string-tightened boxes...Since it was past 10:00 P.M....there wasn't many people in the biggest building I'd ever seen... Dimple called it Central Terminal... Then...at the end of a great hall...I saw it...a big shaggy animal with long...rough hair...standing high... frozen ..."A stuffed Buffalo"... Dimple said...after my three bad guesses... Then the three-dollar ...sleepy... cab ride to Lackawanna... stopping at a place called...17-A Albright Court...This would be where... once again...we would see Lula...my grandmother...at the family's new northern home port...Confused ...and struggling slightly...to pronounce Lackawanna...I wondered if... Lackawanna was in Buffalo...or was Buffalo in Lackawanna...

I was to learn later…that wherever Lula went…some or most of her brood would soon follow…Now after years of bitterness…and fighting… Lula had left my grandfather…Papa… behind in Charlotte…Her trek to Buffalo was no accident…since her brother and sisters …long before in the 1920's…like so many others…had started the outflow…from down south…They too…were all caught up…in that steady migration of poor blacks…out of the bitter south… to something better…up north… More than anything…they were fleeing American apartheid's …heavy racial burdens on their backs…and on their souls… They ran from brutal sharecropping… and white folks' hot kitchens… and cruel rules…They ran to new aspirations …and hopefully fairer wages…and a chance to grow…and prosper…from then on…

At 17-A Albright Court…they were glad to see us…Grandma Lula… Uncle Bill…and my young aunt Ruth…Later came hugs from…next door relatives…Janie…Lula Belle and McGee…In the next few days… we huddled together…like ancient-day Gypsies… encouraging and… collectively supporting…sharing floors and space…until each one could be free…We were clearly a poor clan…mostly uneducated…somewhat naive of northern ways… unsure refugees… gingerly picking our way through… the mirage of integration… up north… After a few weeks…moving from Grandma's …to a rooming house on Ridge Road… Dimple … duty bound…continued the ever tough struggle for parental dignity…Youth and inexperience kept me from seeing… and feeling her burden and heavy load… but she dutifully took it up…even though…the full weight…of what she faced…none of us…could fully see…

Within days…there was school for Gwen and me…and baby sitters for little James… Like a mouse overcoming a maze…I soon learned my way… through Lackawanna's snowy streets… Dimple…rode buses… and cleaned white folks houses …She did lots of things back then…I learned to fix lunches…wash clothes… and iron sheets …As I shivered and trudged … through that first New York winter…I also learned to whistle new songs … with white breath …and cold… puckered lips…I also often wondered if Dimple…like me… ever yearned for the far off…long ago …warmth of Carolina …where the skies seemed clearer… and the air was certainly purer … where each day…for a little boy…it seemed…so much freer…so much finer…

Charlotte...Lackawanna...they were certainly different...Now I even had white kids and white teachers...in my new school...some of whom were nasty...Others were friendly and helpful... Dimple told me don't fight them and always stay cool ... She said just learn to count... read... so you can read the Bible one day...When she said that...I thought about Papa...I wondered if he was still reading his Bible...missing Grandma... missing us... Sometimes...I wondered about Richard too...if he owned a Bible...still went for walks... played with new little kids...stuff like that...

At the rooming house...we lived in on Ridge Road...lots of people lived with us...Only a few kids lived there...usually with their mothers.... Some of the men worked at the steel mill... Some worked as cooks or truck helpers...and some didn't work at all...The grownups often had parties... lots of parties ... Well into the night...they would be drinking ... laughing ...and dancing to music ...from a large juke box...in the parlor...I heard Dimple once say... Cookie's reminded her of a "down-home honky-tonk"...The party makers loved to see ...my cousin Libby and me... dance a mean boogie-woogie... Sometimes they even tossed us... nickels and dimes... when we got through...all sweaty...and out of breath... There were arguments sometimes...but people were mostly happy...and got along...back then...

While we lived on Ridge Road...we spent a lot of days...at Grandma's... When the short... cool days...finally gave way to Spring...and warmth...It was a time when Grandma Lula's face brightened...as she returned to her roots...For now she could till the soil...and do her planting thing... In the back...behind the Court...of 17-A...she would plant tomatoes... corn and yellow squash...then cuddle and nurse each of their tiny shoots...to life... Mama Lula...loved those plants almost as much as she loved all of us... especially her own sisters and a brother ....most of whom had come north... to Buffalo ...in the late 1920's...They came to Buffalo...when blacks totaled about 4,000...or so...and they mostly lived...around Michigan Avenue... Broadway...and William Streets...My uncle Frank said...back then a car couldn't...climb the dirt hill...at Jefferson and Best...after a good rain... Grandma Lula's siblings...Tom... Daisey ... Nannie and Janie...all were within car...or bus riding distances from Lackawanna ... Lula was glad she had so much family so close...Only her sisters... Carrie and Annie... and a brother James... chose not to come to "cold" Buffalo...

Then there was Grandma Vynnie…my grandmother's mother… She was there too…with a powerful presence that bound us all…Vynnie was quiet…stoic…rock-like…like Gibraltar… It was from the proud… determined Cherokee…"the people of "Kituwah" …from whom she learned to stand tall…and unsmiling… To me…back then…she seemed to be a hundred… wrinkled-years old…I learned later she was *barely* in her eighties…Today…as I think of her…I wish there had been some way… to get from her long…gray…braided head…a written story of our clan of old…a story that told about the tears…the triumphs…the places and the histories…she and her mama and daddy… had been told…

Family legends …my mother told me…said that Vynnie…was of mixed-blood…and born free…She was the offspring…of a runaway slave… and a Cherokee lady…from the Eastern Band…of North Carolina… They were that lucky…clever thousand…who escaped …the government-forced…1838 Tennessee…"Trail of Tears" …trek west…to what is now Oklahoma…Vynnie married another half-breed named… Ruben Barnes…whose mother …was a thin…smallish white woman with a club foot…Dimple recalls seeing her great-grand mother…just one frightening time… when she was five or six years old…My great-aunt Miss…(Nannie was her real name.)…who was my grandmother's sister… whom I got to know…and love…as much…if not more than… grandma Lula… later told me that…their grandmother… came from Ireland…to this Country… to "keep from starving"…

Vynnie's children were all reserved…cool…soft spoken and very fair… She and Ruben… instead of a legacy of things…left a large…quiet… prideful clan…that possessed a dignified air…that disguised their intelligence…They each acted as if they belonged…to some mysterious… black aristocracy only they knew about…Sadly…a few short years… after we arrived in Lackawanna …we would lose our grandma Lula… to pneumonia and exhaustion …Then just weeks later…Vynnie would go too…With the loss of Lula… however…the whole family seemed to be…suddenly lonely… deflated…suffering a kind of gnawing thirs …for something…or someone to mend their souls anew…For all of us…the sun had dimmed some…even been snuffed out for a few of us … However… the most memorable things I remember…about that sad…snowy January time…of my grandmother's death … were the flowery smells…of those early…Rochester lilacs… and roses… and the quiet prayer …Vynnie… hair braids touching her waist…quietly spoke over her… eternally sleeping daughter … lying in repose at 17-A Albright Court…It will stay with me the rest of my life...

> "You've been a good daughter, Baby.
> A mother couldn't ask for more from you.
> Sleep well and go home to sweet Jesus.
> I am sure I'll see your face again soon."

Lilacs and Roses

Lilacs…they told me…have a wondrous smell…recognizable even in the midst of…and surrounded by…red and white roses…gladiolas… and some other blooms with names…no one knew…Together they perfumed the small living room and the whole of…17-A Albright Court… Lackawanna…New York…January…1946… Lilacs from afar…they said…were a graceful…reminder of spring…a beautiful addition…the perfect conveyer of sorrow…and forgiveness…at grieving moments…They were piled behind…alongside of…and in front of her casket…the pale… purple…cloth covered casket…holding the body of…Lula Matilda Eliza Minnie Stewart…my grandmother…

Just weeks before…before the snow came…she was alive…upstairs in her heavy…medicine-reeked…darkened bedroom… sick…slowly dying… fighting to stay alive…fighting to continue to be the sun…her children… her mother…her whole clan…orbited …and needed… for sustenance… When I saw her lying there…motionless…frozen in eternal sleep…I noticed a foreign…dark spot next to her mouth…I wondered if it was something the Undertaker… Mr. Sherman Walker put there…It was not there the last time I saw her…when I heard her for the last time… when…in a weakened voice…she bade me to… "come closer…let me see you again"…

That night I was encouraged…to stand closer too…to "go on up… you can touch her"…But I did not want touch her…I was afraid…I was struggling to understand the moment…to find some comfort…But fear was overwhelming me…I understood the grief…from losing someone you cared for...but I did not understand my fear...I had never been that close to a dead person...to a dead...still person...who had been so alive...so tender...so firm...so insistent that I eat...that dreaded...yellow squash...I hated so...and refused...

I had heard of dead people before...in Charlotte...North Carolina... There was a cousin...Manuel and Beverly's brother... Albert...killed in the War...and the kid across Renner Street...who fell off the back of a moving...pickup truck...But I had never actually seen them dead... This was the first time...to see death...so close...to smell...to hear... the soft humming sobs...to see the red...tear-filled eyes...of everyone in the room...Everyone that is... except Vynnie Barnes...my great-grandmother...Lula's mother...

She was not sobbing...she just sat quietly... looking at her...gnarled... cupped hands...resting in her aged...slackened lap...as if she were silently reciting... a Christian prayer...or...some ancient Cherokee chant her mother had taught her...Maybe she was remembering...Lula's father ...Rubin... her husband...who died thirteen years earlier... Anyway...I was crying... and ached too...My shoulders kept arching... spasmodically...with every sniffle...and I was hating the sight and smell...of those lilacs and roses... I kept wishing...over and over again...that I had...just once...just once... gone ahead...and eaten some of that dreadful...old...awful yellow squash...Just once!...Just once...for Grandma Lula!....

The Kituwah

They escaped the ingrates Van Buren...and
Jackson's...angry... determined wrath...to
push and drive them...from where they had
been...since more than a hundred grandmothers
ago...My own told me...it was the soil...red
between her toes...a taste of sweet in her dry
mouth...that really betrayed them... They had tried
to be white...even own slaves... create and write...
be "civilized"...Still they couldn't stay...They had

to give up the morning mist...running through the high grass...the fresh drink of Catawba waters ...the sharp belch of the cricket...at early night... everything sweet for the Kituwah...For a brief time...they fought...and called upon the ancient ones...They tried to save the old homelands...But it was...in white eyes...the gleam of gold... pushed from mother earth...that ultimately doomed their try...The war was lost...with Tsali's blood...Still the forest's...arms opened ...welcomed...and gave them shelter...and sustenance...Then the young ones...were saved... right up to me...she said...

Rats

Albright Court had rats...
Gates Avenue had rats....

Brown ones, gray ones
Bold rats...scarey rats...

Lackawanna had some
pretty big...ugly rats...

Bigger than any I had ever
seen...or even imagined...

I don't remember seeing big
rats...before Lackawanna...

They lived in round holes...
under the concrete block

walls of Albright Court...
They lived in the dark house

with us on Simon Street...
Later they would live

with us in lots of houses...
where they would chew

on the Corn Flakes boxes...
and hunt for kitchen scraps

when the lights went out...
Sometimes we fought

them...caught them...
and even killed them...

Robert and Raymond...
caught three rats in a cage...

lit a fire under them...Jumping
squealing...climbing...they died...

Watching that...was the first
time...I ever felt sorry for a rat...

Lackawanna Days

It seemed like soot always fell...A sulfur smell annoyed you on windless days...It was Bethlehem Steel's town...Lackawanna...New York...Rust colored...neatly segregated houses... delineated neighborhoods..."No bootblacks Allowed" signs...At least the kids went to school together...in wartime 1944 ...For us...in many ways... Lackawanna...was like Charlotte... North Carolina...But in 1944... Lackawanna... wasn't as segregated...as it would be in a few short years...Back then though... we knew our place... We knew to stay... on the right side of town...this side of the tracks... near the plant...near the lake...away from South Park...After all...we had

Gates Avenue...Simon...Wasson and...Steelawanna streets...and that was enough...for Negroes...back then in 1944...in Lackawanna...New York...

For me...life in an upstairs...rooming house...on Ridge Road...Cookie's place... offered a new kind of excitement...for a seven-year old refugee...from apartheid-ruled... North Carolina... Ridge Road...that old high ground... Seneca Indian trail... was busy and exciting back then...It was a main drive... with stores...and a movie show...called the Ridge...which you could go to... along with the white folks...The trail was always bustling... with something new ... revealing ...to see...to hear...It was a far cry from...Charlotte's sleepy Renner ... Beatties Ford Road... Freemont...or Douglas streets...

If we weren't on Ridge Road...we were at... Albright Court...that enclave of ...gray concrete block homes...for low income folks...black and white...part of the New Deal...or some deal...from the President... or the Governor...or somebody... Albright Court...clean... bright... straight hardwood floors...but separate...from the red brick...Baker Homes... where only white folks lived...back then...At Albright Court... we darted...back and forth...between 17-B...where aunt Janie and McGee and Lula Belle lived...and 17-A...where my Grandma ...and Ruth... and Uncle Bill lived...My Uncle Frank...came all the time too...There was always... something to do there...with cousins... and uncles...and aunts... and smart-alecky kids outside...who thought they...could pick on...the new...dumb kids in the funny clothes... who didn't know where the store was... until...that is...they found out we could fight!...

Dimple...my Mother...was right...I was happier there...up North... with Grandma and lots of other...relatives and friends...For sure...it wasn't the weather...or the...rust-colored air...we breathed in...every day...I missed the sense of ease...and warmth of Carolina...It may have been... Roosevelt School...where there were... a few white kids...who really liked you... Could it have been...the cowboy movies...at the Ridge show...Saturday mornings...or was it cousins...Wilbert and Libby... my Aunt Ruth...or little Cliffie...who also lived...with us...on Ridge Road...who caused funny feelings...in me... when together...we snuck peeks ...at grownup's calendars...and each other... Cliffie wasn't especially pretty...just a real... fast little girl ...who...at age nine...insisted...that I remember ...and saw...that there really was...a difference... between boys and girls...and how they went to the bathroom...

After living at Cookie's a few months...Dimple...in spite of hard... house-cleaning work for white people...long hours and exhausting bus rides...suddenly began to smile more... Cookie's had a bar...a jukebox... and dance floor in the parlor...where roomers met and got to know each other... In spite of the hard days...Dimple seemed to have enough energy...to dance...with those smooth talkers...in their Cab Calloway hats...pegged pants...and hip pocket chains...After watching her dance I began to think ...My Aunt Janie had McGee... Aunt Ann met John... and moved cousins Wilbert and Libby...to Simon Street...Were we next?...

The answer...would come soon... when a smooth...light brown-skin man...with a thin...Ronald Coleman mustache... started coming to...Ridge Road... almost every night... Dimple liked him...with his... sweet... girly perfume... She called it...Peach Blossom Cologne... Peach!... Geach!... we kids laughed ...except when Steve... (That was his name.) ...gave us nickels... and bags of... roasted peanuts...Steve could talk...and laugh up a storm ...but he couldn't dance... He liked... Iroquois beer...peanuts... and those nasty...little pickled sausages...you had to chew...forever ...and ever... Did I like him?...Not yet...The verdict was still out... Suspicion was still in...

It hadn't been quite a year now...and Richard...my Dad... and Charlotte...North Carolina... were memories fading fast...Dimple hardly mentioned them...anymore...She talked a lot about Steve though...about his funny walk...how he liked spaghetti...and how he was...a father too...He had a boy...and a girl...just a little older...than Gwen and me... Yuk! ...Where was this going...I thought...Getting ready...I asked cousin Wilbert if he called ...his mother's friend John... Dad?...Daddy?... Father?...Nope! ...Nope! And Nope!...he said... Just Mr. John...So that is what I called him too... Mr. John... Unfortunately...baldheaded-son-of-a-bitch... would be what I would call him a few years later...

Time passed slowly...it seemed...and days in Lackawanna...grew easier...and easier to take...Little did I know...that Lackawanna was the beginning...of a decade-long... boarding house odyssey...of shared living... half-emptied boxes...doubled-up roll-away beds... trained bowels... sweet smells...and a few smells you wish you didn't have to know ... Ahead ...beyond Lackawanna...lying in wait...were more dark days than bright... constant little struggles...nagging anxiety...humor...laughter and small triumphs...There would be exhaustion...but never hunger... depression ...but never surrender...It would be that way...for what seemed like a long time for us...and a young single mother of three...trying to find some modicum of dignity...and someone to be happy with...

My Great Grandmother Vynnie

Like every cool, but bright day in Lackawanna,
today too, the sun shone through a rusty haze.
When we kids got tired of throwing rocks at rats,
we climbed the monkey bars, as we did on most days.

Hanging upside down from the highest bar,
little Hilda came up and I heard her say,
"Billy! Billy! Mama Vynnie wants you.
She said don't fool around, come right away."

Mama Vynnie was my grandmother's mother,
who stayed mostly quiet and just smoked her pipe.
She was real, real old and walked with a cane.
Mostly gentle, she was still a quick-temper type.

When I got there she was sitting in her favorite chair,
smoking her pipe like she did most every day.
Her waist-length gray hair was up in Indian braids.
"Come up here closer boy, I got something to say.

I want you to take this here money, go over
to the store, get me George Washington tobacco.
Don't tarry none, because I'm almost out. Bring
back my change and get your coat before you go."

Mookie and me went together to the store.
He didn't wear his coat so I left mine too.
Mookie was my best friend and I had lots. But
none was like Mookie, if you wanted something to do.

When we got to the store, Mookie said brightly,
"It sure would be nice if we could buy popsicles."
Foolishly, with Grandma's change, I did just that.
I thought surely she wouldn't miss just a few nickles.

Popsicles in hand, we took the long way home.
We had to gobble them up before we got back.
I also had Grand mama's tobacco and her change too.
I carried them both in a brown, paper sack.

When I handed the tobacco and sack to Grandma,
she said, "Boy, just where have you been?"
I mumbled a tale about helping find Mookie's lost cat.
Sheepishly, I had to admit the story was mighty thin.

After Vynnie filled her pipe and counted all her change,
She said, "Seems to me fourteen cents is missing."
My answer was, I probably lost it looking for the cat.
Grandma looked at me, and didn't say a thing.

Finally, she said, "Come over here and stick out your tongue."
Puzzled, I warily, slowly walked to her, tongue half out.
Before I knew what had happened, her cane brutally sung.
The pain was so fiery red; all I could do was move and shout.

Well out of reach, I got a stern lecture, I only vaguely heard.
I remember words like, *"don't you," "my money," and "mind me."*
The pain from her cane taught me, that not even a hundred popsicles,
was worth lying to, or disobeying, my great grandma Vynnie.

Family in Buffalo

We all started with Vynnie and
Rubin, long gone, I never knew Rubin.
A couple were called Janie, both were aunts.
But Grandma Lula (minus Lewis) was the real glue.

There were some little cute ones called:
Hilda, Pat, Debbie and Marsha.
And a few well-feds known as:
Earl, Miss, (Nannie) Etta and Edna.

There was a Frank, a Bill, Corine and Lula Belle.
Another Janie, a Ruth, a Joyce, even a Celeste, James and Gwendolyn,
A Billy, a Bobby with a C, Charles, Clarence (Pat), Richard and Monty,
A far-from-flowery Daisey, Sylvester, Ruby and Uncle Ernest.

We had one Ann, a Wilbert and Libby were also there.
Uncle Tom (John), his Nancy and offspring named Shirley, another James,
Rebecca, Jenny, Bobby, Jean, Ophelia, Eli, Elizabeth, Ruth, Robert and
Another John...Can't forget Pat Kye...

Also Missing: Julius, (twice) Ernest, Ulysses, (Sea) Eleanor (twice),
Diane, Randy
Ricky, Sarah, Gregory, Erin, Mark, Sabrina, Lorna and Jackie...

The come Later Crowd: Stewart, Carmen, Donna, Angela, B.J. (Will),
JoAnn,
Christopher, James, Zena, Azalee and Damon
Sherri, Marquita, Andrea, Marcus, Howard,
Tiffany, Courtney, Ray, Bessie, Kim and Larry
Adrienne, Michael, Bobby, Brenndan, Briann, Gloria,
Treavor, Travis, Travena ...Whew!!!

Roosevelt School

My first school in Buffalo...New York...in reality...was my first school in Lackawanna ...New York... Lackawanna ...a long ago gathering place for the Seneca Indians...had become a small...gritty...Bethlehelm Steel... Company-dominated city ... southwest of Buffalo...As recent arrivals... refugees in a way...from Charlotte...the Queen City of North Carolina ...we briefly settled there before moving on to Buffalo...another Queen City of the State...Although we lived...out of district...in a busy...often crowded... rooming house on bustling Ridge Road...my mother...Dimple ...using my grandmother's address ...at 17-A Albright Court... registered my sister Gwen and me...in Roosevelt grammar school...The School was convenient for us... since my younger brother James' babysitter...lived a short distance from my grandmother...In Lackawanna...we were now a single-parent... family of four...since Richard...my father...who never saw Roosevelt ...or Lackawanna...had abandoned us...a few years before then...

Because my mother worked...I had the considerable ...school day responsibility... to shepherd little brother James to the babysitter...and Gwen and myself...to Roosevelt School that long...first year in our...often-snowy...new home... Roosevelt...like most of the grammar schools...I would attend in the next eight years...was orderly and well run... It was ...like every school I attended thereafter... richly integrated... with an assortment of... likeable... and some not-so likable kids...from the many... colorful ethnic groups... scattered around the schools... From Roosevelt ...I remember the sing-song repetition...of phonetic drills... and thin teaching booklets...given to first graders...to read about Dick and Jane ...and their dog Spot...I remember the wondrous magic of numbers...and the often baffling principles...underlying...the many things...you could do with them...

What I liked most about Roosevelt...was the small park...and busy playground nearby...I think...I...along with my cousin...Wilbert... spent more time in the playground ...than we did at school... Roosevelt school was also the beginning...the dawning...of my serious...formal learning... where I would discover that ...most learning came quickly... almost effortlessly ... for me...I would learn that I could compete...with my mind...a little better than most of the kids around me... especially the recent arrivals...like us...from the southern parts...of the great land of apartheid ...This ability was probably innate... since home drills... or special ... concerted...parental urgings to pursue learning... was only mildly present...in my early school life...Back then...surviving was the highest... and the most important priority...for a struggling...young... single mother with little more than a grammar school education...My mother believed in ...and always exhorted us to go to school ...but I always felt...she felt inadequate...to help with our homework...after the early school years... She seemed lost... beyond the Bible...that she read assiduously...when we were kids...

Joey

We (Wilbert and me) went there almost every day,
when the wind died down and it didn't rain or snow.
The playground was where most kids went to play.
Chased from the house, where else could you go?

We would go shoot marbles, play ball and hang out on swings,
race each other, play the dozens and practice dirty words.
Few white kids would challenge us, since we won at most things,
where you ran, jumped, wrestled or mocked humming birds.

One day Wilbert and I wanted to hang out on the swings.
But the white kids filled them up and just wouldn't get off.
So we waited for them, we weren't interested in other things.
We looked at them, shuffled feet and gave hints with a cough.

Finally, we went up to a husky, white kid named Joey.
We had seen him in the playground a few times before.
We knew he didn't like us, a little tough mouth, he tried to be.
So I let him know we wanted a swing, he had ten minutes more.

Joey kept right on swinging but he got a little nervous.
He stopped laughing loudly and his swings got a lot shorter.
Soon he stopped swinging and just looked and stared at us.
He told his friend, "let's go. We'll come back later."

We jumped on the swings, as they walked away.
We said, we'll show them swinging, we're no amateurs.
I had forgotten all about him, when I heard Joey say,
"We ain't scared of ass-holes and go to hell, you Niggers!"

Now that was the magic word for a fight,
and even though we black kids said it all the time,
you'd better not use it around us, if you were white.
To us, white kids who did, committed the ultimate crime.

Bang! We were off the swings in full chase after Joey.
And just as fast, Joey and his friend, hit stride in a gallop.
With their good head start, catching them would not be easy.
Down streets, over fences, we lost them and just gave up.

We spent the next few weeks chasing Ole Joey.
We chased him in the playground, streets, even at school.
The way Joey eluded us was almost uncanny.
No matter what we did, he made us feel like a fool.

Week after week, month after month, just about any day,
if Joey saw us coming, he'd yell, "nigger, nigger, n-i-g-g-g-e-r!"
He'd stick out his tongue, laugh, then make a quick get-a-way.
And once more, his bravado reputation got bigger and bigger.

Nearly a year had passed; we had almost forgotten about Joey.
We just gave up; we thought we were never going to catch him.
Then with a stroke of luck beyond our wildest fantasy,
we spotted Joey through the windows of the school gym.

He had not seen us; we were the last thing on his mind.
We made a plan to catch him right then, that very moment.
The plan had to be good, truly one-of-a-kind,
one that the clever, little devil, couldn't circumvent.

From the school gym we knew which way he'd run,
so one of us would go wait to block his way,
while the other would circle and chase the son-of-a-gun,
into the other's arms. By God! We'd have him that day!

Eureka! The perfect plan, worked perfectly.
Wilbert chased after him while I waited, and

sure enough, we finally, at last caught Ole running Joey.
But everything did not work out according to plan.

Instead of anger and beating up on Ole Joey,
we looked into his frightened and pleading eyes,
and broke out laughing and joking ourselves silly.
We couldn't believe we had him, after so many tries.

We joked about the time he ran out of his shoes.
We rolled about me sliding and flopping in mud.
Joey told us how he gave his mother the blues,
Sewing up his pants, cleaning up his running crud.

From that day on, Joey was one of the best friends we had.
He even took us home with him to meet his dear mother.
Joey got so close to us he was always very glad,
and quick to check any kid who used the word, "nigger."
Except us, of course.

Marbles

I loved to play with them...
but no matter how hard I tried...
I couldn't shoot them the way
other kids...and even Wilbert
could...I loved marbles...I
would spend my last cent
for one I wanted...Swirls...
solids...bowlers...even cold
steel...I had them all...I would
trade them...steal them...
collect huge numbers of
them...get whippings...for
crawling on the ground...
wearing out pants...while
shooting them...in a ring

of dirt…or walking around
all day with two pockets…
filled to burst…even the
firmest…pocket seam…I
wasn't very good…playing
the little buggers…but no
matter what…I was obsessed…
I just loved marbles…marbles…
marbles…

Sycamore Street

It seemed…as if all the white people…in Buffalo…were happy that beautiful…May day… Mr. Korlowski…who owned the nearby fruit and vegetable store…was happy… The old German…who wove baskets… all day…in the dusty…straw laden shop…downstairs …next door to us…was happy… The mailman…in striped denims …almost skipped to each mail box…he was so happy…"Yahooo…Yeah!"…was shouted loudly everywhere… Ragged …mini-parades kept streaming down…Sycamore Street… People…in their cars…were blowing horns…waving flags and crude signs…with blaring …squawking trumpets… Base drums…on the back of pickup trucks…thudded…Fists waving in the air…they came all afternoon… past Sycamore and Mortimer streets… *The war was over!… The war was over!*…I had never…in all my eight years…seen anything like it…We kids gleefully waved back…got caught up…in the spirit… and partied in the bright sun too…We hadn't been on Sycamore Street long…Sycamore was usually a whole lot quieter…a bit more residential… than Ridge Road…where we used to live…in smoky…rust-colored Lackawanna…some miles away…

Dimple…my mother…sister Gwen…brother James… and I…now happily lived with Steve…and his son…Junior…and wistful daughter… Vista…Two families had become one…sharing a one toilet…two-bedroom… upstairs…creaking floors… flat…All five of us kids…sat on the street curb …that warm Spring day…in 1945…watching excited… smiling revelers… celebrate the war's end…Funny…how the war just never meant much to us before...that day...My teacher...at School 47...had mentioned it once or twice...and then there was the time...cool...Uncle Ernest...in his bright...sailor's whites...visited us...and went to the store with us...Dimple...said Ernest...and two other brothers...sailed on big ships...and fought in the war...She said they were war heroes...Korlowski certainly thought Uncle Ernest was a hero...He let Uncle...take an apple... without even paying...It was free apples...for heroes...that day...but not for the hero's nephews...Korlowski... sternly made clear...Ernest had to pay for our apples...from the piles...and piles of apples...dozens I'm sure... in baskets...free for heroes...on the sidewalk...that day...

Most of the paraders on...*War-Over-Day*...were white people...Oh... every so often...some of those...raggedy colored kids...from Jefferson Avenue...came waltzing...and strutting by...waving somebody else's flags...as if they knew more about...the war than us...And then there was a drunk...from around on Eureka Place...stumbling along...with the procession... picking at us...Well...I knew about the war...way back in Charlotte...North Carolina...when Mama put books...around the radio light...when there was an...air raid drill...and all lights had to be turned off...We even had to do it...when we listened to...the Joe Louis fight... or just music...if it was night... But it is true...we never heard a lot about... the war before...from Steve...or Dimple...or Steve's mother...or his brothers...My grandmother Lula...never mentioned it...except when someone's son died..."overseas"...We knew the war was...mainly...a fight... between white people here...and "Germans"...and "Japs"... overseas...

That day... it sure looked like...our white people here...had won...if all those ...prancing...happy people... making noise... were right...Later I asked my teacher...if the war was over...because the President had died... a month...or so before...She said no...in her usual matter-of-fact...very decisive way...When we weren't...celebrating and watching...end-of-war parades on...Sycamore... (There would be another...smaller one that August...after a big bomb fell...but before the Buffalo earthquake...)... and when there was no school...we were usually scouring nearby neighborhoods... for newspaper...or old car batteries...most anything to sell... to old Mr. Saltzman...at the junk yard...Car batteries were prized...Just one would buy you...a half dozen donuts...usually glazed for me...until the day...I ate one before I had washed...battery acid...off my hands…I got real sick… and wouldn't eat a glazed donut…for years… until Freddy's Donuts…came along years later…

It took an equal number of years…for me to figure out…what really… made me sick…back then…on old Sycamore Street…a street where I learned a lot …about white and black…It was on Sycamore…that I think I began… what would be a…life-long study of…white people…White people…who seemed to be everywhere…always there in our midst … (or was it the other way around)…who always seemed to be in charge…who you went to…got from…gave to…measured everything by…They were… the landlord…the mailman…the principal…the store man…the police… the teacher…the junkyard man…the fireman…the people you mostly… feared…but not always…Sometimes you played…with their kids…stole their apples…or threw snow balls at their cars…Sometimes …you liked them…like Mike and Maryann…the white couple…who…while passing by…one hot August day…saw us playing on a foul… old…ratted-out couch…someone had thrown away …

There was always…junk to play on…or with…in the neighborhood… and that day…we were playing on an old …but sturdy couch…no one wanted…we thought…Well Mike and Maryann…wanted the couch…and offered us two dollars…We said a dollar… a piece…They said…O.K… even though there were…four of us…Mike did the talking… almost like a teacher…how he collected old antiques…and stuff… Maryann…tall and gaunt… just looked at us with that familiar… Oh…you…darling-little-rag-a-muffin-Negroes look…You saw that a lot from white people… in Buffalo…in 1946…We promised Mike we would watch…his couch… while he went to get a truck…to take it home…

Then it was…down the alley…up the stairs…through the back door…which was really...our front door… to show Dimple the loot…she couldn't believe…we could make…selling someone else's old junk…off the street…She wanted us to come…get her…when Mike came back…for his cruddy…old couch …In the meantime…she took control of…our four dollars…of which…we would see just 25 cents apiece…come back to us… That is…if you don't count …the beans and ham hocks…Dimple bought for supper…that day…When Mike and Maryann…and another man… came back for the couch…Dimple…in her…Oh…you- nice-white-people way... smiled at them...and agreed to let us...go visit them when Mike... restored the couch...

It wasn't long before a Saturday...after school had started again... when Mike and Maryann...came back for us...James... Gwen...Junior and me... Vista was sick again ...and didn't go...We rode in Mike's Packard...east...to a real nice house...on East Parade Street...I learned many years later... When I saw it again...I couldn't believe...that it was... that same old cruddy couch...Now it was...green and gold...and too dignified...for Sycamore Street again...As we ate Maryann's cookies... and drank lemonade...I thought...to myself...we should have asked for... two dollars...a piece...for that couch...

Later we learned Maryann...had been an army nurse...She showed us a picture...We also took pictures...and we came back...to their house once or twice more... while we were on Sycamore Street...They even took us to the zoo...and on one visit...they gave us new shirts...and pants...and a coat...and long socks for Gwen...Dimple appreciated that a lot...After a while...we lost track...of Mike and Maryann...but I remembered them... often... since... in some ways...they made up...for the many times...we got cheated...or abused by...nasty...prejudice...white people...you wanted to hate ...Remembering ...Mike and Maryann...also reminded me...to always say "some"...before the word people ...in this world...especially... white people...Back then...I guess...I already...did that... when talking... about black people...

Snow Mounds

It was the second winter and the first heavy snow.
North Carolina was gone, it was now Buffalo.

I'd seen snow in Charlotte, just a thimbleful,
But this much white stuff was simply wonderful.

After truck plows came by and made it so neat,
there they were, piled up high from the street.

The white hills, the high stacks, the snow mounds,
created for us, block after block of snowy playgrounds.

Now we could climb them, run and fall down,
tunnel through, jump across, slide just like a clown.

School and chores were boring and often hard to do,
but jumping snow mounds made you feel brand new.

Warm summer days certainly had their happy place.
Football and baseball lovers could make a strong case.

But when it came to snow mounds, forget the ball and bat.
For big city kids, like us, it didn't get any better than that.

Dimple and Steve

Dimple…comely…just twenty-eight then… was my mother… Single mother of three…one year from North Carolina…we kids were all she had…that is…if you don't count Steve… Steve…my mother's…thirty-eight year old boyfriend… was of average height … slender …with… light-brown skin…a thin…short mustache…and soft… thinning hair… on a partly balding head… He loved to dress well… drink Iroquois beer… by the quart…eat filling… Italian food…(especially spaghetti)…and laugh and joke with a loud brood of younger …beer swilling…sibling brothers… The brothers…all slender and handsome… clearly mixed-bloods…they would stand out… in a crowd of pure…beautiful …blue Africans…

They all played…some kind of musical instrument… from boogie-woogie piano…to school-band trumpet…to jungle-rhythm bongos… Every one of them… adored reminiscing and joking… about their rough and tumble days…growing up in mean…tough… Buffalo… New York… Steve's gray-haired…ambling mother…was tall and dusky…with a quiet… shuffling gait and long …bony fingers…She reminded me of…those worn-out…old-looking …cotton pickers…from somewhere down south…in a faded-old photograph…that my grandmother cherished …and kept in a tattered…blue album…from as far back as I could remember…

Steve's mother:…I loved her dumpling-greens…Steve's father… was a short… squat …beer-soaked… red-bone-of-a man…with a blaze-hot temper…and enormous pride...in his clan of five sons…and three daughters…He could easily have been mistaken… for one of the residents… on the nearby Tuscarora Indian reservation…His daughters… Steve's sisters …younger…healthier-looking… lighter-skin versions…of their mother…were stoic and… handsome too…The old man…with dancing eyes…and a polite…but always wet smile … never said much to me…I knew… however…without a word ever being spoken…that I… we…could never belong to him…

Today…as I think about it…it must have been a delicate…and very sensitive move …to introduce and seek acceptance…from your family…of a girlfriend…with three young children…while you are still married…with two kids of your own…But as far as I could tell…Steve's parents… and siblings…for the most part…accepted us…without much more… than an initial snide joke or two…about our hair…our clothes or something…that was whispered…out of hear-shot…However…they were usually kind… always eager…to feed us…and we often went with them…to cookouts or on overnight…fishing trips to Canada …On one hard luck... occasion… for a few months…we actually lived …with one of Steve's brothers…on Division Street…

Upon reflection…they were…always… close and supportive of each other…They were…indeed…a close family…I liked that about them… Dimple…my mother… (Her name was Corine…You can guess why she was nick-named Dimple…) also came from a large family…of surviving siblings…four sisters…five tough brothers… Most …if not all…were born around Lancaster…South Carolina…Most had smatterings of… grammar school…but only one…a younger sister… graduated from high school… They were all hardscrabble…farm kids…who spent…most of their childhoods'… helping their…hard working…sharecropping parents… plow hard soil…hoe rows of plantings…pick cotton…feed animals…and do other hated chores…

Dimple's mother… Lula…was fair-skinned…with soft hair and thin lips… She was strong…chiseled…and charmingly tender… a prized catch for…Lewis…my grandfather… Lewis was tall…and leather-strap strong…with a weather-worn face…a quiet firmness… and easy smile… He…shotgun in hand… would fearlessly stand up to the Klan…but get cheated …year after year…by smiling … greedy… white landowners… who owned…tough-to-farm land…he… and his brood…had to farm to survive…Years of hot…slowly simmering jealousies…and a penchant for violence…finally drove Lula away from Lewis…up to her sisters and a brother…in Buffalo…

Dimple…fresh from Charlotte…North Carolina…was separated… more than two years now…from Richard…a brave…troubled soul… who fought the ravages…of an epilepsy-like illness…all of his life…His illness…and just confusion…fueled by…fealty suspicions… destroyed their fragile marriage…after eight short years…and three surviving offspring…I was the oldest of their off-spring…exactly twenty years… and four months… younger than Dimple…Richard and Dimple…like so many other American blacks…were common people…but flawed victims…of a ruthless system of apartheid…and enforced poverty…that scarred them and…many generations after them…for life…

Steve…with two kids…(Junior and Vista) …was bitterly separated… from a wife…I only saw once…Their issues escaped us…except there seemed to be constant …explosive warfare…over custody…and possession… of Junior and Vista… When Dimple met Steve in Lackawanna… and decided to move us… (James…Gwen …and me) …to Sycamore Street …to live and share with him…he had possession of his kids…His daughter …Vista …was pretty…but shy and sickly… and just months older than me…Junior was also older… by more than a year… but…slighter and shorter than me…Both of them had similar …vacant gazes …in eyes… that softened their presence…but somehow…wedded them together…as if…they shared a dark secret… they alone knew…

Soon after we moved to…Sycamore Street…two doors from…red-bricked … Mortimer Street…on many weekends…Junior…who fleetingly resembled his father…and I…would often… accompany Steve…on junk hunting trips… Steve would borrow an old truck…or station wagon…from a brother…or someone …and go scouring for scrap iron…or copper … anything…that could be sold for…a tidy profit…Back then…in 1946… and still today… scrap metal of all sorts…commanded …good prices…

for the persistent…and resourceful hustler…Steve and his brothers…knew the scrap game well… Most of them… (Steve excluded)…had eight-hour… day-jobs of some sort…but they also… "scrapped"…for junk…whenever they could…I think they deliciously …loved scrapping… almost as much as…they loved fishing… I was told their dad taught them all to fish…I often wondered…if he had also taught them…about scrapping too…

While Steve would do…almost any kind of work…wash cars… shovel snow all day…he loved the freedom…and adventure of metal scrapping… We all called it scrapping …but after one late…moonlit night…I told… Dimple …the next day…that I thought we were…really stealing …I told her how…Steve cut through a fence…at a factory site in south Buffalo… and boldly spirited away…an enormous piece of steel pipe…that Junior and I… struggled…to helped him load…into an old…rusty green van… That pipe…along with a few other smaller pieces…brought Steve…a wide grin… and a fist full of dollars …when we dropped it off at a scrap yard the next morning…

There were other times too …many times…I told her… My story didn't seem to terribly disturb …Dimple…too much…but later I heard her quietly asking Steve…about the episode … Nothing became of their exchange…as Steve shrugged it off and…as he had done…so many times before…playfully grabbed…and nibbled at Dimple's…neck and ear…while he whispered something…and wrestled her to his lap…in the nearest chair…I could see that Steve…unlike me…could get away… with any story…he told Dimple…She clearly… unashamedly…cared a lot for Steve…Maybe even more… than she ever cared for Richard…my father…I often thought…

After a while…on Sycamore…the two families …meshed fairly well… Dimple continued to do day work…when she could…and Steve was the steady hustler…who kept his distance…yet stayed…darkly slick…Still he was also likeable…in some ways… Dimple …early on…set up the rules on discipline…If necessary …Steve would discipline his kids… and she would discipline us…We kids got along because …in spite of being younger …our… (Gwen…James…and me)… natural aggressiveness …and my size… dominated Junior and Vista…

We kids went to School No. 47 then…our principle…and maybe only… source of academic stimulation and encouragement…Some evenings I showed Junior ...how to draw and make crude cartoons...For added emphasis...I loved to write captions ...beneath the cartoons...Junior loved to show off his... drum-less... drumming ability...with two fingers on the edge of a table...He reminded me of my cousin...Libby ...who used to always pretend she was playing a piano...on the top of a dresser...a table...anything flat...God...she looked silly...

Thinking back...I remember that...almost immediately ...I sort of felt sorry for Junior and Vista...but I didn't know why ...There was just a kind of sadness about them...Although friendly and respectful... understandably... they weren't especially...loving toward us...and except for her biscuits... I don't think they ever...really took to Dimple... Still...I wanted to protect them...Dimple did too...Though I wasn't the oldest...I felt as if I was the protector...for all the kids...I guess I was still doing what Richard asked me to do...before he left back in Charlotte ..."Be the man of the house ...take care of the little ones"...

We...and Steve's kids...weren't together for more than a year or so... but for years... long after Steve was just...a painful memory...long after a quiet...sad parting...I remembered ...and often thought about Junior and Vista... Steve and Dimple would be together...off and on...for nearly five years...While there were some calm and amusing times...for many reasons...the relationship was stormy and...a...great deal more "off" then on...Because of Steve's baseless jealousies... fiery temper... a beer-driven combativeness ...and...an always-back-in-your-face challenge from Dimple ... they fought a lot... Sometimes it scared us...but it never got seriously deadly...

It was...however... always puzzling to me...It seemed...despite his meanness...and his size...Steve always wound up on the short end of a fight... Firmly confronted....and challenged back...he was easily intimidated...and especially so when Gwen... James...and I...fiercely determined...weapons in hand...like Gulliver's Lilliputians...threatened to join in the fray against him...Dimple might occasionally wear a black eye...and have to sew up a dress...but she never lost a fight...and I can't... remember Steve...ever rough touching one of her kids...

There was a "not-my-kids"...Dimple's principle...and very firm rule for Steve... Still it was not always... acrimonious between Dimple and Steve... Most of the time...they genuinely enjoyed...being with each other...They were a fight-one-minute...kiss-the- next... couple...It was hard to break the attention...the radar beam...between them...To Dimple... Steve was sort of a new...sophisticated northerner...with an infectious sexuality ...she had not known before ...He liked food that was new for her...He enjoyed things like...all-night bass...or cat fishing...from the Canadian side...of the Niagara River...or hammering out...an almost professional-level ...boogie-woogie...on a piano... Steve adored Dimple...mainly because...he knew he was always on stage with her...He liked her fascination with him...and he liked her fight-back spunk...since he knew...he was usually wrong...and deserved to be checked...I felt that he knew his inner demons ...wanted him punished...for his many sins... and he hoped... that punishment... from wherever it came... would free him...of those haunting demons...

In the five or so years...Steve and Dimple... tried to be a family... sometimes the dollars...got thin and we moved often...from rooming house to boarding house...Like gypsies...we would be at a place...as short as three months ...or as long as a couple of years...It seemed as if...there were always half emptied containers... wooden...window seal cooling boxes...and new kids to get to know...At times...Steve drank too much... and struggled with phantom jealousies...and again...those real...inner demons... Dimple... struggled with her weaknesses... mainly for Steve... and the constant adjustments...necessary to share so many kitchens...so many toilets...with so many strangers...

During that time...my morale roller-coasted...and my opinion of Steve...hit an irretrievable rock bottom...Once...in a family brawl...on Clinton Street...Steve...wielding a razor...from his pocket...seriously slashed the wrist...of one of Dimple's sisters...Later... in Lackawanna... Steve was beaten senselessly...with the top from a garbage can...by one of my uncles...and ...in the worst of bad...we kids...accidentally...discovered that he had been ...sexually molesting his daughter Vista...for years...

No one ever turned him in to authorities ...but Steve's wife reclaimed her kids...after the molesting came to light...After each of those episodes ...Dimple moved us away from Steve...for a brief period... but she always... inexplicably... incredibly...somehow found a way to forgive him...one more time ... Me?...I grew to genuinely... hate the man...and after one of his violent flare-ups...I cursed...and swore to him... that one day...when I could...at my first opportunity...I would repeat the beating he got…from my uncle…He looked at me ominously…but said nothing …and just walked away…

Some years later…after Dimple and Steve had finally parted completely…he saw me…now more than six feet tall…walking toward him on William Street…He quickly crossed the street…and abruptly disappeared through a doorway…It would be the last time I would ever see him…Ten years after their final parting…long after I became a grown man… long after we heard that Vista and her mother…had moved to Oregon…and long after Junior's arrest for molesting…an eight-year old school girl in a school yard…Steve was killed… crushed to death…in an industrial accident…where he worked…

A short time after that…in a quiet moment…when I visited her…I asked Dimple… if she was sorry…to hear of his death…She admitted that she was…and that Steve… regrettably …was the only man she ever really loved…I think I knew all along…that she loved him…Yet I never clearly understood why… until I heard her soft words… resolutely say to me…"I just loved him…I don't know why…It's as simple as that"… It would be the first…and last time.. I would ever hear her say that about a man…any man…

She Taught Me Many Things

She taught me many things,
the obvious that any mother would,
but also the not so obvious….She
taught me how:
to change a baby's diaper,
  to build and tend a wood fire,
  to light a kerosene lamp in the wind,
  to comb braids in a little one's hair,
  to wash clothes on a wash board,
  to iron white sheets and pillow cases,
  to iron a heavily-starched, white shirt,
  to bake six or more kinds of cake,
  to shop for food at the best price,
  to sing hymns in a dozen churches,

to be wary of dark and shady people,
to fight a bully with all your might,
to believe in your own strength,
to pray when all hope is almost gone.

But the greatest lesson she taught me,
she did so without knowing...without
intending that it be passed as it was. By
observing her every being, I learned that,
whatever we are born with, whatever we
learn afterward, most of life's pain starts
with our own choices and it is the sum
total of what we are, when we choose,
that can make a difference...in our lives.

they eat the children

every gathering...every family has one
at least one...whether they know it or not...

he is the dark one...the throw back...
to a time of misty...semi-consciousness...

when amorality reigned...when the
defenseless could be easily subdued ...

when lust and cannibalism mimicked
breathing...and females...like pride

lionesses...watching a trapped orphan...
from another pride...joined the pride's feast...

stamp as hard as we might...collectively
the ugly gene still insists on living...just

like the dreaded vampires of darkness...rising
from hell...to suck the innocents' blood...

all to create another monster in our midst...
where are you god?...oh!...where are you?

Little Sister Ruth

Ruth, was in high school when I was just eight.
She was my mother's pretty, gray-eyed, little sister.
Tall, fair of skin, plump, with a slight, knock-kneed gait.
with mutual respect, my mother Dimple, adored her.

In her sad, third year at old Lackawanna high,
Ruth's mother, my grandmother, closed her eyes forever.
Left with a brother whom she couldn't see eye to eye,
she soon left home and school, to start a brand new chapter.

Hip, street-wise, she worked in restaurants and bars.
With good looks and cool humor she began to draw men,
some hard-working and simple, others slick with big cars.
We watched her quickly mature, as she visited us often.

When Ruth visited us, sometimes we played games.
Dimple, would cook something special she knew Ruth liked.
Often Ruth'd bring a friend named, Phil, John or James,
or let us kids share her drink, she knew was strongly spiked.

Once Ruth said to Dimple, that Billy's as cute as a girl.
Why don't we put a dress on him and take him along with us.
Some dancing flirt'll never know and want to take him for a whirl.
My mother said, "Girl, we can't do that, the boy will put up a fuss."

They asked me if I was willing and if I would be up for it.
Would I wear heels, put on lipstick and play the game along.

I said O.K., if I don't have to dance and can just look and sit,
and by the way, there was no way, I'd agree to sing any song.

So there I was, in heels, prissy and fancy and all gussied up,
Looking, to my surprise, just like a pretty, young, dressed up lady.
In a nearby bar we sat at a table with ginger ale in my cup.
while Dimple and Ruth, danced with men who looked pretty shady.

Then it happened, what I absolutely, dreaded most.
Men, young and old, started coming up to talk to me.
Even though they protected me and played the role of host,
the two still, enjoyed watching the squirms of their little he/she.

There I sat, twisting and resisting for two, long hours straight,
trying hard to keep the whiskey breaths away from my little knee.
While my two protectors laughed and partied, I just couldn't wait,
to get out of there and get rid of that disgusting misery.

For years now, all who hear the story can't help but laugh at me,
as they poke fun and ask, if I still wear heels and a fancy dress.
I guess they think they're being clever, or some other kind of funny.
Well I see nothing funny in what was for me, a painful, stressful mess.

Little Dark Boy

I envy you, happy little white boy.
You don't have to deal with color issues.
Because you're colorless, you can take joy,
in not having to stand or walk in my shoes.

One day I'm colored, the next day I'm black.
Some call me African and I used to be a Negro.
If you ask me, there is one big thing I lack,
one name for myself, just so I'll know.

Why we even got schisms amongst our own selves.
There's that white, black, brown and yellow thing,
where skin hue gets you placed on ascending shelves,
and the lightest, light-skin can make you the King.

We're sure messed up people, as you can see,
with good or bad, Ol' curly or nappy hair.
This peculiar story probably goes back to slavery.
Yup! That Ol' slave master started the whole affair.

You see, white people think dark is evil or bad.
They, with our help, define standards of our beauty.
Unfortunately, when you think about it, it's all really sad.
I sure hope I can soon learn to love and just accept me.

Going to Church

The Church was rocking...spirit...sound and joy smothered...and filled the small... converted ...two bedroom house... Little John pounded and thumped away on the Upright... *"This little light of mine...I'm going to let it shine"*...lifted up and out...soaring through the Pine Street neighborhood... The small congregation sang harmoniously... swayed ... clapped and paid homage...Everything was in rhythm...It wouldn't be long now...Soon the visuals... the sounds...the excitement would blend into...what everyone there...came for...that magical moment...when the Bishop...Bishop DeForest... serene and deliberate ... would step through a blue...silk draped doorway...white robe swirling...ready to cast his blessed... wonderful spell...

Dimple...my Mother...my siblings James...Gwen... and I were there... Aunt Janie Curry...Cousin Ruby Curry... and Sissy Curry were there...We faithful joined the two dozen or so others in worship...on that cool fall...Wednesday evening...on the near... eastside...of Buffalo... New York... Sitting there...with the faint scent of fried chicken ...from the good Bishop's earlier supper...we absorbed the smells...the sights... the sounds of worship that evening...To me...it seemed as if...we had just been there yesterday...or was it last Sunday...Church days back then... seemed to merge and come...oh so quickly...

The sameness of the moments...when you went there...sometimes invited fleeting...but momentary boredom... But we were really devoted... and went to Church a lot...especially Dimple...my mother... and Aunt Janie...They loved to worship God and Jesus...at least twice a week ...sometimes more...if there were special celebrations ...like a holy day...or the Bishop's birthday...Dimple and Aunt Janie...especially... liked the wonderful preaching of the tall...handsome Bishop DeForest... He could sing and shout better than anybody...in any church they'd ever been to...and if you listened...and watched closely ...you might also hear or get a clue for a 3-digit number...to play on the numbers... the next day...

For example...he might say...that Sampson swung three times...at seven Philistines ...in the valley of eight ghosts...and lo' and behold...there you have it...3-7-8...tomorrow's 3-digit number to play...Obviously...you had to pay attention...and keep a pencil handy... Aunt Janie...in reality Dimple's aunt...played the numbers every day...She also read tea leaves... and dream books...for precious clues...on what could be a winning... 3-digit number ...All of my relatives in Church that night...Cousin Ruby and Aunt Janie...who married the Curry brothers...and Sissy... the oldest of them all...(an original Curry)... all played the numbers... hoping to strike it rich one day... Sissy was also the most spiritual...and the funniest...She liked to tell you to..."go kick a brick" ...if you ever annoyed her...

All of my relatives there that night...except Dimple...swore they had hit the numbers ...from some clue...or reference... received from the good Bishop... But that was not the only reason... they were devoted members ...of New Shining Light Tabernacle Church of God in Christ ...The real reason was...the incomparable ...the irresistible... Bishop John Devereaux DeForest...the third...

Bishop DeForest...now he was something...when he stepped through the blue curtain... that separated the kitchen from the sanctuary... He was tall... mustached... goateed...athletic and darkly handsome...Moving gracefully...he looked like an exotic Arab...in his white... silk robe... and pearl-wrapped turban... Little John...the Assistant Pastor...pianist...

and choir master...wore a turban too... I never saw him in a robe... just brown suits and brown or black turbans...The smooth-faced... and delicate Little John... and the Bishop...were very close... They lived in the quarters upstairs...over the Church...I liked them a lot...They spoke softly...good English...and they seemed so kind and caring...They always smelled "good" too...You could understand why Church members...liked hugging... and being hugged...by them...

When we kids went to help clean up the Church on Saturdays... the Bishop and Little John...always had sandwiches ...and something for us to drink... Sometimes they would give us dimes...or quarters...or let us tinkle on the Upright...Dimple and Aunt Janie told us... never go upstairs where they lived...when we went there to work...They said...we only had to clean the Church downstairs...

Most of the time...at the Tabernacle...there were just women... Occasionally... old men... like Uncle Ernest King...my Aunt Daisy's companion...or Mr. Sonny would come ...Janie McGee...another aunt... or other relatives sometimes went to Church with us...They too... like Dimple and Aunt Janie...loved to hear the Bishop sing and preach...It all but seemed as if...he could cast a spell on anybody...who went there... Women especially ... would shake and shudder when he roared..."J-e-e-e-s-u-s!"... Sometimes they got "happy" ...and shouted ...and danced ...and cried...or laughed...It seemed the more Bishop DeForest shouted ...the more happy the women got... and that's what "good church" was...to the women members back then...

After going to Church so much...to me...the service got to be very predictable...I came to know...which songs would make Dimple happy... what sermon would get Mother Jones worked up to... "testify"... You learned that...a low moan from Bishop DeForest ...and a high-pitched... "Lord-have-mercy"...from Pastor Little John...would make Sissy Curry jump out of her seat...neatly avoiding...brown folding chairs...sprint to a spot...any open spot...and just spin like a top...The men had to watch her...if she got too close...to the hot stove...in the middle of the sanctuary...

Often-times...it was hard for us kids...not to laugh at the mesmerizing show... especially if Bobby Curry...and James...started mimicking getting... "happy"...as if they too...had gotten the spirit...If we got noticed cutting up... Dimple...would end all of our shenanigans...with a sharp…cutting glare…that promised painful retribution when we got back home…

From back then…down through the years…until I was nearly thirteen… Dimple made us go to more than a few churches…where the singing and preaching…soared to the rafters… For various reasons…I liked going to some churches more than others… There was Saint John's…Pilgrim Baptist…Tired Stone …Friendship …Calvary… Michigan Avenue and… Church of God in Christ…They all had wonderful singing…and roaring preachers …Gwen and Libby…and Aunt Lula…and Pat…and Hilda… all loved going to Mount Olive Baptist… in Lackawanna …I think they were all…kind of…in love with the Pastor… Reverend Watson… another pretty good moaner…Some of the kids even got baptized there…Not me!…I wasn't going for none of that "foolishness"…water and dipping… and praying stuff…

Dimple said…that was my problem…She said to me…"You just don't believe in anything …do you?"…After a shrug…what could I say?…I didn't know it then…but looking back…I was just a natural-born skeptic… Somehow…I could see through what I thought were elaborate cons… by clever hucksters…who played a faith-game as old as slavery… Through the years…some pretty good…heavyweight believers…took runs at my skepticism… My mother…Dimple …Janie McGee …Daddy Grace…a half dozen…lesser known ministers and preachers…and saviors…and my dearest… Aunt Miss…They all came at me…to convince me…to somehow make me believe in their miracle…believe in their wonderful truth…

Aunt Miss…was really my great-aunt…She was my Grandmother's sister…Short…rotund…and very fair…she and her very…dignified…very steady husband …Earl… (Uncle Billy)…were childless… (Long years later it came to light that Uncle Billy actually had a son… from his wild-oats days…that lived somewhere in North Carolina.)… From adolescence to well into my teens…most Saturday mornings…I ran errands and… shopped for groceries…at Kulick's…on William Street… for Uncle Billy and Aunt Miss… They became attached to me…concerned for my well-being…and from Aunt Miss…a special concern for my spiritual well-being…

Aunt Miss…a deeply devoted Jehovah's Witness…tried as hard as she could…to save my soul…to affect my conversion …to save my soul from the hell of non-belief...Try as she might...it just never happened ...But I never resented her efforts...or lost respect...or loved her less for her sincere beliefs...for her faith... For that matter... all my life I never questioned any human's harmless... loving faith...I accepted all faiths... as potentially ...the comforting refuge for all of us... However...I was... and still am...suspicious of one's faith... when it proclaims possession of the ultimate... and only truth...and they will kill you to prove it...

Later...I would...on my own...read and study all kinds of religions...attend all kinds of churches... mosques...and temples...to learn...to sing...to pray...to enjoy the pageantry ...But even though I liked...and respected most religions...I remained deeply skeptical... and suspicious of the kind givers...the interpreters...the professionals... the self- anointed... intermediaries between me and God...To this day...I remain the skeptic...the doubter...the suspicious... Skepticism aside...however...I think I was... nevertheless... profoundly colored and influenced...by all the professed revelations ...and all the very human sincerity...of the true believers all around me... Many of those believers tried to convert me... Most of them however... just finally gave up... and let me believe...what I believed... But in the process... because of who they were...and my quiet respect for them... without realizing it... they did help me to understand that...even reason...in full blown command... has its limits too...

The God Gene

Humans want and need a Lord...
It is truly... as if they had a God gene...
right there with all the rest...They mostly...
instinctively...yearn to be ruled...To have a
king...or a leader...a benevolent father...or
for some...perhaps a mother...Surely the God
gene...is the most primitive...and ancient of all
our genes...It could almost be called...the Silver
Back gene...We all want to...and need to defer...
to the great Silver Back...whether he exist down

here among us...or in some imagined...heaven...
or green paradise...we...so long and yearn for...
Desperately...we will even anoint some among
us... as emissaries...from the great one...then
confer upon them...extraordinary powers...to
punish or beseech us...to obey...to touch a real
effect...to try to understand...and be at peace
with...the most illogical...of all our genes...

Without Faith

Do not
believe in
God until
you see
God...and
know it...

Likewise...do
not deny
the existence
of God ...
until you
know that too!....

Those Believers

Be wary of faith, you mighty believers.
Faith has two edges, both razor sharp.

One edge cuts softly, peacefully, quietly inward.
The other cuts raw, dogmatic, violent and defensive.

One edge will encourage love and generosity.
The other will proselytize and wield the sword.

One will ask God to admit the unbelievers. The
other will ask her, to slay them, cast them out.

Whichever the edge, one thing is certain, if it is
God's word, it came from a man…yes a man.

Is that man, any man, bigger, greater than you?
I think not you faithful believers, I think not.

Faith

The shallowest people I have ever met…are
the rigid ones…who are absolutely… convinced…

that they are…right…correct…beyond the slightest
doubt…that they are…imbued with a righteousness…

that leaves…no doubt about…the veracity of their
beliefs… They are steel on copper…hard… They are

convinced …that they have the…truth…and that they
have the…miracle of life…and deeds…and scripture

to…support it… Most thinking people …would call them…
fanatics…and the cheap price…for being a fanatic…is

simply…submission… However…fanaticism…comes in
muted…degrees…shades of purple…and it is not always…

easy to detect… A challenge to a fanatic's belief notions…
always becomes a challenge…to their faith…A fiery red…

challenge to their devotion...and creed...is hard to argue
with...just as it is...hard to argue...with the will...of a

faithful...human being... who leaps from ...a ten story
building...fully believing...he or she...can fly away...to

Heaven!...

Faith can be...positive...inspirational...It can also...be
the...refuge for unthinking people who...refuse to reason...

or question...the source of...their faith... Faith can also
be the...answer...for weak...timid...or lazy minds...who

are always...looking for an easy way out...a cheap answer...to
all that troubles them...all that keeps them...from happiness...

as they define it... Make no mistake...faith can be a powerful
elixir...for the searcher...who finds it...It can help the...most

faithful...to gain powerful advantage...to proselytize...even
prevail over large...populations of mankind... But I would urge

the faithful...to avoid being...so full of faith...that you cannot
challenge...your faith...For faith is a choice...among many

choices...none of which commands...absolute truth... Even
the sun...may not rise...one morning... To avoid stupidity...

do not always trust your brain...or your heart...to give you...
absolute truth... To question is to keep you... open...and mentally

flexible... That should be enough...to sustain you...through the...
worst and...the best...of your life...in spite of your

Faith!...

The School Yard Fight

Leading up to...the fight...the pre-fight ritual dance...had spilled over...from the School 32 playground...past the steps of Technical High School...across Bennett Street...past the Arthur's house...where George lived...to the little park...at Clinton and Pine Streets... This great showdown...was going to happen here...not at all by special design...it was just on the way home...It would happen not far from...the park's care taker building... where you usually found...dear Mrs. Freeman...keeping order... knitting...or just listening to the stories we kids told...It was the same park...the nearly all white...Tech High kids...used as an... outdoor gym...when the weather was decent...It was also my neighborhood... where we played baseball...and tennis...with bare hands...phantom nets... and small- face... wooden racquets...someone threw away...It was where we lived on the second floor...of an old...red brick...apartment building across from the park...upstairs... over Sonny and Stella's small store...

The fight combatants... angling to get it on that afternoon...were a tough little... cocksure bully... named Charles...and a skinny... nervous... but game me...Charles was popular...with a lot of kids at school 32...Almost two years older...and a grade ahead of me...he was sturdier... taller...and maybe...some thought...better looking than me...I had watched him...a couple of times...destroy other kids...who bucked-up to him...He was fearless...and usually got his way on the playground... Me?...I could usually hold my own... with most kids...but would always look for a way...to avoid a fight if I could...Look good ...turn your collar up...be a smart student... win the girls...that was my game most of the time...

Fighting wasn't for me...but unfortunately...and to my surprise...I had turned the eye...of a mutual favorite...and Charles was upset with me...But the fight... wasn't about a girl...No self-respecting...grammar-schooler... with a pair of shades...in his shirt pocket ...on the east side...of Buffalo... New York...in the mid 1940's... would be caught dead ...fighting over a girl...of all things...The fight...this day...was about "honor"...whose...for the life of me...I cannot remember...I just remember that the squabble... had been building for days...I had received signals ...and I had tried my customary diplomacy...In school...when Charles was near...I had... assiduously avoided my usual...peacock-like...courting rituals...with the young lady of our mutual interest...I had even picked him...to be on my team in dodge ball...but nothing I did worked...I really wasn't angry with him...but this kid...clearly ...couldn't stand me...

Earlier ...that fight day...we had physically bumped into...each other... without apology... but with equally sharp glares...of threatening contempt... Sensing the inevitable...I decided to try to weaken his confidence...so I let the word out...to the surest snitch in school...that I was ready for Charles and would..."kick his butt any time ...any place...any day"... Now the bell had rung...school had let out...and we...Charles and me... walking together...had threatened... pushed and shoved each other...for two blocks... Soon ... there in the little park...with my nervous stomach... and dry mouth...at the risk of disturbing...all the homeless vagrants...who slept under bushes in the park...and at the risk of ...upsetting the health workers...from the nearby... Emergency Hospital...we had to get it on... The weather was beautiful ...there was no excuse now...the scuffle was on...

In a cloud of dust...and grit...we came together...It wasn't pretty... Punching... grabbing... tearing at clothes...we flailed away...at each other...We were egged on by the small... encircling crowd of excited... yelling...and yapping kids... as curious onlookers ...and passersby... wondered ...what the fuss was all about...Wrestling...sweating and snarling... we traded blows and...tried to throw each other...The longer the fight went...the less nervous...and more bolder I got...I took...a few telling blows...and could taste... blood:...my own...

But I felt the tide was...turning my way...when my knee...found Charles' stomach ...and he groaned...and went down...on one knee...He struggled to get up...as I pounded away... girly... windmill style...Just as he finally scrambled ....back up on his feet...a streak of blur...came up from behind me... flew by me...and swung at Charles...I was startled... for a moment...I turned...I focused and looked...It was Gwen ...my fierce ...fearless little sister ... wielding a little...short stick...of some kind... yelling..."You leave my brother alone... you bastard" ...The crowd howled and swayed ... Wide-eyed Charles backed away... with a whoaa!... and a...I'm-surrounded-by-Indians look ...I grabbed Gwen... and held her back...as she shook... and waved the stick at Charles... threatening more... where that came from...

Well that...was the end of the fight...No whirlwind posse came to help him...No brave Charles-admirers...stepped forward...so Charles was beaten...and wanted nothing but out of there...As for me... while I was...to say...somewhat embarrassed...I was relieved ...and glad too ... I mumbled something to Gwen...about why she shouldn't have done that...that I had it under control...and that tough little sisters... shouldn't interfere...in their big brother's fights...stuff like that...As the crowd... from school quickly dispersed...I hoped the next day...they wouldn't say...I needed my little sister to help me handle Charles... After all... handling Charles...could help make you...a pretty big man...in the old school playground...I also hoped no one...would tell...you-know-who... that my little sister had to help me subdue Charles...Darn that Gwen!... Darn her meddling...I thought to myself...

As we grew up...down through the years...we often laughed...about "the fight"...And I was always reminded that there were other times... when "battling Gwen" and I...and my younger brother...James... and my Mother...would take them on...Like the time...all of us ...pots and broomsticks in hand...hemmed up...Mr. John Johnson...my Aunt's "woman- beater" mate... out on... Bradford Street...near the old refinery... The bald-headed bastard... changed his mind quickly... about bullying my Aunt...that day...And there were...more than a few times... when we took on...Steve ...my Mother's jealous...coward-hearted boyfriend ... and as my Mother used to say..."put a knot on his head too"...Funny... how it is when you stick together...like Mama said...you can back up a lot of would-be-tough bullies ... looking for a fight...

Fourth Grade Humor

Trust me...I tried not to be cruel...
I tried to remember...the Sunday
School lessons...the admonishments
to never make fun...of another's
misfortune...to be kind...helpful...
not destructive of spirit...In the
fourth grade...I tried...but failed...

I couldn't help it...I laughed at
Kermit for two days...You see
Kermit was fat...He was not only
the largest kid...in the fourth grade
...he may have been...the largest
kid in all of School 31...Kermit
was in my swimming class...an
integrated...mosaic of...black...
brown...and white kids...We were
also a mixed quilt...of all sizes...
short...tall...fat...thin...straight...
bent...We had no clue about our
covered...less obvious differences...
until swimming lessons...in the
nude...Clothes off...the warts...rises
...scars...flat feet...pigeon-toes...
fat rolls...and shriveled protrusions...
stood out...testifying loudly to our
diversity...also...by the way...
confirming our sameness...At the
first lesson...our squeamishness...
and naked shyness was obvious...
We made jokes...asked where
were the girls...I...in fact protested
their absence...and just poked and
laughed at foibles a-plenty...as
we looked...compared...measured...
It was at the second lesson...that
poor old...Kermit...took the full
brunt...of our fourth grade humor...
A little devil-of-a kid...named
David...presented Kermit with a
two-foot long baton...with a small
mirror on one end...so Kermit...
could..."finally see what his penis
looked like"...The class cracked

up…for days…it seemed…Poor
Kermit…hurt at first…soon
laughed too…took it in stride…
and quietly swore to a regimen…
that would…by the middle of
high school…win him his first…
body building contest…David…
lost swimming class privileges…
the next week…and me…I am
still remembering…and I am
still laughing…and laughing…
and…

young beasts

even the children can be beasts…

before more than a dozen years here…

they can perfectly mimic the violence…

we teach them…or on their own, succumb

to that dark gene...humans have known

since time began for them…jeering…

mocking cruelty is how it begins…

contagion feeds its path…running

in packs of like-minded thieves…yes…

even rape becomes a man-sport for them…

and so on…and so on…and so on…but

dare not… don't expect it to just go away…

there is no religion…no constitution that can

save us… could it be that it all begins with us…

all of us?…i think so… i think so…i think so…

blues songs

blues songs from just a babe

are we there yet?

the sun will know and tell us so

then birds will eat only raw carrion

rocking chairs will no longer rock

a centipede's segment will lose a pair of legs

locusts will never be sweet again

the sun has spoken… we missed it

we are there now

Errol Flynn

As was our custom…buddies…Bobby…James..
and me…eleven…seven…and ten…wise men…
shine boxes in the closet now…show money

was made Saturday...This was Sunday...after
the picture shows...We had done the Academy...
the Keith...and the smelly Hippodrome...two rounds....

each of Gene Autry...Errol Flynn...and James Cagney...
Tired of stale popcorn...and stretched-thin sodas...in
a warm evening...we walked down quiet Main...to

Division Street...east...straight away to lively...but
humming Michigan Avenue...After 9 hours in movie
show darkness...the real night sky...with stars...was

fast approaching...So was the witching hour...to
be home by...screamed at us before we left...273
Clinton Street...earlier that day...That day we didn't

have to go to some damned hot Church...with poor
pitiful fools...praying to heaven...to lift us...to save us...
At Eagle Street...before the Sugar Bowl Delicatessen...

or the Club Moon Glo...Flashing police cruiser lights
startled us...There were three...One blocking the
sidewalk...fancy a big...crouched...hungry panther...

which had cornered its prey...Headlights lit the
scene...of a tall Negro...wielding a menacing
pool stick...outside of the glass fronted...crowded

pool hall...that I had also hoped to play in...one
day...Six drawn guns...and six black nightsticks...
challenged back...The husky Negro yelled...

"I didn't start no fight...why should I go to jail?"
...In a way...he reminded us of Errol Flynn...
in an exotic land...wielding a sword...before the

evil King's dirty...villainous guards...keeping
him from his love...the King's beautiful daughter...
who had begged to be kissed...Quietly we joined the

handful of lookers...across the street from the standoff...
The growing whine of another panther...grew louder and
louder...in the Summer twilight...Someone muttered...

"honky bastards"..."Drop the stick!"...yelled...
the Gang of Six...Tense moments...glares...then
the frightened eyes of the Negro...slowly softened...

He dropped the sword...As five of the King's
white guards rushed in...One was grabbed by Errol
Flynn... the sturdy one...and hurled through one of

the large beckoning windows...Four others pounced...
clubs and .38's swinging...Howling...yelling...choking
...swearing...cursing...bloodily they fought to subdue

Errol Flynn...One of the King's guards...pointed his
.38 at us...the un-approving onlookers... "Get back...
get back I said!"...yelled the occupier...with the gun...

from another neighborhood...from some other foreign
land...Beaten...stomped...and kicked to a glass-strewn
sidewalk...they dragged Errol Flynn to one of the

big cats...just as another panther screeched up to
a sudden stop...Semi-conscious...with bleeding...and
swollen eyes...Errol Flynn was trundled into the back of...

one of the panthers...by the King's heroes...They helped
the wounded guard to his feet...As they drove away...we
could see Errol Flynn...still kicking and screaming in

the back of the big cat... Making our way down Clinton...
to 273...We hoped we had enough bread...and mustard
to make baloney sandwiches...when we get there...

Then Bobby asked..."Do you think they killed him?"...
James...the youngest...answered..."Probably!"...I
said softly..."I hope not...dirty bastards...I hope not"...

Ghetto Kids

Ghetto kids grow up fast...real fast...
There ain't nothing they don't know...
There aren't many things people do
that they haven't seen...by age 12...
They instinctively know if you
care or are a phony...They watch and
see... everything...and everybody...
and most are grown...way beyond
their years...before they are 10...
Most...are senior citizens by age 20...
Too many are dead...before they are 40...

Bristol Street

Our Bristol Street...with its quaint...old...cobbled red bricks...a mix of aged...small gray bungalows...two story double-toned flats...and mostly brown faces...was just one city block long...Oh...there was another Bristol Street...over between...Emslie and Lord Streets ....but it wasn't like our Bristol Street...which ran between... Spring and Jefferson ...just one block north of Clinton Street...on the near east side of Buffalo...New York...

Our Bristol Street...in the late '40's...and '50's was also more than a typical...big city...mostly black people's enclave...It was more than just a place to live...a place to grow up...It was a unique experience...in a childhood of many neighborhoods...of many memories ...of many experiences...You couldn't just live…on Bristol Street…you had to become a part of it… to interact with it…blend in…like the iron railing…yard fences…the voices…the dust…the smells and sounds…all that was of Bristol Street…

12 Bristol Street …just a few doors from Spring Street…was a single family…3-bedroom bungalow…with a large fourth bedroom…in a half-finished attic…reached by a narrow stairway off the kitchen…Dimple…my single Mother…with three children…had recently separated from Steve…her erratic boyfriend…whom we previously lived with…12 Bristol was now our…newly rented space …in my mother's flight….to escape from a trying relationship… That relationship…was one that saw periodic separations…between two people…tragically in love with each other…but who were never able to overcome the holes …and missing threads …that are so necessary for a stable…and lasting pairing… Bristol Street was the next to last time… Dimple would try to get on with our lives…without Steve…the man she loved… almost as much as us… Yet Steve was a man I hated…and despised…and I was glad he did not live with us on Bristol…

At 12 Bristol…in the beginning…three families shared rooms…in the one bathroom …living space…until Trannie…and her two daughters…moved away…Prior to Trannie leaving…three months after we moved in… my sister Gwen and…Dimple…shared a small bedroom…while my younger brother James…and I…slept on a couch-bed…in a small…open room…between the living room…and the dining room…After Trannie left…we kids…moved to the large upstairs bedroom…she vacated…a much more comfortable…and private arrangement…for James and me…

The other family consisted of "Scrap"…whose real name was Martha…her sister Granny (Louise)…and Granny's daughter…Delores…For a lot of reasons…I always doubted that Granny and Scrap…were sisters by blood…but instead had chosen to be sisters for whatever their reasons…Both "sisters" in their early sixties…had been together for years… …Just months after we moved there…Delores …who was single…gave birth to…a little girl…Judy…Judy's father… Delores' married boyfriend…came around every so often…but even when he sheepishly came by…he really wasn't there…

In spite of the…sometimes…cramped living…the two families got along quite well… Bristol Street was the sixth house…we had lived in…since arriving from Charlotte…North Carolina …some years earlier…By then…we Bailey's…had learned how to share a kitchen …or a bathroom… how to stay out of the way…and how to be good "roomers"…with the two aging sisters…Delores…and the baby Judy…Unlike some other places… we had lived in… since arriving in Buffalo…Bristol was the easiest for us… almost like a real home…

The two families supported each other too…sometimes even sharing food…almost as if we were one family…It was impossible to cook… create smells…or visual impressions… without affecting every nose or eye…within distance…All of the women…loved to cook large pots of beans…stews…greens…foods that reeked up the neighborhood…but also filled many hungry bellies…On holidays…we chipped in to make large celebratory meals…that we kids loved …This was a big help for us…since for months…at a time…the Bailey's only income…was a monthly welfare check…or the few hustle dollars I could I could scrape up… shining shoes… or whatever…Welfare temporarily became necessary…when Dimple had to have a serious operation…and couldn't work for months…

Adding to the sense of family…we naturally commented on clothes… laughed at goof- ups…we all made from time to time…and watched the 12- inch TV…our first…Scrap brought home one day.….We kids…ran errands…carried delivered piles of coal into a rear storage room… and… on cool days…kept a fire going in a huge…pot-bellied stove in the parlor… We helped clean windows…baby sat…and I felt….brought a sense of security…to a house without a grown male…on the premises…

It was easy to like the three women…and little Judy… Delores…in particular…with a slow shuffling gait…and an elongated speech pattern… endeared herself to Gwen and me… the very first week we were there…At that time…I was a sixth-grade student…still attending School 31…a few miles away…on Sherman Street…Once again…I had gotten into a school yard tussle…over a young girl…at School 31…After my fist…got the best of a young rival…he rounded up a small gang of seven…to seek out revenge…

That gang of seven…followed Gwen and me…all the way from School 31…to Bristol Street…considerably more than just a few miles…threatening to do us bodily harm…Along the way…they were held at bay…by two ugly ...but handy…sticks of wood…wielded by Gwen and me…When the yelling…and threatening…gang of seven…refused to leave…from the front of 12 Bristol…gangly Delores…with fierce …twenty-something…

piercing eyes... came to our rescue...With blood curdling...screaming curses...and a pot of scalding hot water... she scattered that gang ...in laughing quickness...

Not long after moving to Bristol...we kids transferred to School 6... and began to get to know our new neighbors...Next door to us... was Reverend Wiley...the lanky...painting and singing preacher who...when it warmed...occasionally hired me as a helper...to paint in the high... and low places...of the houses he worked on...The good Reverend was mostly harmless...however...I always felt... even at my age...that I was ahead of him...and I used simple reasoning...as an insulator...against his proselytizing ways...

Directly across the street was the Henrich Lumber Company...It was the source of the smell of cut lumber...and gasoline...that permeated the air...on our end of Bristol...The Company kept its enclosed premises as neat as hey could...but you could not miss the sound and goings ...of its delivery trucks during work hours...We...somehow...were never terribly disturbed by Henrich...and in fact we kids...got to know and like...a number of the everyday workers ...and drivers for the Company...all white of course...We also liked to play handball ...or a wicked game of dodge ball...against the big...Henrich garage door...that shut tight... every evening and weekends...

A few doors from us...was the Barr family...with four rugged boys...and a dirt basketball court...with peach basket rims...in their front yard...I...and the Barr's...Jimmy and Theron...especially...spent hours...practicing jump shots...and imitating Sweetwater Clifton...on their makeshift ball court...The Barr's "front" yard was in the rear of a house... just across from another rear home...occupied by a family of five kids...and a single mother...named "Spunky"...I was surprised to learn... that Spunky...and her five young kids...didn't have much more than an ice box...chairs...a rug and a cooking stove...in her place...Shy and skinny... doe-eyed Spunky and her kids...could have easily gone...unnoticed in a Bombay slum...in far way India...or on an unpaved street...in a sewer less Tunica ...Mississippi...

On the other side of us...toward Spring Street...lived the McDuffys...a fairly stable...and intact family...where there was a mother, a father and three kids...I remember ...Johnny Junior...Jean...and Reba...as friendly...

likeable neighbors…who were eager to share whatever they had…The girls…especially pretty Jean…stirred the gonads a bit…but other choices… and greater prizes…always seemed to beckon me…Gwen and James… loved playing with the McDuffys…I preferred the rugged…rough and tumble…of the Barr brothers and Donnie and Cab Brown…who lived in the middle of the block…a few more doors away…

I had an up and down relationship with those Browns…playing and getting along… some weeks…battling and arguing…mostly about neighborhood girls…or athletic prowess …at other times…The Browns also lived in a single-parent house…with what …I thought …was a pretty good-looking…almost sexy…mother… I liked hanging out at the Brown's house…I had one of the most vicious fights in my childhood… with Cab Brown… whom I heard many years later…became a policeman in Philadelphia…I completely lost track of his brother Donnie…

Diagonally, across from us…was a large white/gray…multi-storied tenement Known as "500 Clinton Street"…It was filled with families and kids…almost all black…of course… 500 Clinton Street…which stretched from Clinton to Bristol Street… was where the snazzy flirts…Myra… Loretta and Myrtle Burroughs lived…They were the objects of pursuit… for kisses and caresses…in the dim hallways and stairwells of 500 Clinton…500 Clinton…was really a stacked ghetto project…with a small… glass-strewn playground next door…It had monkey bars…and space where we actually played…"tackle football"…500 Clinton…was also where…two Herbie Campbell's lived… I was quite fond of…one Herbie…The other Herbie thought he was better than…most of us neighborhood kids… and I…then…and forever…thereafter…stared through his presence… with a permanent disdain…Later…my favorite…Herbie Campbell… ultimately…went on with me…to the same high school…

I also remember the Peterson's…Ken…Lawrence and Lorraine…They lived in a single-family house…further down Bristol from us…with their mother and father…The head of their house…King Peterson…was the Councilman for the Ellicott District…His kids… Lawrence and Lorraine were friendly and easy going…Ken…their older brother…was an arrogant stuck-up…who briefly had a fling with my cousin Shirley Barnes… We never interacted with the Peterson's…much beyond polite play…and respect...But we gladly had a King Peterson sign...somewhere on the 12 Bristol Street property...whenever he ran for office...

The large Barnes' brood...who lived a block and a half away...on Spring Street... were the offspring of my grandmother's brother...Tom... and Nancy Barnes...For reasons that escaped me...in spite of the family connection...we were not particularly close to the Barnes's...when we lived on Bristol...It could have been because...the second-cousin Barnes kids... were older than us...and we just did not have that much in common...It could also have been...because we were a poor...rag-tag family...headed by a single mother... whom they deliberately chose to know little about ...It was later...after a few more neighborhoods...and after I had left home... that Dimple...Gwen and James...got to know the Barnes clan...a lot better than I did...

June Carter...my brother James' godmother...also lived on Bristol... We first met June in the last neighborhood...we lived in...before Bristol Street...June...then a single woman...with a small baby...lived in an apartment above a small...branch library at William and Sherman Streets... We lived in a rooming house...at 648 William Street...and I was hired by June to paint two rooms in her apartment...While she was more than just a few years older than me...I thought June was one sharp lady...and I usually...melted in her presence...It was during that painting episode... that James started babysitting June's young...baby son ... Lamont...and she eventually became James' godmother... June became a fairly well known socialite...and later a reporter...for the Buffalo Challenger...a local...weekly newspaper... started mostly by Assemblyman Arthur Eve... She was...and remained a friend of our family...for nearly half a century...

Bristol Street was a human menagerie of colorful kids...and grownup characters...that proved to be a fish bowl of learning...and interacting... that would be forever remembered ...When the smell of food...pierced the air...we loved to guess what food was cooking...at whose house...and if there would be a welcome for us...Sometimes there was...Sometimes there wasn't...Two doors from us...was a wizened-up...old lady...we kids called..."Mama-Doo-Doo Fingers"...She had a small store...of sorts...in the covered porch...of her small bungalow ...She was a gruff one...who really did not like kids...but she was eager to sell them pop... candy...or stale potato chips...for the nickels and dimes...she collected in thin ...

wrinkled... brown fingers...We never bought much from...Mama-Doo-Doo Fingers...but devilishly annoyed her...occasionally...by hanging out ...loudly...on her steps...

Then there was "Mama-Let-You-Live"...as the neighborhood girls called her...She was a slight...older white woman...in her 50's...is my guess...She ran a small...musty...re-sale store...on Spring Street...a few doors from Clinton...beside the Henrich Lumber Company ...If you needed a brassiere...a used bathing suit...or a short-sleeve shirt...and had only 75 cents...You could probably find it...at Mama-Let-You-Live's... One day...I heard Johnny McDuffy say...he thought Mama-Let-You-Live...might be related to...the owners of Weintraub's Men's Store...at William and Jefferson Streets...Weintraub's...now that was the place...if you needed a pink...Billy Eckstein shirt...a blue...tear-drop...pea-green... or loud Yellow suit...with pegged-pants legs...

Every day...Bristol Street...was a daily churn of school...play... excitement...tension and growth...There was never a dull moment... Bristol had its own bouquets...sounds and life rhythms...It was from Bristol Street...that we explored the magic...of that William Street mile...from Jefferson to Michigan Avenues...William Street...in the '40's and '50's...was like Detroit's Black Bottom...Baltimore's Pennsylvania Avenue...Atlanta's "Sweet" Auburn Avenue...or Tulsa...Oklahoma's... Greenwood... Every city or town in the Country...with a population of blacks...had one...It was where the parties began Friday night...after a long week of work...in segregated America...

Buffalo's William Street...didn't match those other ...famous urban places...in colored-world USA...with as much black entrepreneurship... but in all other aspects...they were quite similar... Weekends...in particular...were a constant party...of restaurants... bars... music... Negroes drinking...fighting...sometimes dying...and there were lots of opportunities for...a kid with a shoe-shine box...and a cool hustle... If I could...I would hit all the bars... and hangouts...on William Street... looking for customers...I can remember conning the old doorman... at the Vendome Hotel...at Clinton and Michigan...to let me just walk through the lobby... with my shine box...I was always hoping to catch a glimpse... or a job...from some celebrity ...like Duke Ellington ...Count Basie... or Joe Louis...They all stayed there...when they came to Buffalo ...They sure couldn't stay at the Castle Inn...the Lafayette or the Statler hotels...

It was either the Vendome Hotel…or the Little Harlem Hotel…for black people… back then…in segregated Buffalo…New York…

As for the Bailey kids…we were constantly on a thin line…on Bristol Street…It was a thin line that…if crossed…one of us might be arrested for fighting…upbraided for taking advantage of a neighborhood flirt… or being abused by some pervert…or sloppy drunk… Luckily…none of that ever happened…to us…But there was always…some kind of drama… if not danger going on…Once on…Bristol… Dimple…beat my brother James…to within an inch of his life…for stealing trinkets from the Five and Ten Cent Store…on William Street… and Gwen got into a ferocious fight with…Roberta…a neighborhood girl…that later became one of her best friends…Despite it all…I excelled…as a 7th and 8th grade student at School 6…and was named President of the graduating 8th grade class…

It was on Bristol that Dimple…began to explore becoming a Jehovah's Witness…and continued to go…off and on…up and down with Steve… her very criminal…and very jealous boyfriend Steve… Although trying hard…to impress Dimple…he just couldn't seem to get his life together… However…I can't remember him ever being on Bristol Street…more than a couple of times to visit…and to my knowledge he never spent a single night…on Bristol … After three and a half years…we finally left Bristol Street…when Dimple and Steve…tried to live together… one last time…We moved to another rooming house…on Pratt Street…for a very brief…and final time…with the hopeless Steve…Once again…I hated Dimple's weakness for Steve… and I hated leaving Bristol Street…By then though…I had gotten used to being an urban nomad…and resigned to wandering through…and growing up…in shared houses…in the many neighborhoods…of the near east side…of Buffalo…New York…

Painter's Helper

Hey boy! You want a job?
Yes, Sir. I need the money.

Are you scared of high places?
No, Sir, I am very brave.

Good, because I am a painter.
I paint houses and I need some help.

I need somebody to go up the ladder.
You know, paint in the high places.

I'm your man, Sir. I know how to paint.
And as you can see I'm very tall.

Good, meet you right here in the morning.
Don't bring nothing but a sandwich.

Hey, up in them gables you pretty good, boy.
I never had a better, quicker helper.

You're not afraid and your paint stroke is fine.
Why it's almost as good as mine.

But I am also worried about your soul.
You go to church, boy?

No, Sir. My Mama said I didn't have to go.
After I told her that I hated it so.

You got to serve God, if you want to go to heaven.
You do want to go to heaven don't you?

I'm not sure, Sir. Do you know about heaven?
The real heaven, not just up in the sky?

I sure do. I'm a preacher, boy.
You looking at a child of God!

I preach the word of the Lord every Sunday.
Look, next Sunday come to this place.

Don't be disturbed because it used to be a store.
The Lord walks and works there now.

Come and get saved. Save your soul.
You might learn how to spread more than paint.

Well, how did you like it? The preaching?
The singing? The good folks you saw?

Oh, it was all right, I guess.
You were really something.

And I never knew you had a Cadillac.
Boy, that's some mighty fine car.

Yes, it is boy. Yes, it sure is.
Most folks can't get one like me.

Do you think they all want one?
Most people who came walked to the store.

Church, boy! Church!
They came to the Church!

I got a Cadillac because it's a symbol of hope.
If my people see me with a great big ride,

One with fins, all shiny and stuff;
They'll believe I know where I'm going.

They say, Reverend Wiley know where he's going.
They'll believe I can get them there too.

But then they'll all have to be preachers, right?
They'll have to learn how to shout and yell all night.

Naw, boy. Not everyone gets the calling.
But faith can get them some nice wheels.

It might be a Ford, a Plymouth or a Chevrolet.
Any old way, they'll ride in grand style.

What do you think about that?
Me? I think I'd rather have a Cadillac!

the little thief

mama beat james without mercy that day.
i had to grab her arm to take the stick away.

i had never seen her so angry before.
he had stolen toys from the five and ten store,

she found them in a drawer of a bedroom dresser.
and felt he had completely disrespected her,

she swore and vowed that she would kill him before,
she would let him grow up a thief, and darken her door.

james continued living in mama's house after that day,
and grow up he did, indeed, i am very happy to say.

School 6

After Lackawanna...and Roosevelt...the number of schools I attended... equaled exactly half...the number of rooming houses...apartments...and relative's flats...we had lived in...in Buffalo... After Lackawanna's... Albright Court and Ridge Road...in the next nine years...we lived on Sycamore... Broadway... Swan...Clinton... Walnut...William... Bristol... Pratt... Glenwood... Bradford... and Adams streets...I attended Public

Schools 6... 12...31... 32... 47...and Buffalo Technical High School... My brother James...and sister Gwen... attended a slightly...different mix of schools...but their nomadic and learning experiences ...closely mirrored my own...At each stop...the learning...friendships... struggles... opportunities and successes...were typical for black school kids...growing up...in prejudiced...but livable ...Buffalo...in the '40's...and '50's...

We had good teachers...and good experiences... and we had bad teachers and bad experiences...It was rare to see a black teacher...but I remember Mr. Reynolds...in fifth grade...at School 31...the only black teacher...I ever had in Buffalo...I liked him...but he would seriously... hit you with a ruler...(for nothing of course) ...At School 6 at the corner of Hickory and North Division streets...I also remember...the many young ... idealistic...white teachers...who were boldly...determined... to make a difference...who made you believe... that they were true surrogates...who cared and went about the business of helping me...and others like me...to learn... Then there was Mr. Muto...the Italian...gym teacher/coach at School 6...who...even though you sensed he liked you... he said he didn't believe black kids ...were intelligent enough...to play baseball well... track ...basketball for sure...but not baseball...(As I grew older I often wondered if that was just a ploy to motivate.)

Because we moved frequently...we Bailey kids...quite often...found ourselves out-of-district...or logistically challenged...to get to and from school...We always...however... found our way to school 6...At school 6 we met...studied and grew up with...mostly kids like ourselves ...friendly... some poor...but not always fatherless...We were...what today's social commentators...would call..."the under privileged"...There were few... family legacies of academic achievement...or path finders to guide or inspire us... and hardly any...close role models...to set examples ...for us...

We were expected to... always go to school...do your best ...and stay out of trouble ...That seemed to be...enough for...Dimple...my mother... Stay out of trouble...She preached it over and over...I understood her concern...because...whether we were in school ...or out...we lived in the streets...as much as...we lived in...the many shared homes of our childhood ...We scrapped...and fought our way... at times...but... happily...avoided any serious trouble...I feel fortunate to ...have developed...and still have...many warm... fond memories ... and life-long associations...with friends...from my childhood days...in all of the Buffalo schools I attended...

The fondest of those school memories...mostly happened at School 6...the last elementary school I attended...I spent seventh... eighth...and part of the sixth grade at 6...In many ways...it was a time of maturation...of coming out...for me...Major interests... academics... sports...girls...bloomed and became important...for me...at 6...I recall so many moments... like writing my first speech...competing with Malcolm Erni...to paint stage props...playing the old witch...in a Hansel and Gretal Play...and falling in love with... ah...ah...well falling in love...

There was...learning how...to say good morning...in Italian (Buongiorno!)... or... Polish (Dzien Dobry!)...how wine and tomato paste...is made...and what the word Mafia meant...A few steps away from 6... on Hickory Street... I learned how to eat Bocce's pizza... which... from thenceforth...you would compare...to every pizza...in every city... you would ever be in...for the rest of your life...I learned that Bocce was really...a game...played with wooden balls...and not the name of... the smiling...young guy behind the counter... serving up... fifteen cent slices...or was it twenty-five cent slices?...

At School 6...there were kids with names like: Lawrence...Barnes... Muldrew... Rich ...Pepe...Carloni...Briggs...Brown...Aquila...Hayes... Billups...Forma...Barrett...Montana...Richardson...Evans...Cieri... James...Stacy...Incardona...Young...Flowers...Davis...Smoot...Jones... Washington...Redd...Martin...Luche...Fairchook...Warr...Mitchell... Mullens...James...Maclin...Hooser...Sutton...Hightower...Marshall... Briggum...Lewinski...and teachers with names like: Wyatt...Raffauf... Muto ...Becker...Clampet... Barth... Gentile... Ballard...Donovan... Saunders...and a Principal...named Gordan Higgins...

Academically...in my early years...I was usually...an above average student...and I am told...even excelled at times...In the seventh grade... owing to the efforts of a wonderfully ...dedicated white teacher...Ms. Martha Becker...I placed second...(or was it third?)...in a city-wide... public speaking contest...In June, 1952...again with inspiration from teachers... and the help of an untiring...homeroom teacher ...Ms. Ella Raffauf...I became the top student in the eighth-grade...graduating class of School 6...For such...I was elected President of the Class...and received a medal of achievement (Number 3924)...from the Trustees of the Jessie Ketchum Memorial Fund ...That eighth-grade achievement...helped to qualify me...for acceptance into Buffalo Technical High School...at that time one of the top high schools ...in the City of Buffalo...

Each day at School 6...was an interruption of anxiousness...of yearning...and learning ...always singular in its beginning...unique in its outcome...School 6 was there when...the fluids and muscles... awakened for the next maturity...in spite of how we lived... and where we lived...Our lives then...and later...were not necessarily drawn to fit the schedule...of parents...bureaucrats...politicians...or undertakers... but more nearly...to fit the shifting...unfolding and scheming...of forces we didn't even know...or imagine...existed at that age...Those forces... though unseen...were human...most times impersonal...but specific enough...to be grafted onto our souls forever...For some...it could have been a person...a place...a word...a thing...For me...it was Bristol Street and the whole experience of School 6...It was the time...and the real beginning of my early maturation...

With all due respect...to Tech...and the University of Buffalo...which I would also attend later...clearly...my time at School 6...was the most enjoyable...educational experience for me...The rich mosaic of humans... at School 6...shielded me...from the harsh reality...of prejudice and school segregation...so prevalent... elsewhere in the Country in the '50's...

The violence of school integration...was telling around the Country... and sadly to be ... glaringly so...in Buffalo...in the '60's...and even later when the number of blacks...in the City exploded... In the late 40's and early '50's...in spite of...the designed clustering...of our ethnic neighborhoods... and the occasional neighborhood flare-ups of racial tensions... around the City...we...the children of the near-east side of Buffalo...came together serenely ...most of the time...especially at School 6... The experiences... the learning...the peaceful integration...would serve me well in the coming years... Looking back...I wish the whole racial integration experience... in the entire Country...had been as peaceful and as rewarding ...for every student in the Country...as it was for me...for all of us...at School 6...

From The Last Page of a Battered 7th Grade Notebook

"She is a very kind white lady I really, really like.
I mean it's like she could be in my family. Miss
Becker reminds me of Dimple, except she is
older and has gray hair and more wrinkles...
But she don't take no stuff and she seems to
always be looking at me. She made me stop
pulling brassier straps and to pronounce the
word Pen-nel-o-pee...instead of Pen-a-lope
and how to pronounce the word li-brar-y
correctly. She also taught me how to speak to
a crowd and not be nervous and how to write
speeches and how to respect myself. I hope I
never forget Miss Becker..."

Third Baseman

I wish he would just...
Shut the hell up!....I tried
to stop the freakin' ball...
It skidded by me...just
like it does...to other kids...
---Why is he picking on just me?...
Just me!....As if I have to be
perfect!
Nobody is perfect...asshole!...
I'm not perfect....
Nobody is perfect!....Damn!....

Tom Thumb Wedding

I remember her from Swan Street
and my favorite grammar school.
Smooth of skin...pretty dark hair...
shy and unassuming...I always
thought of her...as really my wife
...after all we got married...in a
mock...tom thumb wedding...one
weekend on Swan Street...I was
just ten...back then...I tried
to keep track...of her growing
up days...School 6...high school...
far away Tonawanda...her early...
mistaken marriage...to a conceited...
little chicken man...children...a
sad illness and...banishment to
a dismal...lonely place...I then
finally watched...a cruel death...
from a deadly fire...that so broke
my heart...Very few ever knew...
that I loved her...that I cried
for her...that I prayed to her
memory...and that sometimes
I still do...to this very day...

That was Close

In the year of our Lord...
1950...I did something at
School 6...that could have
gotten me lynched in North
Carolina...It was done in
semi-darkness...on a stage
...but out of sight of most

...if not all people nearby...
In the eyes of some...I am
sure...it may have been a
sneaky act...worthy of some
punishment...but lynching?...
I did it with humor...smiles...
tingles...and lots of gusto...I
had planned it carefully...but
forgot about it...and then
it happened...suddenly...
...like a hobo...upon a $20
bill...I seized the moment...
I could not help myself...
Like Rudolph Valentino...
Like the Sheik of Araby...
I kissed...Mary Cieri!...
I put my lips to hers...right
there...at School 6...It...
It was the first time...I had
...had ever done such...to
Mary...Why no one ever said
don't do it!...Mary did not
object...No one bled...No one
fainted...and I don't believe...
in fact...I know it never...ever
happened again...Thank God!...
I got away with it!...Just think
...I could have been lynched for
it...in North Carolina...*lynched!...*

Second

Is it important to finish second?
Yes, since you cannot be first
until you secure second. But you
never start out to be second. The
goal is always to be first, to be
the best...to lead...Yet the greatest
outcome of all, is to have competed,
been there, tried. That is better than
being first, because when you compete,
to the best of your ability, you create the
possibility for a winner. Winners are
always made by those behind them.

North Carolina Justice

Shame on you mighty North Carolina,
for your narrow, blistering, hateful prejudice.
Your racist skirts are showing, they couldn't be finer,
than your silly reaction to a little girl's kiss.

In a playful mood, a little Carolina daughter,
placed a white kiss on blacks, Hanover and Fuzzy.
Little did the boys know it could lead to their slaughter,
until authorities tossed a rope over a tall poplar tree.

But alas, alas, North Carolina justice prevailed.
They decided not to hang the two nine-year olds.
Instead, 12 and 14 years they were sentenced to be jailed,
and they told the miscreants they better learn some controls.

After all, Carolina don't allow that kind of funny stuff,
blacks kissing whites is getting a little too bold.

Hiring them and funding schools is more than enough,
but good old southern tradition they had to uphold.

Thank goodness a little national wisdom seeped in,
and the sorry little kiss episode wasn't quite done.
But it took a presidential pardon to forgive the kissing sin,
when old Ike showed some wisdom, and Carolina had none.

Edward and Eugene

*"Ace boon coons"..."running buddies"...
That was Eugene Brown and Edward
Lawrence...at School 6...and during my
early high school years...Edward...who
could spend 24 straight Hours... at lower
Main Street theaters called...the Little
Hippodrome...the Keith and the Academy...
watching every movie at least 3 times...
became...what else but an actor...A dozen
times...I wished I had had as many...large...
older brothers to help me fight...as Edward
had...*

*Eugene loved bike riding...basketball at
Welcome Hall...and fishing for carp...in placid
Delaware Park Lake...We liked eating Freddie's'
doughnuts and playing horseshoes...anywhere we
could find them...I loved his mother and his sister...
Mary Lee...and stayed up all night with them...the
night we graduated from School 6...We drank red
wine...that night...Eugene went on to Emerson High
School...and became an honest...hard worker...I
lost track of him...when he moved...back to Bessemer
...Alabama...where he was born...Seen him once
since then...*

I followed Edward...to Technical High School...and introduced him to Libby...my cousin...whom he swears ...mates aside today...and some 50 years later...he loves still to this day... I kept in touch with him...supported some of his career stops...and still talk to him...every other week or so...He introduced me to James Earl Jones...Abbey Lincoln...and all of August Wilson's plays...

My favorite thing to do with him...is to sit on the edge of the raised court yard...at the corner of 9th and 42nd streets...in New York City...drink...laugh and comment on the traffic and fools...going by below...and tell tall tales...about the so-so girls and fine foxes...we knew...and grew up with... long ago... in Buffalo...

Wheels for a Working Man

There it was again...in the crowded store window...of Main Auto Supply...on Main Street...The magic moment was a heavy inhale... exhale... then relief...for me...The perfect bike...was still there...In simple...13-year old words...it was a shiny...dark red... gold and silver... full-size...knee-action...balloon-tired...heavenly Schwinn...It was like Roy Rogers' Trigger...the Lone Ranger's Silver...It was the baddest...the absolute baddest ...two-wheeler in the land...and I had to have it...just had to have it...

From my first eyes on it... just days before...my dreams were now consumed with riding it... I bored siblings...James and Gwen...and my friend Eugene...with conversation about it...I couldn't wait to mount it...to do a "wheelie"...or jump a curb...Everywhere I went...I looked to see...if there was another one like it...owned by some other kid...plying Buffalo's mean streets... So far not one...not one like "my bike"...Oh...I saw a couple of...knee-action Schwinn's...but they were different colors... different models...or different something...Not one...was quite like the bike...my bike...

At home I hinted to Dimple…my Mother…that it sure would be wonderful to own a bike…that bike… I told her how much faster… easier…effortlessly…I could fly to Roland's store for her…and how I wouldn't need bus fare anymore…to go to Cold Springs …or anywhere… with that beauty…I gave dozens of reasons…why that bike…should belong to me…to us…to the family…But truth be known…to all who would hear …I really wasn't expecting much … Mama…just matter-of-factly said…there was no way…she could afford to pay…$49.95… for a bike to play "dilly-dally" with…She said besides…she had never heard of…"a darn bike costing that much anyway"…

Of course…I knew that would be her reaction…I was never hopeful… because by then… since I was eleven…or thereabout…I had been buying my own shoes…and most of my own clothes…I knew Dimple could just barely afford…to feed us everyday…but I still wanted to plant the seed… gain a little sympathy…for what I had to do…I had to let her know…what I wanted to do…I always knew…deep down… that I would have to pay for that bike…by myself…

A week before that day…I had gone into the store…to get a price for the bike…and I had also asked the clerk…if the store had a layaway plan…that blessed tool…we…our family…often used…to buy anything costing more than $20.00…He said…"yes… one third down…pay the rest and…pick it up…in two…weeks"…Now I was back…to pay $13.75… all that I had …I hoped that the store…would accept that…let me put it in layaway…and come back in two weeks…I was very apprehensive…had been for more than a few days…I didn't quite have a third to put down… and even worse…I didn't know if I could get the rest…in two weeks…

With a lumpy throat…and a promise to return in two days…with at least $3 more…they agreed to put the bike…in layaway… Heart pounding …I watched the clerk…take the bike…my bike…out of the window…and roll it to a back room… with my name on a tag…hanging from its shiny handlebars…I could hardly believe it…I stood for five minutes…and imagined riding it… But now I faced the hard part…On the long walk home… I asked myself…over and over...from where…and how was I going to get…the rest of the money…the precious money I needed…to get my bike…

While I wasn't the cleverest kid…at making money…like some kids I knew…I was always willing…and eager…to work for it… Like most kids…I would run errands for money…do chores for neighbors…and somehow…I always seemed to keep…a few nickels in my pocket…I would do things like…carry coal into somebody's coal bin…shop or clean windows for elderly folks …shovel snow…and help out on paper delivery routes…almost anything for money…I was proud that…Dimple…often borrowed from me…

For years…ever since my… first pair…on Ridge Road…in Lackawanna…I had shined shoes in bars…on Jefferson Avenue…or up and down…downtown streets…in Buffalo… And then there was Sophie… loveable…superstitious…old-as-my grandmother… Sophie… When I first met her…she lived around the corner from us…on Sherman Street… with her sister and grandson… Pookie… For years…I had a standing job to be the first one…to ring Sophie's doorbell… on New Years Day…Year after year…a few seconds past twelve-midnight…on New Years Day…I would earn the easiest three bucks…and cookies… I ever earned…You see… Sophie thought the whole new year…would be filled with bad luck… dark days…devils and witches…if a female …was the first to darken her door…the first day of a new year…So I became her good luck charm… for five straight years…

Then there was the painter…Reverend Wiley…the tall…thin… gangly…singing preacher …from Bristol Street...He hired me to help him…paint the high places…and gables…and hard-to-reach corners of… mostly old houses…and chipped paint garages…Of course…I was the one… who went under the low porches…or high up the shaky ladders… while he held or propped them up… I liked painting…but I did not like…the good Reverend's constant…flock recruiting…for his store front church…I learned loads about painting from him…but usually clicked off…the moral sermons and the save-me-Jesus… songs…

Lord I had had… enough of that…the first ten years of…my life… when Dimple… took us…or made us go to some body's church…I did a lot of small…paint jobs on my own …too…and once Miss June Carter hired me…to paint her living room… "passion pink"…if you can believe it… June…who eventually became…my brother James'… godmother… would become… and remain… a close friend of our family…until the day she died...half a century... after that oh...so curious...and mysterious pink room...was finished...

In the days after...bike-down-payment day...I thought of money constantly...and kept asking myself...how I was going to pay for the bike... my bike... I kept regretting that I wasn't sixteen yet...There were lots of jobs...I could get...I thought...if I were just sixteen and had a work permit... But I couldn't...let that stop me...after all...some people didn't make you... show a work permit...all the time... Like the many times I got on...farmers' trucks...to go out for a day of grueling bean picking...And some of the kids told me...old man...Lou Jacobs...from Sportservice...would sometimes... help you get hired to clean up...Offerman Stadium... at night...without a permit... Anyway...those kind of jobs...you could only do on weekends... or after school...or in the summer... I had to get money right away...$33.20 in two weeks ...that was my mountain...and I was desperate...

That weekend...I told my Aunt Miss...my grandmother's sister... for whom I went to the store...every Saturday... about the bike...my bike...and my dilemma...As was her custom ...she didn't say much...just listened... and finally quietly said...maybe I could earn... some money running errands...for Uncle Billy...her beloved husband...She promised she would speak to him...when he returned home...from managing the Willert Park Credit Union...

When I came back from Kulick's...with her groceries...that day...she gave me four... tightly folded...dollar bills... from the small... smooth... leather change purse...I had seen many times before...It was double what...I usually got...for weekend errands...except maybe when there was...a hard rain...or a snowy day...In fact...she doubled up...three straight weeks...in a row... For that...I vowed I would never charge her...for going to the store again ...after I'd gotten my bike...of course...That afternoon...I went back to the store...on Main Street ...and paid $3.00 more on...the bike...my bike...

In the midst of an anxiety-filled weekend...I learned that my cousin... Wilbert...had made a major decision...in his life...Wilbert...the shy one... the quiet one...almost four years older than me...had decided to quit school...and join the Army paratroopers...This puzzled and saddened me...since we were almost like brothers...and I always enjoyed the long... bus rides...to Lackawanna...to spend playful weekends...with him...and Libby... his sister... Now I was looking forward to...riding my...wonderful bike…from where we lived in Buffalo …to Lackawanna…a long…traffic-laden challenge…for an adult…let alone a 13-year old…

But the more I thought about it…Wilbert's decision probably…had a lot to do…with being sick of…and just fed up…with his bald-headed… intimidating…woman-beating… bastard-of-a-stepfather …John Johnson… At that time…Wilbert worked after school…and on weekends …as a pin setter in a bowling alley…on Niagara Street…He invited me to visit him on his job…the next Sunday afternoon…We would talk more…about his enigmatic decision …about his soon-to-be…new life…about jumping out of airplanes…and whatever…

I enjoyed visiting…with Wilbert and his friend Riley…I also met Mr. Joe Illos…the bowling alley owner…who…with Wilbert's encouragement… offered me a pin setting job… like Wilbert and Riley…even though I was only 13-years old…Wilbert showed me how to… stab pins on pegs…to make them stand up for the next ball…how to jump from alley to alley… dodge the flying pins…It looked like…and was…hot grueling work…and I really wasn't… too thrilled… until I was told you can make… $3.00 for two and a half hours of work … and maybe more…with tips…if you got fast…and stayed late…for the big money matches…

Mr. Illos… encouraged me to come back…in the afternoon…when the kids bowled …Learn the ropes…with the slow rollers…is how he put it…The next week…I skipped out of school twice …worked for the slow rollers…and learned how to be a pin setter…By the end of the first week… after a few days of work…I had $11.00…after bus fare…and expenses… (food)…I was disappointed so I begged Mr. Illos…for more work…He said…"be patient… Junior…Learn… get faster…Speed and quickness… will get you into…the starting line up …let you make the good money"… He then fed me Mrs. Illos' chicken cacciatore before I left for home…

What was once…a motivation for money…to pay for a bicycle…now also became a moral urge…to redeem the faith of a man…Mr. Illos… who decided to believe in me…Then I also recognized…that once again… beneath it all…was a personal drive for the satisfaction… of competing in…a world of work…reserved…mainly for men a lot older than me…Money was the object …to help me own a bike…but it also helped me to bring home… vanilla ice cream or Chinese food…after a night of pin setting…

As I look back with older eyes…I now believe…that it was also… an attempt to fill a void…to look normal…to respond to a growing impatience …with a childhood…filled with the angst of poverty… the undeniable burdens…of a single parent family…facing the daily uneasiness …of not knowing…what the next day…what the next week… would bring… Owning a shiny…new bike was…for me…making a statement in the neighborhood… It would be a statement…that said…we are like other families…with kids who owned bikes…

Shorn of the slightest doubt…soaked with an empowering sense of determination…I put arms…legs…and mind…to the whirling task of becoming a pin setter…The money was very important…I had to have the bike…but now the prize…also included a satisfied…Mr. Illos…who gave me a chance…The difficulty of the work…soon eased…loosened…and yielded to…a smooth rhythm…speed and quickness…that confirmed my ability…and my mastery of the job…I could do it…and do it so well that… for the next three years…I was told…I was one of the best pin- setters…to ever work at the upstairs…Bowl-Mor Bowling Alley…on Niagara Street…

But the first few weeks…of my new career…Dimple was not happy… when she learned what I was doing…Skipping school…working late…I seemed to be forever sleepy… tired…tense …She relented when I explained… when I promised…it would only be for a short time…On the final…long awaited…last day of the layaway…I was $6.20 short of my goal…After frantically trying… and failing to borrow… from anybody…I thought had money…I begged the clerk…at the store…for a few more days…He gave me another week… and after three and a half… long… tiring… anxious and grueling weeks…I finally rode home with…the bike…my bike…my precious bike…

I was a proud…and grateful…kid… I was especially grateful to Wilbert for showing me…a way to win…for showing me how to make some…"real money"…When I saw him…before he was off to…the 503rd Airborne Infantry Division…at Fort Campbell… Kentucky…I was straddling my bike… Just four years later… I…a pretty good pin setter too… would repeat what he did…and be off on my own…military adventure…But in the meantime… there would be lots of… "wheelies"…curb jumping… racing…and just…plain old cool…bike riding…on my bike…

pumped up pinboy

god…it's a great feeling…great feeling…
when they want you…only you…you
always doubt …always wonder…if you
are good enough…if your will is known…
if they sense how hard you will try…if they…
believe that you are up to it…you are…you
know you are…you have the knack…the hop…
the jump…the swing over the railing…down pat…

then softly they ask…for you…junior…only
you…you then step up…and get to it…go…
pound…stab…leap…go…the pins belong to
you…nothing hurts now…you're bursting with
infectious…pride…your rhythm is smooth.. your
heart is pounding…you can say it now…"damn
right!…bring it to me!…let me have it!…now i
am ready!…*NOW…I… AM…READY!…*

Coming From Roland's

Pedaling uphill in the Fruit Belt…white eyes see and hate me…
Maple Street I think…
A sack of groceries on my handlebars…not more than $22.50
from trusty Roland's store…
A gust of wind lifts my 5 and 10…Brooklyn Dodgers baseball cap…
for sure…no stinking Yankees…
Just enough to cover my big…brown…usually looking but
now totally unseeing…eyes…
Panic sets in…I jerked the bike to the left…determined…confident…
A car was passing on the right…
I slammed into an immovable car…not a tree…not a curb…It was…
a damn blue Chevrolet…
Down I went with pain in the groin…God it hurt…hurt so bad…

Just missed the family jewels...
The groceries were all safe and sound...in cans and brown paper...
still scattered all around...
Not so for my beloved, faithful bike...that I worshiped almost alive...
My gallant...sturdy steed...
Its frame was bent out of line...ready for a bullet...like in the movies...
God...that thought hurt me more...
So it was limp and drag all the way to Glenwood...bike and food...
Not a soul offered a helping hand...
I prayed...get me through this...the world can be next...It got in line...
and believe me...damn it...it hurt too...

Marathon Bikes

Sometimes...the distances would rival a marathon...
mimicking...perhaps a city leg of the French Tour...

Grownups marveled at how far...we...Eugene and I...
would pedal our bikes... Just getting to each other's

house...he lived on Seneca Street...I lived on
Glenwood...was a leg cramping jaunt... that even

young...13-year old limbs would feel...They were
our customary...beginning points... for bike riding

adventures...on a school-free...dry summer day...
A model day of...string-on-cane-pole fishing...

might start from my house...after a quick backyard
dig for crawlers...then a rapid dash...past the Albright

Gallery...to the lake in Delaware Park...It was there
that I first heard the word "abstract"...after a yellow

bus ride…from School 31… A joyous fishing result
would be five or six…silver carp…to toss back…or

bury in someone's flower bed… Carp were too lowly
for Mama's hot skillet…which always eagerly welcomed

pike…catfish or perch…Every trip to Delaware…going
or coming…yielded to the amorous call…from Freddie's

Doughnuts…for a half dozen of mixed…jelly…glazed…
or cream delights…divided evenly… devoured quickly…

sticky fingers…then wiped on pants… Often a fishing
day…would begin from Eugene's…on Seneca Street…

down Michigan…over the tracks…by the warehouses…
through Fuhrman…down to the blue Erie's edge…at

Times Beach…The prize was crawdads…by the dozen if
you could…with beaconed hooks…or minnow nets…always

alive…Eugene's Mama said…"no good if they're dead"…
Seldom did we catch enough…but it was still fun…lots

just trying… Other days…we aimed our trusty wheels…
for William and Fillmore Streets…to watch or play glove-

free softball…with white kids… who had gloves…or "Wow!
…Stan Musial Spikes"…On our bravest days…we boldly

challenged…the length of Fuhrman Boulevard…south
to Lackawanna…dodging dangerous traffic…by nasty

people…all the way to Ridge Road…From there it was a
short…quick fly…down Steelawanna Avenue…to Wilbert's

house...A cool drink...maybe a snack...then back again...
for Seneca ...where...exhausted...I would spend the

night...if it was OK with Mama... Once or twice...we
pedaled the short...for us...trip to Bradford Street...near

the old Elk Street refinery...to join the local scavengers...
digging for bits of copper...or other sellables...in open

lots...where factories once stood...On very hot days...
Eugene and I...would meet half-way...and join the

teeming throngs...and daring swimsuits...cooling heels
in the Civic Stadium pools...or playing shirts and skins

basketball...nearby...Always on those long biking
journeys...between destinations...we would...at

the drop of a hat...play horseshoes...pickup basketball...
or race and flirt...with any young foxes...we saw...along

the way... Those were the good summer days...linking
days of work...and hustle...that I also had to do...if I

wanted any money...to buy Freddie's doughnuts or a
replacement tire...for my well used...and trusty Schwinn...

She Lived Next Door

I used to see her every day...in pedal-pushers...jeans
or a sleeveless blouse...maybe a pale ribbon...tied to a

twisted pony tail...just riding a bike...or trying to stay up
on shaky skates...She was the little girl next door...who

played with Gwen...and winked at me...with a wide smile...
and a sassy flirt...I thought she was cute...in the family...

I stayed busy...chasing other kisses...and hugs from fancy
prizes...I thought...more worthy...more valuable to catch...

With fickle...and bravado...I charged from one...to another...
like Bessie looking for taller...greener...sweeter...something...

But slowly...gradually...in passing time...she pulled my
eye...my notice...so much so...that I had no choice...but to

stop...slow the dash...take note...of the beauty standing...
right there...before me...Surely this too was a prize...worth

winning...desirous of having...by even such a conceited rake...
Like a puppy in training...when its leash has been jerked...

my heart jumped to attention...melted and conceded...to a life-
long care...genuine concern...and an undying...love...forever...

A Beetle's Call

A new day comes...no difference...
just dull...flat...dry...very brown...
There is nothing but sameness...
Even kids playing...scream the same...
The sun comes up on time...The
night will be swift...black...promising
nothing...A beetle's call...makes me
sneer...What can that creature's bleep
tell me...to relieve the yearning...the
despair...Thinking about her...or him...
all of them...just people...around me...
without a hint... I promise...I will be

happy...one day...tomorrow...the next
day...soon...In spite of what happens
...whenever...I will insist...and I am
determined to be...happy...again...
Even if...only for just a single day...

Bean Picker

It was little more than ten years ago...
I was a twelve year old bean picker...

Bean pickers start their day in the early
morning hours...when dew is still on the

leaves...when the air is still moist...or when
the moon still shows its ancient face...Ok...

second and third shifters have later starts...but
it matters not when your bean picking begins...

Bean pickers start in a crouch...bent
over...or on their knees...OK...you do it standing

...sitting at a desk...or behind a wheel...Postures
may be different...but the grind is still the same...

Bean pickers fingers fly...as they crawl down
rows...singing or daydreaming...hoping it ends

one day soon...OK...tell me you're not crawling
down or up...trying to get to the end...with maximum

poundage...as your reward...for the long hard day...
Bean pickers often curse the scales...and are convinced

they're rigged...to favor the boss...or somebody
else...just not them...OK...you have a wonderful

boss...They all treat you well...you know you are
loved...every day...can't wait to get back...Right?...

A Bean picker's body tires...withers...bends...and gets
racked with pain...OK...that has never happened to clean

finger nails...suit wearers with ties...or carefully quaffed
skirts with doily trimmed blouses...from Sears...Right?...

Bean pickers hope...and pray...for the day it gets better...
for the end of the last row...for that last sack on the scale...

But that ain't us...we're through slaving...we are satisfied...
happy and glad..." we ain't no bean pickers"...Right?...

High School

I once lived at 273 Clinton Street...at the corner of Pine Street...in a large...tired... old...red brick...apartment building...where thousands of dreams...some my own...were born and died... Further down Pine Street...was the Catholic-run...Emergency Hospital...Just across Pine... there was a small park...a tiny...ghetto refuge...with benches...a softball field...and tennis courts... Beyond the park...further down Clinton... loomed Buffalo Technical High School...the City's proud...old emblem... of secondary excellence...Kids... rumored to be...Buffalo's brightest... went to Tech... from all over the Queen City...Before the 1940's ...true to Buffalo's usual segregation patterns...those kids...were almost...always deserving white boys...

Weather permitting...the Tech kids...in neat conformity...shorts and tennis shoes ...would have...physical education classes ...and play touch football... softball...tennis ...and chase...in the little park...

We...the pre-high school...neighborhood kids...would sometimes stop... and watch...the bright Techies...with their crew cuts...red noses... and puffy pink cheeks ...We were always bemused by their surprising...and we thought rare... athletic competence...or laughed at their...gangly slowness...their clumsy throwing ineptness...or whatever...they did...we thought funny...

Most of the time...I lived on Clinton Street...I believed that black kids...with their brown noses...swift legs...and huge...athletic vanity... would never be...allowed at...proud old Tech....and they weren't...at least not in great numbers...They were rare...indeed...until one day...in the mid-forties...on a crisp...Fall...school day...I finally saw a lonely... cherubic... black face...playing in the park...with Buffalo's brightest... Unmistakably black ...he was...cavorting awkwardly... un-handily...in the park...with the...pale legged... "Ofays"... as we used to say...I didn't know...the skinny...black kid...He sure wasn't...from the neighborhood... not running like that...I thought...I learned later...that it was...Robert T. Coles...a later-to-be...well known...very competent architect...He was one of the earliest... of the black Techies...In later years...Coles would tell me... that Tech...in the 1940's...had an official limit of 12 blacks...maximum...

In those days...in segregated Buffalo...most of the black kids...in our eastside neighborhood ...went to Hutchinson Central...a co-ed...near west-side...high school...not far from downtown...The near east-side... on the other side...of downtown...where most blacks...had lived...since the 1920's...was clustered mostly between...and around... Michigan and Jefferson Avenues...Genesee and Seneca Streets...It was a contiguous flow of old neighborhoods...previously claimed by...mostly Polish ...German... and Jewish immigrants ...Solid black schools...southern-style...may have been desired...by most of the narrow-minded whites...in Buffalo...but the rather small...black population...would have made it...very costly...and impractical...So the City...for more than 100 years...did what it could officially...and unofficially ...to "group them"..."contain them"...as much as possible...

But sitting in the middle of the black enclave was Tech...From its creation...Tech had been reserved...for the brightest...for the best...for the "buckra"... A few years before I graduated from grammar school... the enlightened Board of Education had decided...(before the 1954

Brown versus Board of Education decision ...mind you)...that at least... some of the high schools...should be further mixed...and there was a concerted...very genuine effort...to try to integrate...a few ...of the high schools in the City...Oblivious of such official-dom ... personally...I had been ...resigned...to the notion of attending...Hutchinson High... and even if I could...I never thought...I would wind up at Tech... mainly for two reasons...Tech was too lily white...and it had no girls... Since about fifth grade...maybe even third...girls ...girls...girls...had become ...increasingly...important to me...But in 1952...encouraged by teachers...and Gordon Higgins...the Principal at School 6...to reach for the sky...instead of brassieres...and bobby socks...I listened...I thought... agonized...and finally...agreed to apply...for admission to Tech...

As a hopeful eighth grader...I thought...perhaps my deep interest... in sketching... painting ...and drawing...might lead to an architectural career...or whatever...Like most...at that age...I wasn't sure about too many things...My application for...the Building Construction and Design Class...at Tech...was accepted...While there had been...a token...a sprinkle of blacks...at Tech since the early1940's...the year...I went to Tech...1952...it admitted...the largest number...of minority kids...in the School's history...up until then... The old...official excuse for excluding blacks...and others...was that...we were too dumb... We just could not... qualify for admission...Suddenly...dozens upon dozens of black kids... from the eastside... overnight ...were now declared bright enough...to be Techies... Just like that...our IQ's improved... That...of course... helped to eliminate one of my original hesitations...about going to Tech... But...alas...still no girls...no brassieres...no bobby socks...Damn!...I muttered...

On my way to Tech...the very first day...after getting off a bus...I walked...to my old home...at Clinton and Pine Streets...Then I deliberately walked down Pine...on the sidewalk...past the first entrance...to Catholic-run...Emergency Hospital...As I walked...I recalled...the many times we kids...had curiously ambled...those same old sidewalks... following... tracing the bloody trails...leading up to the Hospital door...Almost every Monday morning...after a weekend ...we kids had a game...we played...We always tried...to guess if the leaker...of the bloody drops...had just received a knife prick...and was sent home...in time for work... or did the poor owner…of what looked like a real gusher…make it…survived the trauma… the bloodletting… At that time…we didn't know it…but those bloody trails…were a testament to the anger…violence…nihilism and pathology… that so often…sadly infected …who we were…where we lived…how we lived…jammed up in the eastside…of old Buffalo…New York…

But bloody violence…was not always…the only signature…of the old neighborhood …The whole…near eastside…also had a rhythm…a blending of joy…colors…sound and beauty… mixed in with those quick…explosive cuts…and stabs…of rage… In many ways …our neighborhood mimicked the hues and strokes…of an abstract painting…you have to sometimes stand away from…to really see its beauty…Typically…like most black people… wherever you find them…we were a colorful… talented…easy-to-laugh people… Every gathering had the potential…to instantly become a party…a happening… We also suffered first…and most…when domestic calamities… like unemployment…or joblessness struck… But most of us…kids and adults…were too close…to our own reality…to understand …that behind… the drops of blood…the uncompensated sweat...the little understood…real source …of so much of the violence…and self-hatred…was a quiet rage…at a forced-upon…way of life… that stoked the pain…the anger…the pent-up frustration…in so many of us…back then…

As I walked down Pine Street…headed to Tech…that early Monday morning …there were no story-telling bloody drops…on the side-walk… leading up to Emergency Hospital… There were no clues…to a spent weekend of anger and disagreement…For some reason…that helped to make me…feel better…I felt as if…the missing…bloody crimson drops…that morning…was a silent signal…that the old neighborhood… perhaps…was breaking out of containment…cutting loose…from its mental shackles …Maybe now…I too…could be confident…about what was now…about to unfold…in my life at Tech…Maybe I too…like the neighborhood…had matured enough to now…also cut the shackles…and make the next step…

I continued across Pine…through the little park…almost hearing again…the voices from the pink faces…from the future engineers…that we used to watch…and make fun of…But that was before…Now things would be different…Now I was going be…like Bob Coles…and Leland Jones… and the other flies…specking the buttermilk…cavorting with the Ofays…

in the little park...Now...I too...was also going to be one of those... instantly recognized... Tech kids...hopping from the bus...carrying their tan canvas cases...holding their T-squares... and drafting boards...Now...I also thought to myself...you are going to see...some real athletes... in that little park...After all...we know...where all the roots and stones are buried...and how the ball...takes the seams...on the tennis court...We'll show them Ofays ...how to run with style and sass...I laughed to myself...

Smiling...as I walked up the steps of the entrance to Tech...I glanced over at the evergreen shrubbery...and high entrance steps...James...my brother...and Bobby Curry...a cousin ...and I...used to hide behind... or jump from...while playing cowboys and Indians ...We always had our cap pistols...and holsters...we got every other Christmas...from the ...Goodfellows Christmas Charity...Sometimes...play on the Tech grounds...was with Errol Flynn swords... fashioned from slats...torn or ripped from some abandoned...plastered wall ... That day... walking into Tech...I smiled and quietly thought...I'll never tell anyone here...not a soul... that I was once quite intimate...with the bushes and evergreens... the steps ...the trees... scattered around and hugging this old building... Not a soul...would I tell that to...not a soul...

The Only Real Truth

From the moment......it is born or conceived,
be it a plant, an animal, a man, a clan, a city,
a nation, a world,
a universe, a moment, an hour, a day, a star,
a light, a word, a poem, a
book, a feeling, a taste,
a sound, a thought, ...an idea, a theory, a sunrise,
a sunset, a moon, a wave.......a
state, a belief, a smell, a religion, a song, a
note, freedom, liberty, bondage, insanity,
a ray of hope, an angel or even a god,
they all begin to die....the instant they are born or created....
There can never.....be life..............for anything

without death. ...
There can never be existence..... without nonexistence.
It is just a matter of time...all things...everything dies. ..
That is the ultimate and........only real truth. ......

Just Bake a Cake

Mama was sad...She would be sad when worry...
mostly about us...her kids...overcame her...Most
times this happened...when we needed something...
a pair of shoes...a winter coat...next month's rent...
Mama...being sad made me sad...because I was
the man in the house...and I always asked myself...
what would Richard...my absent dad do...if he
were here...sharing the dry days...the hardness...

I was never able to know...what Richard would do...
and I always came back to ...what I could do...
I learned that sometimes...it was little things...
Chinese food or ice cream...on my way home...from
night work at the bowling alley...or just bake a cake...
a yellow...or chocolate...or coconut cake...come
Saturday morning...I loved to bake cakes...and
my mother loved it too...I often wondered...if
Richard could bake a cake...and make Dimple
a little less sad...like I did...many times...

Hurry Up

Look around you!/...
Right this moment/...you are alive!/...
You can see/...feel...touch...smell!/...
You are alive!/...It is a gift!/...

You are conscious!/...Without
it...you would be dead!/...without feeling!/...
without even the realization!/...that you
are here!/...were here yesterday!/...alive!/...

You will get there!/...one day!/...
some hour!/...that moment of
truth!/... for all living beings!/...
But you are not there yet!/...Celebrate!/...

Do it!/...make it happen!/...as if you won't
have tomorrow!/...Hurry!/...Hurry up and
take your time!/...Be excellent today!/...Right
now!/...Do it and don't stop!/...Do it every day!/...

until it comes!/...Hurry up!/....Hurry up!/...

My Time at Tech

Looking back...my time at Tech...was a glazed...often hazy mixture... of good times ...and sadly...discouraging times...Good because... as always...I still enjoyed learning ...Discouraging...because the time learning...being there in school...seemed to grow harder and tougher... as the days went by...Learning subjects...for me...was not especially difficult ...or uninteresting...in spite of...often being tired...drowsy and sleepy...I thoroughly enjoyed ...the magic...and discipline of mechanical drawing...I loved the basics of building design... writing...trying to play basketball...I say trying...because I also worked ...after school...and summers...and I just never...seemed to have enough time...to do it all...

Conditions at home...also weighed on me... Dimple...my long suffering mother...had a new husband...that I thought was the laziest doofus...I had ever seen...and there was ...growing tension between Gwen...my sister...and Dimple... Dimple...was worried about Gwen's female blossoming...("fastness"...she called it...) and she constantly harangued and restricted her freedom...They bickered a lot...and I felt like so many…in their teenage… formative years….that things seemed to be rushing at…and past me at blinding speeds…

I didn't know it then…but looking back…with today's eyes and awareness…I do believe …at some point…I became mildly depressed… Looking at old photographs today …it is so obvious…I remember trying to do…so many things…maybe too many…Tech required …a measured amount of study…and drawing…after school…If you played basketball… for conditioning…you also had to run…the Cross Country in track… Also at that time… if you wanted…very much…to be the number one pin setter…on Niagara Street…as I did then… you worked hard and fast… often till midnight…

But the deepest cut of all…the greatest sacrifice…was that my time for girls… shriveled…almost dried up completely …This reality … unfortunately…forced me to… ah…well…stretch the truth a bit…about the frequency …and number of female conquests…I could boast of…to the joshing fellows …at the school lunch table every school day…

While at Tech…my good scholarship…begun in grammar school… continued in the beginning…but then slipped a bit…I made the Honor Roll…a few times…but most of the time…without trying too hard…I was just an average B-student…like most…of my fellow black…and white students…A phenomenon of our…integration experience…was the fact that we blacks…like the…"school integrators" who would follow us…in the coming years… usually huddled together…at separate tables…in the lunch room…It wasn't…that we were not welcome…at other tables…so much as it was a cultural "thang"…We had our own… flowery…maybe…sort of peculiar way…of communicating…of joking and jiving…and playing the Dozens…in a manner…that those white boys…just could not…begin to "dig"…to understand…We did…however…have one unifying thing in common:…a loud…roaring cheer…from black and white students… whenever someone dropped a tray of food in the lunch room…

Yes…we blacks hung together…Why?…I think I know…and I'll be honest…It is just sometimes hard…to forget about "your place"…to walk freely…to walk… unencumbered by the fear…hesitation…the caution… and fearsomeness…of racial discrimination…You can feel racism…even if you can't always…touch it…or scream at it… I could be mistaken…but in the few years before…and during my time at Tech…I do not recall…

any black kid...being elected...an Officer of a class...Things changed... of course...but back then...in the early 1950's ...it was mostly reality for us...In later years...Bob Coles told me there were one...or two non-whites pick to be leaders...before we attended Tech...

For us...you were...in the building...but not fully there...accepted ...to a degree...but not completely...and you knew it...and accepted it...On more than one occasion...in my life...I have tried to explain...the phenomenon... of racial scarring...of quiet victim acceptance...of feelings of inferiority... and smothered assertiveness...My efforts usually had mixed results... with American whites...who know everything...of course...but who have never...had to deal with ...the psychological damage...of any thing like the victims of... black American race discrimination ... I might also add...on many occasions...I have also tried therapeutically...I thought... to highlight the same issue...also with mixed results...to fellow blacks...

We blacks...at Tech...hung together for personal familiarity...for comfort and ease... At Tech...blacks and whites...were integrated...We played on teams together...studied together...but we still lived...in different worlds...I am convinced...the greatest sin...of American racists...wasn't the measurable violence...the vile... openly physical brutality ...against us...that happened so often...so long...all across the Country...The greatest sin was the quiet...many-generations-long...psychic-lynching... of nearly all of us...To be uncounted denigrated...left-out...that was the worst...the most lasting cut...white people... put upon the souls...of their fellow black citizens...

But it wasn't just us...Looking back...with new eyes...and new understanding ...other ethnic groups...such as...Jews and Italians... were also...integrating the "Techs"...the many work places...the sacred institutions...and Waspy enclaves...of the white males of Buffalo... That was also...an unfolding story back then...blind to most blacks...who understandably focused and defined the world...mostly in black and white terms... Nevertheless...our early racial integration experience...in the 1950's...at Tech...was an atypical precursor...to the many ugly scenes... and stories...at high schools...and colleges...then about to unfold... around the Country...

During my time at Tech... we were just approaching...the bitterly explosive...13 or so years of the...civil rights movement...in America...

At Tech…long before the violence elsewhere in the Country…we wrote… our own chapter on integration… Thankfully …ours was a relatively… peaceful chapter…

At Tech…individual whites…who resented you being there…or didn't like you…usually just stayed their distance…Others were pointedly friendly…I will never forget Henry Brodowski…a tow-headed…blond Pole…who sat behind me…in one of my homerooms… We struck a warm friendship…and Henry even invited me…to a Saturday party…in the Walden area of Buffalo…It was there…that I learned that a polka… wasn't that far from…the old two-step… (…just add a "skip")…There were other friendly whites…I easily took too…like Italian lover-boy… Sergio Fornasiero…and the Armenian…Evan Bagdasarian…I had…almost universally good…relationships…with my fellow black students too… Some I had grown up with…in neighborhoods…long before Tech…playing sports… going to movies…sniffing around girls…I can recall little…if any…real rancor…or bitter animosity among us…at least not at school…

Like most black kids…long before high school…I loved sports…and I tried my hand…at everything…Baseball…football…basketball…track…I was determined to be… Robinson …Motley…Sweetwater…and Owens… all in one…I can remember racing… swift kids…on the red bricks…of Bristol Street…tackling tough little…recent arrivals…from Alabama…in glass-strewn lots…next to the Projects…on Clinton Street…I remember helping to make…the dirt holes…under the… baskets…at Welcome Hall… deeper… I also remember puffing…and huffing…a half mile behind…Cross Country champion…my schoolmate … Mike Finnerty… and dozens of others…in Delaware Park… Unfortunately…running Cross Country was a requirement to make varsity basketball …But for years…I tried to forget… about the time…I was knocked unconscious …at the Bennett High School football field… trying to make the Tech varsity football team… Without regret…I didn't…

Then…one evening…I proudly high jumped a bar…set at five feet… in the School 75 playground …across the street…from where I lived… That was…just minutes before Harvey Austin…that athletic terror… from Emerson high school…practice-jumped…six and a half feet…over the bar…And I even once…had the impudence…to challenge…some "show boating"… basketball shooting…kid named…Chuck Daniels… to a game of H-O-R-S-E…one Saturday morning…at Broadway…and

Spring Streets...Daniels just happened to be all-city...at that time...I even played ...second-string...(or was it third-string?)...varsity basketball at Tech...and tried...to keep up with...fancy Joe Bolden...on the brown gym floor...at the Chapel...an eastside community center...My point is...while growing up...I lived...and hung out...in a lot of...old...eastside Buffalo ...neighborhoods...and played a lot of sports...with a bunch of wonderful...young athletes...that I could...not even once...begin to compare to...I enjoyed being out there though ...I sure did...I sure did...

At Tech...I remember kids...with names like...Lawrence... Lomeo... Brodowski ... Gianadda...Hammond...Maggiore...Tillman...Turnage... Rush...Williams...Evans...Nolley...Daniels...Gary...Dixon...Demps... Jeter...Davis...Hewitt...Gayle...Burroughs...Willoughby...Austin... Reed...Mitchell...Godfre...Redd...Thompkins...Ross...Traylor... Herrell...Garrett...Echols...Godfrey...Commodore...Clark...Finnerty... Whittaker...Barr...Bolden...Kirchberger...Caci...Black...Scaffidi... Taylor...Scott...McGhee...Fenty...Luchey...Johnson...Hill...Hipp... Wing...Lee...Draper...Coffey...Brown...Bush...Van Story...McCarley... Woodbeck...Campbell...Barker...Christopher...Dipasquale...Roberts... Bagdasarian...Fornasiero...Hall...Washington...and teachers with names like... Zabo...Hoeffler... Soukup... Burkhalter... Benham ...Smith... Witmer...Zeferjahn...Brooks...May...and Principals...Kuehn...and Ryther...

While at Tech...in 1954...that precociously enlightened ... ever searching...Board of Education ...was at it again...They...partly responding... to money pressures... demographic patterns...and predictions...about the black density of the eastside...made another neighborhood-changing decision...They decided to...scatter the kids...at Hutchinson Central to... mainly ...East High School...but also to...a few other City schools... such as Bennett and Riverside...Along with emptying Hutchinson... they decided... that Tech would be better off...if it was more...centrally accessible...in a newer building...in a whiter neighborhood ...and better reached...by all bus routes...going downtown...Tech...on Clinton Street...was also... increasingly ...becoming an island...of the brightest ...surrounded by...a growing population...of black migrants...from all around the Country... Hutchinson Central... would become...the new Technical...in fact...the new...Hutchinson Central Technical High School ...in a mostly...stable... older...near west side...white neighborhood...

Many of us in the neighborhood ...thought this decision was a bone to the racists ...who saw the near eastside...becoming blacker...and that trend alone...to some...would diminish the sacredness of Tech...It was one of the many political moves...by the Board of Education... and others... that would...in the next decade...help fuel the accusation that Buffalo's schools were the fourth...most segregated school system...in the North... True or not...it would take...two more decades...(until approximately 1988)...to change that... unfortunate perception ... Not long after that decision...sadly...we bid farewell...to the old building ...and the School 32 swimming pool...across the street...where many excellent... Tech swim teams practiced...I ...personally...bid goodbye to the little park...on the corner ...the memories of...cowboys and Indians... hiding in the green shrubbery...and the initials ...and names...I carved in the old desks... [CARMEN NADINE]...Wherever we were going...I was convinced... it just wouldn't be the same...to me...

Playing the Dozens

Scene: *INTERIOR...Tech High School cafeteria. Students making it through the food line. A steady buzz above the clamor, as students wolf down whatever they are having for lunch. CUT TO: A table with six black students enjoying lunch. Another one comes up...*

Mitchell
(At the table)

What's happening...Bailey? Come on in...have a squat.

Bailey
(Sitting down)

What's up?

Mitchell

You're up...How you handling it today, Baby?

Bailey

Under control...brother...Under control...

Mitchell

You mean like your sister was under my control...under me last night... *(The challenge is made.)*

Bailey
(Starting to eat)

At least she was acceptable enough to be under you... Your sister couldn't get under me...unless she put a muzzle on and covered her head with a brown paper bag... *(Raucous laughter at the table)*

Mitchell

Be careful...son... Be careful...Don't be disrespectful...Me and Yo' mama was so close...you could've been my son...*(Laughter again)*

Bailey

Speaking of sun...It looks like you've gotten a little too much sun lately...
Why you've gotten so black...you could leave finger prints on coal...
(Again raucous laughter)

Mitchell

Not bad...Not bad...for the tiniest *dick* at the table...

Speaking of tiny dicks…your dick's so skinny…if it was two feet longer, you could pick your own teeth with it…
(Table pounding laughter)

And so it went…until interrupted by a loud roar and a clap for whomever dropped a tray…in the food line…or until the bell rang…ending the lunch period…for this group of students… some playing the dozens…at lunch time…at Tech High…

A Fateful Evening

1954 and there I was…at his knee again…listening…Well…maybe not quite at his knee… like I used to be…ten years before…in North Carolina…I was just seven back then…and I always loved listening to Papa talk…Not just talk though…I loved all sounds…any sound from…Lewis Andrew Stewart…A belch…a cough…a long loud sip…of bitter black coffee…in the early morning dark of the back bedroom…on Douglas Street…I remembered all of the…sounds…prayers…and quiet hisses from Papa… When I was six years old…he was a man that I so dearly…wanted to be like…a man like Richard…my father…a man just like Papa…my grandfather…

The last time I had seen Papa…my mother's father…before that August evening…on leafy Woodlawn Avenue…in Buffalo…New York… he had just bent down…hugged and kissed us all goodbye…On that day… we…my mother Dimple…siblings…Gwen and James…and I…were about to join… the great black migration north for Buffalo…New York…Just as I was…when I was a six-year old back in Charlotte…that day…I was still mesmerized by the… tall…tan…weather-worn …now 68 year-old black man…from Charlotte…That day…in 1954…he looked much the same… except maybe grayer…a bit shorter…than I remembered him…or was it just that…his height really hadn't changed much…and it was I…who had now grown to over six feet tall…

I always had fond memories of Papa…He had encouraged me to be a "big man"…to stand as tall...as he did…to help out at home…and be a good "school student" too… Papa moved in with us after grandma Lula …"left him"…Just about all of his family…but us…had also left Charlotte for somewhere else by then…However…he hadn't lived with us very long…in Charlotte …before we also left…It was the first time…I had ever lived with Papa…but I was always glad he was there… Now I wasn't the only "man" in the house…to look after us…But when he was there… with us…I also wanted his approval …his blessing… on anything I did… on just about everything…

I was always eager to show him…that I too…could make a big roaring fire…in the big stove…that I could pull his big…black shoes off all by myself…or light a kerosene lamp …in the wind…And I loved his chipped tooth smile...when I showed him how fast…I could pedal my little red fire truck…with the clanging bells… and riding seat on the back… He always softly chuckled when I put James…or Gwen on the back…and went careening down the sidewalks of Douglas Street…ringing the little truck's fire bell… pretending I was off to put out a great…roaring fire… somewhere in Charlotte…

Back then…Papa was usually quiet…plaintive…but I knew he wasn't happy… Some days he was openly sad…mostly after…he talked about my grandmother …Lula…who had "run away"…up north to Buffalo… After talking about Grandma…for any reason… he would usually…go off and read quietly…hesitantly…from a tattered…old-looking bible…as if looking for confirmation …or reassurance of the righteousness…of what he had just said to us…

Papa was…as church people say…"god-fearing"…and I knew he prayed a lot…A few times… he went to church with us…and he always reminded me of the times when Richard …my daddy…used to take us to church…Papa knew Richard well…but I don't remember him saying too much…especially nice things…about Richard…The last time I saw them together …as I recalled…was in Huntersville…at Papa's farm… The year Papa…came to live with us… Richard had run away too… up north…to Washington…D.C…Once I heard Papa say…to Dimple… that he…"didn't respect no man…who would run off and leave his own chaps…for somebody else to raise."…

Now Papa was in Buffalo...for his first..."wide-eyed"...and to my knowledge...only time...to visit part of his considerable brood now living in Buffalo...Of his nine surviving children...out of 14 by my grandmother Lula... six:... Ann... Bill... Frank...Corine (Dimple)...Janie ...and Lula Belle... had followed my grandmother to...and still lived in...Buffalo... Three others... Julius ... Ernest and Ulysses...lived in New York...and Chicago...Four others died in childbirth...or early childhood...Ruth...the youngest of them all...had died tragically...at age 25...just three months before that evening...in Lula Belle's living room... Grandma Lula...whom Papa hadn't seen since 1943...had died in nearby Lackawanna...eight years before that evening in 1954...

That night...my uncles...Frank... Bill...and I...along with Salister O'Daye...my aunt Lula Belle's...long-time companion...were sitting listening to Papa reminisce about events in his life...his children...his tender memories...his regrets...Those moments were magical for me... There... in that room...were the men in my life...my role models...They... more than anyone else... with all of their obvious weaknesses... were the collective surrogate for the long missing Richard...from my life...As I listened to them...they temporarily pushed aside ...that nagging little emptiness...that feeling that something...or someone... a father ...was missing from my life... I listened very closely to their every word...that fateful evening...

Like the temperature outside...it was a warm...and cordial exchange between the men...in Lula Belle's living room that evening...While Dimple and a pregnant Lula Belle... fried chicken...in the kitchen...and the younger kids chatted away...a couple of the men drank beer...Papa... Frank and me...enjoyed iced water...They told jokes...discussed the many differences they saw between...New York's...Georgia's...and North Carolina's weather...churches...farming and politics...Papa recounted the awe he felt looking at mighty Niagara Falls...and I could tell that Frank and Bill...like me...had missed Papa too...It was the first time...I had seen them defer...so politely...to another man...It was as if...they too...were once again...at Papa's knee...like me...listening...learning...

That evening there was also talk...about what had happened...in their lives...since they last saw each other ...They talked about their wives...or their women...their jobs...their dreams...They especially...expressed great sorrow…for what had happened to young Ruth…a few months before…that evening… Ruth was the youngest of Papa's children… She was also Grandma's and Dimple's favorite… Ruth the wayward …the pretty…gray-eyed …pudgy 25-year old…who dropped out of high school…at age 17 in 1946. She left home…just months after her mother died…when it was just impossible …to live in the same house …with her oldest brother…my uncle…Bill…

After seven years…of off and on relationships…with an assortment of men…in the Spring of 1954…Ruth found herself in Cleveland …Ohio… with a smooth…sweet-cologne-wearing operator…named Phil…Phil had been to our house a couple of times…and it became clear to me that Dimple…thought Phil was a pimp…Pimp was a word Dimple had to carefully explain to some of the younger kids…when she used it… Of course I knew what it meant… However …because she loved her so… Dimple…always carefully avoided passing judgment on Ruth… and her life…Still she was anxious and concerned…when she learned…in 1953 …that Ruth…was leaving Buffalo for Cleveland…

In May of 1954…Ruth was shot to death… after a bitter dispute… with another young woman… who lived in the same Cleveland rooming house…with her and Phil…The tragedy was a sharp…deep blow to all of us…It also deepened…the quiet resentment…Dimple had been feeling… for some time…toward her oldest brother…Bill… She resented Bill mostly for…in her opinion…driving her little sister away from home…seven years earlier…It was a resentment…that would never leave…and one that would fester and infect…all of Dimple's children forever …especially me…That evening…my uncle Bill didn't say too much…but he sheepishly expressed sorrow…when they talked about Ruth…I remember that…in an awkward pause in the conversation…at that point…I quietly chimed in…that I… too… remembered …and loved Ruth very much…

At one point…that evening…Frank…my favorite uncle…surprised me…when he politely …almost apologetically… said to Papa… "Daddy… why couldn't you and Mama get along?…That has bothered me…to this day…Y'all used to have some pretty rough fights" …Papa paused…sighed heavily…as if that anvil…he used to pound on…in North Carolina… had been placed on his chest… Then he said…"I guess we had our share of spats…your Mama and me…You know…your Mama had a kind of… way of …well … provoking you…Some women just……I don't know what it was"... My uncle Bill chimed in..."Was it jealousy?...Mama was good looking...and a lot of men knew it"...Papa responded..."Naw...That wasn't it...I knew men...had an eye for her...

You right...Your Mama was a fine looking woman...But most of the time we got into it over silly stuff...little things...Sometimes it was about you kids...Y'all was some of the laziest chaps...I ever saw...and when...I got on you about work...your Mama acted like she didn't like it...sometimes... and you know your Mama...she'd challenge an alligator"...All of us smiled at that...Then Frank said..."Papa...I don't think I was lazy...maybe some of the others...Julius and Dimple...and all...deserved those beatings...but not me...I worked my butt off...in them cotton fields... plowing behind those...old...damn...farting mules"...All of us chuckled at that...

Papa...in a slightly defensive tone responded..."Y'all just don't get it... There was a lot of pressure on me and your Mama...Them white people wanted production...money ...from their land...and there was no way...I could work those farms...by myself...We had ten chaps... five strapping boys...and we had to plant...and harvest those rented fields...and feed and clothe everybody...and at least try to break even...for the year...or we might as well been back in slavery...absolutely working...for nothing...

All them years I sharecropped...working white people's land...I never made no money... Them crackers...wouldn't let you...You always owed them...no matter what crops... cotton ...tobacco...you brought in...you still owed the cheating dogs...And if you objected ...to their cheating... they'd want to hang you...like they did Brother Crawford... over there in Abbeville...South Carolina...I think it was the year...your mother was born Billy...I was a young man then...in my thirties"...O'Daye ...asked softly..."Did they really hang the man?" ...Papa answered..."A whole gang of them...shot him full of holes...and then strung him up over a sign post... just because he challenged the price they offered him...for his cotton... And Crawford wasn't no poor man...like...my daddy Abe was...like I was...He owned his land...before they killed him...and took it all away from him"...

Feeling more confident to speak up...I asked Papa...if he was ever afraid for his own life... "Sure...more times then I have fingers and toes"... sliding forward in his chair...and pointing to his palm...as he answered..."I was deathly afraid of small pox...and white people ...I saw a lot of both... The whites were the worst...Them white crackers...was something...I tell you…They came after me…for nothing…one morning…down there in… Chester County …I knowed they was Klan…But I had my shotgun…in my wagon…and I pulled it and told them …I would use it…They backed off…but we didn't stay…around there too much longer…too dangerous…

Fact is…I been running from…and fighting off…white crackers all my life…All of us!…My brothers Ben…and Wiley…and Heywood… we all had to fight them devils…I suspect your Mother had to fight 'um too"…"Mama…she fought too?"…asked Bill…"Darn right"…said Papa…"She never said much…but I suspect so…My greatest fear…was always worrying… about your Mama… or one of my girls…getting put on…by one of them white devils…while I was in the fields…or gone somewhere…Why they'd rape your women…and think nothing of it…I tell you…a Negro's greatest fear…was his woman getting pregnant… and nine months later…having some strange…light skin…young 'un…land in his basket…Wasn't nothing you could do… Nothing!…It was a terrible life…a terrible life"…

I then asked him…where did the name…"Stewart"… come from. "Where did we get it from?" He said…"Oh…I don't know… my daddy…Abe…said we probably named after some white man… somewhere back in slavery…I never knew Abe's daddy…One thing for sure…wasn't no Stewarts in Africa"…That's the way it went that night… Papa remembering …telling powerful stories…relating and exchanging experiences…with his sons…educating all of us…about his life…as a sharecropper…in North and South Carolina…O'Daye…who had said least…that evening…proudly contributed… that his mother was a school teacher…in Valdosta…Georgia…but they too…his family…were terribly afraid of evil-doing white men…

The evening spun on with funny…and sad tales…about always packing up and leaving…in the middle of the night…and how somebody…got kicked in the head…when they spooked a horse…trying to mount it… from the wrong side…There were sorry tales about… razors and pistols… and brutal fights… with other black men …There was talk…about the time lightning struck…and killed a mule…in the yard of the farmhouse… and how…when it happened…the dog ran under the porch…and wouldn't come out… There were regrets about not getting… enough education… or equal regrets about…too much schooling …for his children…when crops...had to be tended to...I remember fondly...tales about flirting... and what women liked...or didn't like...and what women saw in men... Frank and Bill...told how they couldn't wait to get away from home...and all the hard...brutal farm work...they gladly fled from...

It was a fascinating journey...listening to them that evening... For me... it was satisfying in so many ways...but it was also an evening...that helped to create further impatience...a rushing...stifling impatience...in my life...It was an evening of decision too...After that evening...I no longer wanted to be a bored...too-often depressed...high school kid...who was losing patience with the way he lived...and the direction of his life...I was convinced ...it was a life...that would surely become dangerously bereft of optimism... if things stayed the same...I wanted my life to hurry up now...I felt grown up...ready...I no longer felt unsure... uncertain ...about facing life on my own...and I wanted to get on with it...I wanted to get on with new challenges...new faces...and new places...After all I was nearly 17 now...

Message to a Slave

To all of you...who would be slaves... I say...
why do you choose to be so?...Why do you
accept your condition... bow to the enslaver
...and offer up your being?...Why are you so
valueless...so hopeless?...Why do you not
prefer freedom?...Think about it...A slave
chooses to be so!...There is no other answer....
It is simply that...If you are a slave...you have
chosen to be one...Yes...you have chosen...
to be a helpless creature with...limited vision
...a reduced urge...to be on your own...Why?
...Why have you made this choice?...You do
have a choice...you know...You do indeed...
You can choose...to be a free soul...Listen to
me slave...it begins in your mind...It begins
with...your understanding...of what it means
to be free...Freedom comes...when you first ...

free your mind...when you explore your soul deeply... and conclude...that you were not put... on this earth...to be a slave...for anyone...Your feared tormentor...has no power...that is greater ...than your wish to be free...The enslaver... needs your submission...your deference...even your love...Freedom will begin...when you withhold...each of these...when you despise... when you defy...with every fiber of your being...You can put sand...in his motors...poison in his baby's milk...fear in his night of sleep...and ultimately ...deny him...your very presence...For when you resist...even the worst punishment...can finally...

set you free!....

The Honor Student Drops Out

With all the work..."civil rights" yelling and goings on...inside Tech... and out...I was a very...busy young man......But with the issue of race...in the 1950's....increasingly becoming a powerful subject that you could not escape...I... somehow...on my own... found time and began to read...about history...politics...me...us...black people...I began to ask questions...seek answers and form opinions about slavery... Reconstruction ...Jim Crow laws...Socialism... Communism...and something I knew absolutely... nothing about ...It was something I would eventually call "Americanism"... Up until then...well-meaning ...but equally un-knowing teachers...had taught me a lot about...the Founding Fathers ...cherry trees....and the new..."under god"...Pledge of Allegiance...At School 6 and at Tech ...I learned about Abraham Lincoln...the Emancipation Proclamation... and the absolute wonderfulness...of American capitalism...I was taught about...the Nina...the Pinta...and the Santa Maria...the heroes...Lewis and Clark...Christopher Columbus...and Theodore Roosevelt...

Thinking back...I wish they had...also taught me about...the real heroes of black emancipation...the abolitionists...and brave blacks...who demanded...and fought for their freedom...from the human destruction of slavery... I wish I had learned more about the genocide...practiced openly...against the Indians...or even about ...Buffalo's own...Jean-Baptiste-Pointe-du Sable equivalent...*Joseph* "Black Joe" *Hodges* ...He was reputed to be the first...non-Indian settler...in the 1789 Seneca Indian gathering by the Lake...later called Buffalo...In the coming years...I would also come to regret ... that I did not also know...or learn soon enough...about all the forces...that were slowly... shaping... creating a personality...and setting the stage...for my life to be...

In my third year at Tech...depression...exhaustion...and pessimism... finally became too much...I could not see any hope on the horizon...Some of us...sitting at the lunch table every day at Tech...began to talk about the recently integrated armed forces...about the announced ...soon-to-end G.I. Bill...America's World War II...and Korean War...veterans benefit programs... I became...specifically interested in the college assistance provisions of those benefits...and began to feel that...if I quit school...and joined the Air Force...maybe I could qualify for education assistance...As I saw it...it was the only way...I could see getting into college...

College was a stretch...for most of we blacks at Tech...It was not talked about much... not at school...and certainly not in my immediate family...There wasn't one... college attendee ...let alone graduate...in sight...in my family...that I could relate to...Most of the black kids who went to college...in those days...went under athletic scholarships...The others were mostly the kids of black professionals ...or wealthy black business people...I wanted desperately to go to college...and I had come to conclude that... college...some how...no matter what...was going to be an experience in my life someday...

The notion of quitting school percolated...escalated...and became an obsession...The move from the old Tech building to the new...west side building...didn't help much. either... School ...somehow wasn't quite the same...We had the same teachers...and administrators ...but I still missed Clinton Street...Finally...swearing that I would continue learning...no matter what happens...with my mother's very reluctant permission...ten years after...arriving in Lackawanna...as a seven-year old migrant...from Charlotte...North Carolina...I dropped out of Tech...and joined the... United States Air Force...My last day at Tech...I said good-byes to my buddies...and leisurely walked home...alone...from Tech...to 85 Adams Street... The walk was a good deal more... than just a few city blocks...I think I cried…a little…along the way…but I didn't know why… After all…I was doing exactly…what I thought I wanted to do….

Joy With Green Skies

Lift me up out of the morass of …winless…joyless living…
Let me know what is better…than… this I see…this I feel…

this melancholy…this dry…almost hopelessness… The
solution cannot be…death… because death is the end of

it all…the ultimate…surrender…To die is to not know…
if you won or lost.…No…I want…a new kind of life…a

new kind of consciousness…a fulfilling life of joy…and
giving…and brightness…and sunny days…But if this

kind of existence…is impossible…and there will be…bumps
and craters…green skies and yellow foul rivers…forever

in my path…My choice…for life itself…becomes clear…being
…living…is still better…than not being…not living…at all…

Evil Gene

Why has it happened once again?

Is it to be every day now?

What is the madness, the cruelty

the insanity, the total depravity?

Why do we eat our children?

Why does that evil, brutal gene,

scream to the top of consciousness and

fight to once again be paramount?

Why do so many males, who walk in

our presence, succumb to the urge to rape

and kill the meek? Are they answering a

long ago, beaten down instinct? Is there

truly this kind of savagery in all of us?

Will it ever go away, recede, flicker and die?

Oh, God! When will they be honorable men?

I think not ever, she answered. Annoyed,

she repeated, "I think not ever, human being."

Religious Soldier

I don't believe the truly *religious* can ever be peaceful…
at rest…content within themselves…and their beliefs…
For to be so…is to concede that they may not truly be…
the sole possessors of…the ultimate and only truth…
that there may be a competing truth…worthy of at least
equality…if not superiority…somewhere out there…
lurking…challenging…blaspheming…

To be genuine…real and fundamental…the
truly *religious* must be on the march…proselytizing
… carrying forth the message…to the unbeliever…
whether they want to hear it or not…It is not

enough...to turn away...to just write off the
unbelievers... to silently condemn them to their
worst end...for non-belief...their greatest sin...

The truly *religious* must be aggressive...on guard...
always prepared for the...unstated...but sure to come
...challenge from the unbelievers...This is the only
way the truly *religious* ...can know that they...alone...
possess the one...and only truth...I believe that this
obsession has been ...at the root of most...if not all...
human conflict...since the creation of humans...

Life Ride

Once again the madness comes.
Lies and unrighteousness reigns again.
Blood has to quench and fill the cavities.

Will it be as Niagara or the Rio Grande?
Victims will put chains on their legs and wrists.
God will be annoyed, her ears will bleed.

Tears, laughter, pain, ecstasy, even time will hurt.
Beauty and relief will come in small things,
a soft breeze, a seagull's squawk, a baby's skin.

When? When? Oh God, when?
Never you fool! Who are you?
Just shut up, and enjoy the ride of life.

The Air Force

The train ride from Buffalo to Geneva...New York...was not that far...
It was my third ride...of any distance on a train...It was not...however...

as pleasant...or as wondrous as my second long train ride... Nearly a year earlier...with a pass from my uncle Frank...a dining car waiter with the New York Central Railroad...I had ventured to Chicago to spend a vacation week with Frank's brother Ernest...That was the butterflies-in-the-stomach trip...my growing up trip...On that trip...I would see my first major league baseball game... (Chicago White Sox verses the New York Yankees)... visit my first college campus... (Northwestern) ...and thanks to another young uncle...Ulysses... learn how to be at ease...around pretty ...young white girls...

But this short ride to Geneva was...in some ways... like the ride from Charlotte...10 years earlier...This was the beginning of real adventure... Real ...permanent change was coming...I was now free to control my daily life...and free to decide what kind of man I would be...This would be my ride to freedom...It was my escape from the dry anxiety...and poverty...of a little nomadic...single parent family without much real stability...and certainly limited dreams... Maybe now I would...finally have my own bed...my own space...I certainly wouldn't have to stomach any more...of that bloated...food gobbling excuse for a stepfather...that Dimple married...or should I say...allowed to move in with us...

Earlier...when Dimple "married" Louis Johnson... (They officially married after I left)... Gwen ...James...and I...saw our long held hopes for a real father...come crashing down... Louis and Dimple had known each other in Charlotte...He was a guitar plucking... member of a gospel singing group...that Dimple had a brief liaison with...before we left Charlotte... 10 years later...he just suddenly showed up...in Buffalo... He was jovial and likeable at first...To this day I can pluck...a couple of blues cords on a guitar...thanks to Louis...

But the man was lazy...beyond description...and he ate like a horse... You can imagine his impact...on our little...penny-counting family...when he contributed so little ...and ate so much... It was one thing...when Gwen had to stop sleeping with Dimple... and move to the couch at night... but something else...making room for Louis at the dinner table ...That was truly a personal...and major sacrifice for us kids...I even learned to choose ... very carefully... the times I brought home ice cream...or my favorite restaurant sandwiches ...My rule was...to always be sure Louis wasn't around...or no one...sadly...would get very much of the feast...

As the train...to the Air Force...cut through the growing darkness... the thought of leaving Gwen and James behind...had bothered me... Before I left...I had agreed to have $25.00 a month... deducted from my Service pay...as an allotment to my mother Dimple...I thought this might help...to make up for the hustle dollars...I had regularly contributed... to the family before I left... The small allotment could be increased...or decreased...as my pay changed...I left with a full intention...to increase it as my pay increased...Later when I learned how quickly $80.00 a month... my starting pay...disappeared...I declined to increase it when I received... my first $20.00 raise...My reluctance had more to do with...negative reports about Louis' continued laziness...than anything else...

Now Louis...and years of anxiety...were behind me...After a flurry of medical exams ...oath taking...and a skimpy box lunch...19 of us had been given vouchers...marched to a train... and told..."From now on you're in the United States Air Force...and you'll be told what to do...and when to do it"...My enlistment commitment was for 8 years...at least four of which had to be active duty...Eight years seemed like a lifetime...back then...but I shrugged ... swallowed hard...and thought...Oh well...so much for freedom...Curiously...I was the only black person in the group of recruits on the train...This seemed odd...given all the neighborhood and school talk...about joining the service...from buddies and guys I knew ...When I decided to join the Air Force...I only mentioned it to the one or two of the close buddies I had... none of whom...felt as compelled to leave home...as much as I did...

To them...what I was about to do...was too bold...too drastic...I guess they didn't feel my pain or face ...the same dry...hopelessness...that I felt... As for my mother...she genuinely agonized over my decision to leave.... It was a tough decision for her...but sensing my resolve...she reluctantly gave her permission...With that I walked away from Dimple ...Gwen... James...and the old neighborhood...And as always...when you leave the neighborhood...people who looked like you...who made you feel comfortable...thinned out considerably...This did not bother me greatly... but I sure would have felt a lot better...if I had had a few of those brothers... from the Tech lunch room table...riding that train with me...

When we finally arrived at Sampson Air Force Base...near Geneva... New York...It was pouring cold rain...Two bus loads of us recruits...

were joined together...and put under the charge of Airman First Class Saragusa...our Training Instructor (TI)...Once more...we were sternly reminded...that we no longer controlled our own lives...Saragusa's first words to us was..."Put those God-damned butts out...From now on you'll smoke...when I tell you... you can smoke...and talk when I say it's OK to talk...Is that understood?"...He then taught us how to yell..."Yes Sir"... at the top of our lungs...He told us that from then on...we would be known as Training Flight 3972...of the 3651st Basic Military Training Group... and that we had better get to know...and like each other...because we were going to be doing everything together... eating...sleeping...even going to the toilet together...I remembered Saragusa's stern speech very well...and ironically ...I used it precisely three months later... when I too... became a Basic Training Instructor...But that's another story to come...

In the beginning...Air Force basic training was...like all of the armed services...a brutal... sometimes humiliating...stripping of personal habits... and behaviors...that were antithetical to group cohesion...The object was to mold...unquestioned discipline...into individuals... who may come with...less than stellar credentials...when it came to doing what they are told to do...Some free spirits find this difficult...Not me...I took to the discipline and training very well...I had always been eager for a challenge... and eager to show that I could meet it...no matter what it was... That first bewildering night...in Uncle Sam's Air Force... however...proved to be a real test for me...After being forced to stand...in the cold rain for 20 minutes...without talking or smoking...we were double-file...marched to a dining room... (Chow Hall) and fed...Then we were marched to a supply room...to pick up two sheets...a pillow... blankets and our first issue of shoes and fatigues...Already struggling with a stuffed duffel bag...six of us were also forced to carry pails...filled with brooms ...mops and soap...

Exhausted...we finally arrived at our barracks...We learned immediately why it was called barracks...It was a bare...wooden...double-story dorm... with small rooms lining long...middle halls...Six-commode toilets ...and showers...butted each end of the building ...Each single window room... had room for eight men...with double stacked...iron cots...to sleep on... In a quiet moment...I wondered how many future sailors...before us... had slept in those barracks...since five years earlier...Sampson was a Naval training base...It had been a training facility...for the military since just before...the Second World War...Nestled close to the southeast side of Lake Seneca...it would be a training facility...for the Air Force...for only six years...from 1950 to 1956...

As we all eagerly flopped down...on our assigned cots...sleep was all we wanted... But that wasn't...what Saragusa wanted...We were summarily whistled to attention in the hall...and told we had to sweep and mop the floors...before we could sleep... Saragusa... brutally cussed out...and threatened a couple of complainers...whom I felt sorry for...I also ached and felt a little sorry for myself too...It was nearly 11:00 PM...when we started sweeping...mopping and bitching...I remember...whispering to a couple of guys... that I didn't think the floors were that dirty...I was also surprised to learn... how inept...some of the guys were with a mop...

Saragusa...pacing the hall...kept an eye on everything...He told us... we had to clean "every damn thing"...to his satisfaction...and reminded us ...over and over again...that the longer we took...the longer it would be before we could sleep...We cleaned...and cleaned...It was almost 1:30 A.M. before Saragusa finally stopped yelling...and let us go to bed...I am sure everyone was as happy as I was...to finally get to sleep...Four hours later...he was back... yelling and pulling us out of our bunks...for a chilly15 minute... raggedy march...to a sleepy...but welcome...Chow Hall breakfast...

Of the 42 individuals in our Flight...about a third of them were black or Hispanic ...Seven years earlier...before President Truman issued the order integrating the military services... in 1947...this would not have happened...But during my basic training...I do not remember ...an overt instance where race became an issue...From all appearances... we were equal... Race would ...however...subtly become an issue...later when career and Tech School training assignments...were passed out... But Saragusa never once... showed any obvious favoritism ...After a few days...he chose...from among us...who our airmen... assistant Flight leaders would be...The First Assistant Flight leader was a young ... prior service...ex-British Army veteran...named Copeland...To my surprise...I was chosen the Second Assistant Flight leader by Saragusa...

Flight leaders assisted the TI...with such things as marching drills... moving the group from place to place...or filling in when the TI was sick or absent...Being leaders...Copeland and I...were treated just slightly better than the others...After a few weeks or so...we were allowed to go to Saragusa's room…to get a few necessary leadership points…enjoy a beer…or a soda…Some of the guys resented this favoritism...shown us…but they soon learned that…in the military …"rank always has its privilege"…Privilege …however… wasn't enough to make up for the unwanted smells…dull routines…classroom boredom…and loneliness… that was inevitable for us…The marching… which I loved…the class room study …field exercises…and arms training were challenging and exciting… The same could be said for payday…($40 every 2 weeks) …and spending at the BX (Base Exchange)…or seeing a female anywhere …anytime…

In the evenings…after long grueling days…we played cards…joked with each other… and …despite the inevitable racial cliques…bonded well as a unit…Some of the guys in the Flight…got mail from home…Not me…Once in a while…I would call home…and that seemed to be enough for me…I didn't officially have a girl friend then…although…I sort of…felt close to Sheila Sutton…a former school mate and neighbor…and especially close to…Beverly Callahan…the girl next door…Still I eagerly looked forward… to getting that cherished…3-day pass…we earned after 6 weeks of training… Three days…would be more than enough time to get to Buffalo…take in a movie…or two…or whatever…When that 3-day pass finally arrived…I quickly bolted Sampson…After a short military bus ride to Geneva …another train ride…and a total of three and a half hours later…I was home…

And God Said

And God said……

Really?…Are you sure it was God?

Of course…Just read the holy book.

Really?…What is the holy book?

The word of God!…

Who wrote the word of God?

God!…Not a man?

Yes…a man…He was inspired

by God…

Can another man

interpret…be inspired by God?

This God?…Another God?

That Man?…Another man?

The intermediaries are endless.

They line up everyday…selling God.

When you stop and think about it…

We buy a lot of God snake oil…don't we?

6-Week Transformation

There is something about wearing a uniform…Uniforms…instantly say something about you…Whoever looks at you…without knowing your name…immediately knows something about you…Uniforms also transform…the wearer of the uniform…People looked at me differently…when I wore my dress blues…and spit shined shoes…I also felt different …I stood taller…looked straighter…and focused more sharply on the moment… Maybe it was the training…the self awareness…the new discipline…Whatever it was…in just 6 short weeks…I had been transformed…into a proud new person with more purpose…and a ramrod focus…

My family sensed the change…my old friends sensed it …and I believe that trip home…was an early thresh-hold moment in my life… But it was way too short…The 72 hours flew by…I didn't have enough time to visit…kiss…or talk…to everyone who mattered…The weekend became a whirlwind of visits…with family and friends…A movie date with Beverly Callahan…was especially enjoyable… A highlight of the visit…was seeing…for the first time…my Aunt Lula's new baby girl…Joyce… Joyce's father…O'Daye…(His name was really Salister O'Daye.) was my Aunt's… long-time companion… He so trusted me…that at age 15-years old… he allowed me to drive his car…He later asked me to be Joyce's God father…I was very proud to accept… and she has been special to me…ever since…

When I returned to Sampson…my training situation changed quickly…Officially…at that time…basic training was supposed to be for 11 weeks…but my co-flight leader… Copeland and I…had our training periods cut short…Both he and our Tactical Instructor … Airman Saragusa …were "called up" early…Saragusa was given a multiple Flight training assignment … and Copeland…was promoted to Airman Third Class… He was quickly given a new Flight of recruits for training…I was asked to take charge of our Flight 3972…and complete the final 3…or 4… weeks of its training…Needless to say…I was stunned that the Air Force thought so much of my ability…at my age…and degree of training…that they felt I could lead a flight of grown men… most of whom were older than me…

All this happened just before the traditional…Drill Competition …that we all had been looking forward to…The "Drill Comp"…was a marching competition between rival… graduating…Training Flights…and it would be quite an honor to win the marching contest… Before I gave my answer to Saragusa and our training Commander …I asked for permission to talk to the Flight…The Commander said to me…"Bailey…I know what you want to do…Don't do it…In the Air Force we don't ask subordinates…if its OK to be their superior… You just go to them…tell them you are the man…and that's it…whether they like it or not."…I got the message…On my way out…Saragusa said…" By the way…go buy yourself some stripes… You're promoted to Airman Third Class…effective tomorrow"…

Most of the guys accepted me without reservation…I had to get in the chest of a couple of Ohio buddies…but it wasn't serious…We worked hard those last few training weeks…and my love for marching and singing… infected the guys…We practiced our marching moves over and over… and…astonishingly…finished first in the Drill Competition …We were all ...as proud as hell...that we won...Up until that day...I had not had a happier moment in my life...and I reveled in the special commendations and attention we received... I was extremely proud of my flight... and what they helped me to do... Some of the members of Flight 3972...that I remember were: Pete Copeland...Alton Austin... Clarence Quick... David Draper...Henry Hughes...George White...James Bowman... John Strother...Ed Blake...Byron Shindle... Frank Weber...and Denny Hickey...I loved those guys...

Just before basic training ended...for Flight 3972...each trainee was given an Air Force Specialty Code (AFSC)...which designated your next career training step...Career assignments...supposedly based upon...aptitude... scholastic...and psychological testing... ranged from Officer Training School...to mechanical...clerical support...supply room management...or other less glamorous careers...To me it seemed that...race now had crept into our destinies...Not one black or Hispanic airman...in our Flight was given...one of the more glamorous...technical training assignments... Most were to be further trained as cooks...mechanics...supply and motor pool assistants...I was given AFSC 70010 which designated me for clerical training... I...like a number of my fellow blacks...was very disappointed at my next...designated training assignment...I told myself ...maybe I should have stayed a little longer...at Tech...and finished high school ...I also wondered if...maybe there really *was* an intelligence gap...between blacks and whites ...If there was...I firmly concluded...it sure as hell did not show up...going through basic training...

When I finally announced their promotion...to Airman Third Class... and dismissed Flight 3972...for the last time...everyone scattered for a short leave home...and their next training assignment...at bases scattered around the Country...I felt a little empty and sad... saying goodbye to Flight 3972...Not only was I not leaving with them...but later that night...I had to pick up Flight 4083...a brand new flight of recruits for training...A few days before...I had been officially designated a TI ...and would not be leaving Sampson...for more training anytime soon...As hard as I tried...I could not overcome my disappointment...In some ways ...I liked being a TI ...but basic training... wasn't all the Air Force is about...I told myself... Surely there was more adventure ...excitement... learning and things to do...than yelling at a bunch of scared recruits... looking for healing...or trying to qualify for a changed way of life...Reluctantly...I acquiesced to my fate...

I had mixed feelings...as I started my first training flight through basic...I was very confident...but not very happy...I enjoyed leading... but hated being a tough bastard...I...too ...made my first group stay up almost all night...I got in their faces...threatened and challenged them...I did everything by the book...just as my half dozen training sessions... said a TI should do...But being tough just wasn't me...and I dreaded the thought of being...a TI the rest of my career...After weeks into the training period...for my first flight...I told my Commander I wanted out...a new assignment...He seemed very piqued and annoyed at my request...

At that time...the Spring of 1955...the Air Force was over run with young recruits...who joined before the...then effective GI Bill was set to end...A great many of the recruits wanted...like me...to take advantage of the highly valued educational assistance...the GI Bill offered to qualified veterans... As a result...all of the training bases...around the Country... were jammed with recruits...and there was a great need for Tactical Instructors...Still I wanted out...I just did not feel that I wanted to stay in a training command...Suddenly my personal evaluations...which we received every other week or so...became just average...Compliments quickly stopped coming my way...and I could tell I was in somebody's dog house...Waiting for an answer to my request...I took my assigned flight through normal training... but there was nothing outstanding about the effort...Nevertheless...I was determined that the flight...would be...at least...an excellent... marching and singing group...But weeks before the Drill Competition...and flight graduation...which I had looked forward to...I was relieved of my position...

Even though...I had asked for reassignment...I had mixed feelings about being replaced...before the flight finished training... I regretted not emphasizing that enough...to my superiors...But they followed through on my request...and I was relieved...and forced to sit around the barracks...without a job...for those last weeks at Sampson...When I finally received orders... for my next training assignment...once again I had mixed feelings... I was happy to be leaving...but not very excited about...training to become an Air Force Admin Specialist...at Francis E. Warren Air Force Base...in Wyoming...That was to be...unfortunately... my next assignment...However...with a determined resolve...I sucked in my stomach...shouldered my duffel bag...and headed off to Wyoming... It was a little more than 9 months...after sitting in the lunch room...at Tech High School...and I wasn't quite 18 years old...

Bailey's Duckworth Chant

All right men...Listen up...

Hi...Ho...here we go...

Set 'um in now...Set 'um in now...dig 'um in...

Left...right...left...right...go to your right...

Let me hear you!!

Right...left...right...left...go to your left...

Keep it tight...keep it tight...on your right..

When you get off...don't rush to the phone...
Jodie's done got your girl and gone...

Hi...Ho...here we go...

Set 'um in now...Set 'um in now...dig 'um in...

Left...right...left...right...go to your right...

Let me hear you!!

Right...left...right...left...go to your left...

Keep it tight...keep it tight...on your right..

She got real lonely and there was the skunk...
Licking and lapping and all that junk...

Hi...Ho...here we go...

Set 'um in now...Set 'um in now...dig 'um in...

Left...right...left...right...go to your right...

Let me hear you!!

Right...left...right...left...go to your left...

Keep it tight...keep it tight...on your right..

Left oblique...Huh!
Right oblique...Huh!

Hi...Ho...here we go...

Set 'um in now...Set 'um in now...dig 'um in...

Left...right...left...right...go to your right...

Let me hear you!!

Right...left...right...left...go to your left...

Keep it tight...keep it tight...on your right..

I don't know...but it's been said...
Airman Basics can't get no head...

Hi...Ho...here we go...

Set 'um in now...Set 'um in now...dig 'um in...

Left...right...left...right...go to your right...

Let me hear you!!

Right…left…right…left…go to your left...

Keep it tight…keep it tight...on your right..

Our Lieutenant is a real big slob…
He's the only one…can buy a blow job….

Hi…Ho…here we go…

Set 'um in now…Set 'um in now…dig 'um in…

Left…right…left…right…go to your right…

Let me hear you!!

Right…left…right…left…go to your left...

Keep it tight…keep it tight...on your right..

Right flank……Huh!…
Left flank……Huh!…

Hi…Ho…here we go…

Set 'um in now…Set 'um in now…dig 'um in…

Left…right…left…right…go to your right…

Let me hear you!!

Right…left…right…left…go to your left...

Keep it tight…keep it tight...on your right..

ETC…ETC…ETC…

The TI

They numbered about 32…36 on some days…
Young men…short…tall…black…white..

They came from a number of states…Each
one was unique…yet they were all the same…

To me they all wanted to change their lives…
become something other than what they had

been…It was my job to help them get there…
Some did not realize what it took…Sacrifice

…mental or physical…was new to them…
They were the shuckers…and jivers…Some…

were passive…indifferent creatures…just
sliding by…Some were courageous and tried

very hard…Others were cowardly…weak to
the challenge…I shoved them…bullied and

threatened them…and still…I can honestly
say ….I almost liked….every one of them…

My joy…my reward came with the sound…
and the rhythm of the march…I loved the

cadence…the tight oneness of the Flight…
the hard thump of brogues…on the move…

I loved the songs…sung with joy and mirth…
shouted …to the heavens…but only at…and

by my command…It was the one time…
when we were all changed…new men…

of singular purpose…for that moment…
for that day…maybe for the rest of our lives…

It's Always Tuesday

It seems its always Tuesday,
From soaring spirits...to the
pits of despair...from a winning
day...to where you lost your way
...it begins or stops...it seems...
on Tuesday...Why Tuesday...of
all the days?...Why not Monday
...Most would say...that is the
down day...Why not Friday...
the end of week day...No...for
me...it seems...it's always...
Tuesday...Tuesday...the letdown
day...Tuesday...the need uplift day...
It seems it's always Tuesday...

Pick It Up

All Right!

Come on! Pick it up!

Who are you to think

you can go through life,

without a bump in the road?

Life doesn't work like that.

Every human being on earth will have

at least one bump in the road.

Many will have bump after bump after bump!

So what! You're not dead yet!

If you can feel the pain,

you can rise again! All Right!

Pick it up! Pick it up!

This Thing About Rain

I have this thing about rain... Rain is soothing...nutritious...
and absolutely essential to my being...When I hear the
first crack of thunder...I shudder...and marvel at the
lightening...that flashes across the sky...the shimmering

crescendo that slowly builds...the torrent that soon comes...
There is a quiet joy...and a certain calmness...when I am just
out of the rain...but close enough to feel the chill...the wetness...
the delight...from the few drops that find me...waiting...yielding...

Standing in it cleanses me...It is as if...I am then being born again...
washed of all I do not want...shorn of all the old hurts...physical
and mental...Rain bathes and reminds you...of your chordate
beginning...and why water...like oxygen...is so imperative for life...

I know now...that with every rain...I can be unsoiled ...delivered
again...and reminded ...that my life here...for whatever it is worth
...is being replenished... when it rains...and that the time for no life...
if such is to ever to be... is not here yet...No...it is not here yet!...

Francis E. Warren Air Force Base

After a brief three day stop in Buffalo...highlighted only by a short... but delightful movie date...with Beverly Callahan...once again...I was on a train headed west...I had no idea what was in store for me...as the unfamiliar states...west of Chicago...unfolded before the train...On the way to Wyoming...I wondered what else about me...was going to Wyoming ...along with my assignment orders...I had not left Sampson under the best of circumstances ...After all...I had walked away...when I was needed...by an Air Force...that thought I...even though just 17 years old...could lead men...Would requesting a different assignment be a dark... negative mark...on my record forever?...I left behind a lonely... final few weeks...at Sampson...Before leaving...my superiors...had little to say to me...and seemed distant...and uninterested in my fate...Yet I still looked forward to Tech School...and this new place... called Wyoming...

The train ride west was a familiar one...as far as Chicago...Things changed after that ...I had never seen such vast stretches of flat prairie... open farm land...and just space...as we rumbled through Iowa...South Dakota...and Nebraska...I was struck by the very vastness ... and beckoning of the Country...I continually felt the urge to grab a paint brush... and canvas ...and try to capture some of the wonder I was seeing for the first time...I tried to imagine hordes of Indians storming bluffs... and valleys...chasing herds of buffalo...just like in the movies...back home in Buffalo...To me cowboys just didn't fit out here...This was the Indians' place ...like it had been for thousands of years...Could they... Indians and buffalo ...still be here I wondered...I hoped so...and I hoped that I would have a chance...to see them up close...and to explore some of the open spaces...and sights around the base...

Riding on a bus through Cheyenne...I did not feel as if I was in a big city...Things seemed flatter...smaller...lower than the great cities back east...But you knew you were out west ...You were reminded by the great billboards...announcing the fall coming of the "Frontier Days Rodeo"... the many cowboy hats...and bull horn adornments...that seemed to be every where...After a very short ride... I was checked through the gates of Francis E. Warren Air Force Base...Warren Air Base was originally called...Fort Russell...Built in 1867 to protect soldiers...and railroad workers constructing the Union Pacific Railroad...it is the oldest base in the Air Force...In 1930...it was named after the State governor...who was also the first United States Senator from Wyoming...

I later learned that some famous...and colorful characters...had ties to the old Fort...Military types such as...Captain John..."Black Jack"... Pershing... (the leader of American forces in Europe during World War

I)...General Billy Mitchell... (The "Father of the Air Force")...and General Benjamin O. Davis, Senior... (the first black general in any American military service)... all had ties to the old Fort... I was especially interested in the old Fort's connection to the storied "Buffalo Soldiers" ...those all black Calvary and Infantry units...who patrolled the parched surrounding lands...and fought the Indians...for a largely... white Nation who almost forgot to honor them... Since assuming custody of the Base in 1947... the Air Force had used the Base...mostly for technical training ...For the Next 8 weeks or so...it would be my home ...for training to become an Administration Specialist...a glorified military term for "clerk"...

Riding through the Base...along Randall Avenue...I was impressed by the solid red brick buildings...lining the welcoming streets...Could this be where I was going to live?... No! ...After reporting to the Duty Sargent... in my assigned Orderly Room...I would eventually be shown to my bunk space...in bare...two story wooden barracks...reserved for trainees...From my iron-legged bunk...I could see all the way to each end of the long... open floor quarters ...with communal showers...and latrines on one end... This is worst than Sampson...I told myself...At least we had four man rooms at Sampson...There you only had to cope with one or two snorers at night...not 10 or 15...From that disappointing reality...my morale and opinion of Uncle Sam's Air Force...would start to take a downward spiral...that I would never really...quite completely recover from...

The slow fall of my morale...was tied mostly ...to the attitudes of the leaders in charge...Most were white southerners...or mid-westerners ...who often-times seemed to resent... blacks being there...They avoided overt acts...that might get them in trouble...but they made subtle decisions... that were unmistakably racist... We black and Hispanic airmen felt it and hung closely...when we could...It was our way of coping and reinforcing each other...in a white-male dominated environment...

I quickly picked up on...the training routine at Warren...I was assigned to a unit...led by a First Sargent...who ran 7 o'clock reveille and assigned daily...afternoon work details after formal morning classes... Gone for me...were the little freedoms...and privileges of being a Tactical Instructor...I was once again...just a grunt...one stripper...who went to school in the morning ...and worked on menial tasks (grounds cleanup... painting...KP...or Kitchen Patrol) until the end of the work day at 5 o'clock…Tech School was almost…like super high school again…We were taught military history and regulations…basic math …English… and typing ….For good reason…typing would be the most difficult for me… since we had to learn to type…accurately…at a 55 word per minute speed…before we could graduate…At the time...this seemed stupid to me…and certainly did not fit my images of roaring jets… aircraft dog fights at 20,000 feet…and assignment adventures…in exotic places…

Nope…it became clear…I was training to be a "military secretary"…a support slob…for the real "Air Force" people…manning Uncle Sam's Air Force…Oh…we still marched in parades for inspections…and on civilian holidays in Cheyenne…Some of us were once flown to Seattle for a mid-summer's parade…in our crisp…khaki uniforms…But most week days were gritty… dull and routine until 5:00 P.M. …when you could pursue your own personal interests…We didn't have bed check…but we had 7 o'clock reveille the next morning…I …and my buddies…spent about 4 or 5 evenings a week…emptying and stacking up beer cans…in the nearby Airman's Club… Every day the Chow Hall was open…for 3 meals a day…7 days a week…You just had to remember…to get there before the 2-hour window to eat…closed…After being there a few weeks…if you were on good discipline …you could earn weekend passes…to leave the Base …until reveille Monday morning…

My training unit…was filled with guys from all over the Country… They came from north …south…east and west…I liked and got along with most of them…We were all "one stripers"…mostly in our teens or early twenties…with a few old "coots"… or prior service types…thrown in to keep it interesting…I buddied around and drank a lot of 3.2 beer… with a group that included…Billy Shanklin…from I can't remember… Aaron Cannon…from Harlem …New York…and Jesus Ibarra…from Arizona …For the most part I stayed out of trouble… although I did miss a couple of weekend passes for skipping out on work details… and mouthing back to a redneck Sargent…from Alabama …I used the time to write… draw …and practice that damn typing…

On one weekend pass…four of us took a bus to Denver…"to find some girls"…We didn't find the kind of girls I preferred…but we did find a couple of "hookers"…that cost each of us a third of a month's pay…That weekend was my first experience…with a "working girl" …and while I bragged… with the guys back on the base…I really didn't enjoy the idea of "using" women that way…Up until that time…my sexual experience (not counting my 8-year old tryst with a baby sitter…and a fleeting penetration in the back of an Oldsmobile…) had been limited to basically "very heavy petting"… Of course that was not what I told my buddies…at my old High School in Buffalo…Back then…at the lunch table…I had bragged about… "mowing down ho's left and right…all night"…To reinforce my bragging…I even carried in my wallet a "never used" condom…one of my buddies…at the bowling alley… where I worked…gave me…But to be honest…my Mother's stern admonitions about getting girls pregnant…(or getting pregnant in the case of my sister) was constant…and seriously taken by me…

To break up the monotonous…routine of training…and slogging down cans of 3.2 beer every evening…I looked for every opportunity to leave the Base…I usually went to a downtown restaurant…or just looked for scenes or thoughts…to sketch or put down…in a drawing pad…I constantly carried…At times I would pal around with a buddy…or two… But most of the time…I was alone…On one occasion…I was accompanied by a new found friend …who was a cook… permanently assigned to the Base…I started hanging out with Gates… when he befriended me… by giving me extra special portions of…steaks and chops… when I went through the food line…in the Chow Hall…Gates was a 4-year veteran …Airman First Class…from some where around Chicago…He seemed friendly enough… and had a knack for getting other people… permanently assigned to Warren…to drive us into Town…or to some interesting natural site nearby…I thought he was real cool…

My opinion changed one night…when he invited me to his room…in the red brick …"permanent quarters"…he lived in…I had never been to his quarters before…and was impressed with the much better life style this "cook" had…compared to the rest of my training group…However…my opinion of Gates really changed …when in the middle of a terrific Miles Davis album…and a really cool Miller High Life beer…Gates came out of his bathroom… almost completely naked…I was startled…not from his nakedness…I saw a lot of naked men's asses…every morning…in our lovely barracks…I was startled by the way he sashayed …into the room…turned around…bent over…and asked me…"Do you like this?…I was nervously dumbfounded…I instantly recognized how I had been cleverly set up…and I did not like Gates…or myself very much at that moment…I cussed out

Gates...and called him some names...I think I later...regretfully...wished I hadn't...(the steaks got smaller...) Walking back to my barracks...I kept asking myself..."how could you be so blind...so stupid"...

Not long after the incident...with my gay buddy...I finally completed my training...It was approximately two weeks later than it should have been...I was held back a couple of weeks ...because I could not pass...the typing exam to graduate...My fingers just would not fly fast enough to pass the final exam...until I put in some late night practice...I finally got my typing speed...and accuracy...close enough to 55 words a minute... and earned that coveted certificate...designating me a trained...Air Force Administrative Specialist...At that time I also agreed to be tested for that coveted GED High School Diploma... I proudly passed the GED test easily...exactly one year earlier...than I would have graduated from Tech...

After a few days of suspense...my next assignment came through...I was ordered to report to a newly formed...Troop Carrier Group...stationed at Ardmore...Oklahoma...More specifically...I was assigned to be the payroll clerk and Orderly Room assistant...for the 377th Troop Carrier Squadron...of the 309th Troop Carrier Group....I later learned from our First Sargent...that the 309th was a recently organized...tactical assault group...that flew the newly arrived...Fairchild C-123B...assault aircraft... The Group's primary purpose was to perform ...air transport...air supply... and aero-medical operations for the Air Force...He said...he believed the 309th... was ultimately going to be sent to some where in Europe...This perked up my ears...and I felt somewhat better...a lot less apprehensive... about my new assignment ...Europe:...now that sounded like adventure to me...Ardmore... Oklahoma...here I come!

Buffalo Blue Coats

Their brethren...in this land...stretched from Attucks
in the 1750's...They were excellent fighters...natural

scouts...brave and true...Thousands died for the Union...
ran into canon fire...flung their bodies...stabbed and

tore…at the faces of white men they hated…With aching bellies…and shoes with no soles…they wanted to be free!…

But why did they soldier on…when later they lived…in the midst of people who barely accepted their presence?

Most were refugees…from the hated Black Codes…when they guarded buildings…they were not allowed in…and

people who despised them…But they soldiered on…fighting… dying…even being unjustly lynched…Natives…called them

"Buffalo"…Their superiors called them "niggers"…Yet they and their progeny marched on…believing in the promise…

hoping for a long earned…day of respect…for all the brave… black legs…and all the sturdy…black arms…in blue coats…

and blue trousers…pounding the dust…riding high on a steed… fighting and dying…duty bound…solidly resolved…despite it all…

The Soil of Wyoming

An open soul…cannot be lonely…on the rolling prairies…
hills or bluffs…we call Wyoming…There…it is impossible
to not hear the many songs…testimonies…and utterances of
the ghosts…who stand…follow…and walk with you…They
all talk to you…The prairie grass whistles…and hums as it
bends before a delicate…mischievous breeze…dancing and
cutting its own song…A majestic…screaming eagle will answer…
the howl of a cougar…A lowly rock…will hiss and break in two…
as if a million years together…is long enough…A huge boulder
will move without a wind…a quake…or a single drop of moisture…
A tiny brook strains to mock an ocean…because it knows…senses its
potential…its power to change…deepen…everything before it…The

soil of Wyoming...as most soils everywhere...mistresses of the Sun...
gives and withholds...embraces without a hug...then blows away
with a rakish breeze...wearing a new hat...At the top of the chain...
wind rules them all...even the two legged wanderers...who root and
disturb...and try to sing to us... their song too...Watch and keep
us all...blue sky of mystery...giver of life...Guard us...Let us breathe
forever... at least as long...as the soil of Wyoming yields its life too...

The Rockies

They just sit there...tall...majestic...silent...reverent...
Someone named them the Rockies...But why should

they have a name...that some man gave them?...What
were they called millions ago...before there was a man?...

And what will they be called...a million hence...long after
all men?...Can ever there be an appellation...that befits

what they are?...Will there ever be a statement...an
expression...a murmur...that we can utter...that could

give proper measure...appropriate respect...for their
magnificence?...As they look down...God-like...from

the thin...cold heavens...one wonders...if they have a
name for us...or if we...could ever be worthy of such...

The Team

Every hungry wolf...needs a raven...to tell it where to go...
and when to leave...when it gets there...The raven...
can lead to the pith...they both need...but it takes the
wolf...to set the table...to put muscle to their life...

Every hungry raven…needs a wolf…to do what it can't do…
to satisfy the carrion gene…conveyed from eons ago…The
wolf…has the strength…to feed them both…but it takes…
the raven's eyes…and wings…to know what hill…to climb…
what river…to cross…what valley holds the prize…

One without the other…doesn't mean…they can't live…
that they can't have a time…But together…each of their
lives will be…longer…richer…more sustaining than it
would have been…if they were unaware…of each other…

Land, Ocean and Spirit

***It is still wondrous to think…that they
walked here…climbed these hills…
mountains…trees…and crossed these
streams…They…maybe…even sat on
this very rock…***

***White people said…they were savages…
fought them to the death…My great-grand
mother was no savage…Yet they took the
land…that for billions of years…belonged
to no man…***

***What makes a man…any man…think
he can own land…or that some God…
gave it to him?…The silly whim that
a human being can own a sliver…of
the earth…is stupid…***

***Land is like the sky…the ocean…a
spirit…neither of which can be owned…
They exist…to see…to touch…to hear…
or feel…Then they…as we…just go away…
never belonging to any man…or anyone…***

Ardmore Air Force Base

On a mid-summer...afternoon day in June 1955...dressed in a crisply pressed...khaki uniform of the United States Air Force...sweaty and tired...I stepped off a train...in Ardmore ...Oklahoma...With a duffel bag on one shoulder....and a small suitcase...in hand...I walked through the train station entrance door...and was immediately struck by a sign you could not miss..."WHITES TO THIS SIDE... COLOREDS TO THIS SIDE"...Red arrows at the top and bottom of the sign...helped to show you which way to go...in what would be a small... fan cooled... single story building...I paused for a stunned moment ...looked around briefly... and decided to walk through the side reserved for whites...The sign...to me was almost a joke...Who the hell is going to stop me...I thought...

No one did...The small ...stuffy...main room of the station...was sparsely filled...with mostly waiting benches...separating the two sides... for whites and blacks ...There were ticket dispensing cages...manned by white clerks...on each side of the open room...and a faint smell of sweat and bleach...as I walked through the station...No one said a word to me...but I noticed a black lady...sitting with two young kids...She smiled briefly...as she followed my steps through the room... out through a door...with an overhead "Exit" sign...Outside of the station...a rush of hot...humid air enveloped me ...Close by...but away from the front entrance... there was a free standing sign that said... "WAIT HERE FOR RIDE TO AIR BASE"...

During the blue bus...15 to 20 mile...ride to the Base...I kept thinking about the train station greeting...the sign for blacks and whites...I was still thinking because... I had just never thought of Oklahoma... as a Deep South state...Somehow...I had this vision of Oklahoma ...as a "western" state...an "Indian-Territory state"...with teepees...cowboy hats...and rodeos... I had read about separate fountains...segregated restaurants... and other racial creeds...of the Jim Crow south...back home in Buffalo... Oklahoma just never registered to me...as a southern state...In Buffalo and just about everywhere...I had gone before Oklahoma...I had never come across...a separate water fountain...or a separate entrance for "colored people" ...I do not mean to imply...that there was no racism in Buffalo when I grew up there... There was...but it was more subtle. ..less obvious...Just like mostly everywhere in the U.S.A...in 1955...racism was unmistakably evident in housing... employment...and powerful... meaningful institutions...like the education establishments ...and the Criminal Justice System...

I remembered the train station in Charlotte... when I was a small boy... where there were separate ticket counters for black people...when we went there on the way to Buffalo... But that was Charlotte...I said to myself... After all...Charlotte was as "deep south" as you could get...What could you expect...But my defiant or unhesitating choice...to walk through the "white side" of the Ardmore train station was...I guess...just my way of ignoring...what I thought was a stupid...southern practice...that needed to be challenged...After all...I was a member of a desegregated... United States Air Force...and I wasn't going to take a back seat...for any one... That attitude...for me...I guess...grew out of a smoldering anger...an increasing awareness...of the growing number of Civil Rights protests... around the Country ...and the Supreme Court's decision...to integrate the Nation's schools a year earlier...

Blacks in the Air Force...like me...were embolden by the growing militancy...of young black men and women...like the Freedom Riders... the Birmingham movements...and demonstrators ...everywhere in the Country...We had "attitude"...Then again...maybe my little private protest...at the train station...was a challenging precursor... to the disgusting and hateful feelings...I was unfortunately ... soon to feel toward white people...in the south especially... A few weeks after I arrived in Ardmore...the brutal...lynching murder...of a 14 year-old black boy... Emmett Till...in Mississippi...for supposedly whistling at a white woman... became a world-wide disgrace...That cowardly murder...and the published photograph of his mutilated body...in Ebony magazine... was a singular moment in my life...It was an event ...that would change... for a very long time... how I looked at...and felt toward white people... especially white southerners ...in my own Country...

Before They Killed Emmett Till

I thought I knew what hatred was,
Before they killed Emmett Till.

I thought I had seen the ugliest sight on earth,
Before they killed Emmett Till.

I had never looked at a photograph so long,
Before they killed Emmett Till.

I thought all white people were human beings,
Before they killed Emmett Till.

I thought slavery was over in the United States,
Before they killed Emmett Till.

I never imagined that white people could lynch a child,
Before they killed Emmett Till.

I never dreamed I could ever hate a man,
Before they killed Emmett Till.

I felt there was a difference between white men and white women,
Before they killed Emmett Till.

I never feared white people in America,
Before they killed Emmett Till.

I once had hope for a future in my own Country,
Before they killed Emmett Till.

I used to think Americans were mostly honorable people,
Before they killed Emmett Till.

I tried to sing, "My Country Tis of Thee,"
Before they killed Emmett Till.

I once believed I had rights under the Constitution,
Before they killed Emmett Till.

I once trusted American government and courts of justice,
Before they killed Emmett Till.

I believed in the integration of white and black people,
Before they killed Emmett Till.

I was once proud to stand and sing the National Anthem,
Before they killed Emmett Till.

I never thought I wanted to or could kill a man,
Before they killed Emmett Till.

I thought I would someday grow to love America,
Before they killed Emmett Till.

I used to be proud to carry the flag in a parade,
Before they killed Emmett Till.

I used to be proud to be in the Air Force,
Before they killed Emmett Till.

I thought I would gladly risk my life for my Country,
Before they killed Emmett Till.

I looked forward to having my own son,
Before they killed Emmett Till.

I never wished I lived in another country,
Before they killed Emmett Till.

I used to believe in a merciful God,
Before they killed Emmett Till.

I thought I would grow to be an old man,
Before they killed Emmett Till.

I never feared for my very own soul,
Before they killed Emmett Till.

I hit the ground at Ardmore Air Force Base... delighted that I was finally...in the real world of the Air Force...All that boring training and getting ready was over...Now it was time to get down to business...Air Force business... I was assigned to the 309th Troop Carrier Group ...which included the 377th Troop Carrier Squadron...that I was assigned to...The 309th was a newly re-organized outfit...being readied for later deployment to France... The Group's history went back to 1942...when it trained crews to fly the B-25 Mitchell and the A-26 Invader light bomber aircraft...during WWII... The Group's new mission... as troop carriers...was to support fighting troops... by carrying...men...equipment... supplies and anything else...that needed to get there... In Ardmore...the three squadrons...the 376th...377th ...and the 378th Troop Carrier Squadrons...making up the Group ...were housed in contiguous...but separate barracks... Each... air conditioned barracks...had its own Orderly Room... (administration room)...on the first floor of three...two story buildings...I lived and worked in my barracks... Our living accommodations... to me...were sumptuous.... compared to Francis E. Warren's or Sampson's sparse... barracks's living...

We enlisted men lived in...two-men-to-a-room dormitories...We had freshly painted rooms...privacy in latrines and showers...and my work station...in the nearby Orderly Room...was extremely convenient... The Chow Hall was a short ten minute walk away...and ten minutes in another direction was the Base Exchange (BX)...where you could buy just about anything you needed... Within the BX was a small...sit down/ takeout ...restaurant that stayed open until 10:00 P.M... The all-around convenience...and a warm weather... slow... southern pace was...a pleasant enough surprise...but to my greatest surprise...my roommate ...Curtis

Mitchell… from Freemont…Michigan… was white!… After that jolting arrival at the train station…I guess I just did not expect that there …in "deep-south Oklahoma" …I would wind up with a white roommate…

In 1955… Air Force Squadrons were organized…and composed of personnel to support crews…assigned to fly a certain number of aircraft…A squadron may have 7 to 10 aircraft assigned to it… Aircraft would have flying crews… (pilots…navigators… enlisted mechanic crews…and/or mission specific specialists)… and ground support staff such as base flight operations and personnel administration…. Flying crews were also supported...by base-wide functions....such as food service…equipment and merchandise supply…a motor vehicle pool… finance and health administration…The squadron Orderly Room… where I worked …as an admin specialist…was the center for…squadron personnel administration… and all other …non-flight related issues…

Back then…Orderly Rooms were usually staffed…by an Officer (pilot or navigator) on a revolving assignment basis…and a First Sergeant… They reported to the Squadron Commander…who was usually located in another building…The leaders would be assisted…by a number of administrative assistants…depending on the size…and complexity of the squadron's business…When I arrived for my assignment…there was no First Sergeant …and no other administrative personnel with me…There was an officer (usually a first or second lieutenant) assigned to the Orderly Room…but I was to learn very quickly that most of the officers…considered Orderly Room assignments…the most boring and uninteresting…part of their Air Force life…I also learned that they were not very well trained… on personnel or non-flying…squadron related issues…and relied heavily on the admin people they worked with… Needless to say… my first weeks and months…were very trying…since I was expected to know…a great deal more than I did…

I spent a lot of time learning…from the admin personnel…in the other two squadrons of the Group…Both had experienced sergeants…with a lot more service time than I had… Then there was also help…from some of the more experienced officers…when they were assigned to Orderly Room duty…Because my work was vital to all of the airmen in the Squadron…I gradually grew to know everyone…and to enjoy my work… One of my duties was payroll… In those days…the Air Force paid airmen with cash…

every month…It meant that once a month…an officer and I would pickup cash from Base Finance…a kind of Base bank…

To protect the cash…we had to be armed…It was the first of only two assignments… where I had to carry a firearm in the Air Force… My weapon…which I had to qualify on… every three months… was a very heavy…and I thought cumbersome…45 caliber automatic… Some of my fellow airmen …would make fun of the big 45…strapped around my thin waist…with comments like… "Hey Bailey…that gun looks like it weighs as much as you do"…Others started calling me "Cisco"…or the "Rico Kid"…Nevertheless…being the Pay Master…in charge of pay and per diem reimbursement…also earned me a little extra respect…and I liked that a lot…

A few months into my assignment…my second promotion to Airman Second Class occurred …I was very proud to get that second stripe…It made me feel as if I were a little more senior… once again…a little more appreciated…This feeling was reinforced… especially since most of the one strippers around me…from then on…called me "Sarge"… I liked the implied respect I got…as an Airman Second Class…and I eagerly looked forward to getting 2 more stripes…and becoming a real First Sergeant… doing a First Sergeant's job…

As I caught on quickly…my days at Ardmore…grew increasingly routine…A lot of my admin activity…revolved around…preparation for the May 1956…deployment to France … After work…I spent my leisure time…listening to jazz music…drinking 3.2 beer…reading and writing… Occasionally I would venture outside of the Base…with a sketch pad…or go to a small bar outside of the Base…called the "Last Chance Saloon"… If I could hitch a ride with someone …I would go to nearby Ardmore… or some other little one-stop-light town…like Sulpher…Springer…or Gene Autry…(Yes there was a small town named after the famous… cowboy screen star..)… Still fancying myself as a potential star athlete…I would play pickup basketball games…or join the ragtag… Base team…and play against… local high school or community teams…Early on weekends…I would scour for a decent local newspaper…but I finally gave up and started taking Time magazine…a habit I would keep for more than half a century…

Once my drawing and sketching ability…became known around the Squadron…a couple of 377th pilots came to me…with an idea about a Squadron logo…They asked for my thoughts and…along with their suggestions...I sketched out a flying donkey...standing on a military stretcher ...circling the globe...Soon thereafter...some of the pilots from the 376th Squadron ...also came to me about drawing up their Squadron logo...For them...again using their ideas...I sketched a soaring eagle... wielding a sword...in front of a flaming-red arrowhead... Those logos... soon started showing up as proud shoulder patches...or as symbols on squadron paraphernalia such as German beer steins... I was proud of my work...since it earned me special recognition... and some notoriety throughout the 309th Troop Carrier Group.... (To see those logos today... lookup 377th and 376th Troop Carrier Squadron in Wikipedia [http://en.wikipedia.org/wiki/377th_ Troop Carrier Squadron])

Some weekends...I would get invited to ride the fairly short distance (about 35 miles)...across the Red River... to Texas...Many of the Ardmore airmen would go to Texas ...on weekends to get hard liquor....At that time Oklahoma was a "dry" state and there was a steady stream of airmen...going to Texas...to get the "real stuff"....We were always careful on any trips to Texas... since confrontations with redneck hunters... or other racist types... were very common.... Many of the black guys...on Base...always carried concealed pistols...when they went to Texas... After one redneck...menacing threat...at a hot dog stand...on Highway 35... I too...started carrying a small...22 caliber automatic myself... Thankfully...I never had to use it....

Indian Territory

So this is...the Indian Territory...that convenient...
open...red land...that became the repository...for a

conquered and stolen...eastern people...no longer
worthy of life...in the midst...of the more virtuous...

whose new steps...now fall...where others had been...
since eons past...Was it punishment...from an angry...

slighted god...or the aggressive will...of a proselyte's
march for a new deity...with a dark heart...and an empty

soul?...Whatever its design...the pain was deep...and
cutting...continuous and unforgiving...even when later

the given land...was re-stolen...for the voracious
destroyer of the pristine...looking for favor...looking

for the extra privilege...and the lowest goal...Surely
there must be a reckoning...for such...Is there no power

to confront...the theft...the blood thirst...the shame?...
No!...Our specters have no power...Justice is our own will...

however it is reconciled...however it comes...The dead
spirits cannot save us...We always have to redeem ourselves...

The White Man is God

In America...the white man is God...To him the
Country was created by him...for him...his chosen
kind only...Never...for a moment...was democracy...
others to be welcome...equals:...not women...not
natives ...already here thousands of years...not black
slaves...nor their children...not Chinese...nor other
brown peoples...not even poor...white...landless
men...It has been clear...in America...that every
petition for redress...inclusion...equal rights...must
be made to God...the white man...All human symbols...
creeds...religions...economic outcomes...are his...It
is only he...or his designees...that can grant privilege...
or inclusion for other than white men...In America...
every law...every statue...every image...every legal
reference...has to mimic...or reinforce white males...
as God...This day...this hour...I say to hell with God!...

Sister Rosa

She just had a tired heart…that day…If it had come up…the day before… or even the day after…it might have been different…She may have given in…and let the arrogant bastard…have the seat…reserved for just white people…if they wanted it…But not today…not that day…She wasn't moving a lick…and Lord…she didn't care what…that old white man said or did…He had better get out of her face…and go find somewhere else to sit down…if he knew what was good for him…No matter…she was not going to move…for him…or nobody else…not with her longing disgust…There just comes a time…when you get tired of white people… so tired of their foolish acting…tired of their lording it…over you…just like they're…Jesus Christ… himself…You would think…they would have learned by now…that some of us…just wasn't going to take it…no more… She was tired…of their damn selfishness…period…Her mother had been tired…Her grandmother was tired…Her great grandmother too…had been tired…and they took it…A long time…they took it…..But not her… That was it…she said…She wasn't taking it!…She said…she wasn't taking it no more…and she didn't…And Lord…that day the sky opened up… Gabriel blew his horn…the devil started running…the chains broke…and a whole new people got born again!…Thank God for you…dear Sister Rosa!…God bless your tired soul!…God bless you…Rosa Parks!…

Ode to Jazz

There is absolutely nothing like Jazz.
It is the ultimate rhythm, the sound to soothe the soul.

I know all of us have roots, what we think is our own first music,
our first toe-tapping, hand-clapping, stringing of words…feelings.

But I repeat, there is nothing like Jazz.
It bores into the very soul of the maker, the hearer…the poet.

Even a skeptic will succumb, if they listen long enough.
Jazz is truly the mother of melody, the father of rhythm.

Jazz was there at the very beginning of music.
The first sound we ever heard was the heart beat,

the gurgle, the moan, the sweet stream of wet heat.
Even then we knew warmth and cool, hot and cold.

Some try to get beyond the sound of Jazz.
They venture off into their structured musings,

the sophisticated linking of written words and sounds,
that they think is superior to their primitive starting roots.

Then they hear Jazz again, and are reminded once more,
for it has invaded even their complicated, digitized world.

They are then brought back down, once again to their essence,
back to Jazz, the first and only real music in the world.

The Chicken Man

How do you re-discover a willow....
When it turns brown...and sags to the ground...
life gone...laying dead...unseen...

Who picks up a
wilted leaf...or a failed blossom...now flaccid...
delicate...vulnerable to any wind...

I did...I did... I sure did...
when I heard the last song...of the willow...
his last forceful breath...his last testimony...

It was enough to
crave and want to follow…the trail back…
through all of the breathing…back through all
of the blows…whispers…some joyous…some
bloody painful…

Yet every one was
a pure extraction…of the wonder…and newness…an
unmistakable…sap of genius…pulled from a short…
tragic life…that gave…and left so much…to all of us…

I found the legacy to be…
indescribably rich…like honey from a virgin comb…
so delightfully filling…satisfying…so able to comfort
the musically….emaciated…like me…

Sleep well…sleep well…and
thank you…for the wonderful melodies…. and quick…
sharp 3-notes…Chicken Man…Thank you…Thank
you…Charlie Parker…

The Rico Kid

At Ardmore…as we often did…when the Chow Hall closed …and hunger pains still gnawed at us… my buddies…Curtis…William Wiggins… and I…were having a late evening sandwich…at the small…cafeteria-styled restaurant…in the BX… Sitting at a table…Wiggins said to me…"Hey Rico…how come your ham and cheese…has more of both… than mine?"… Amused …I answered that…both sandwiches…looked the same to me…He insisted that mine…was bigger…nicer than his… My roommate… Curtis agreed with Wiggins… They insisted that… my sandwich was healthier… more scrumptious…than Wiggins'… I laughed …and continued to insist that the sandwiches…were the same... Curtis then said… "This isn't the first time…I've noticed that he seems to get…a little extra something… every time that little cutie…named JoAnn…is working on the grill here… Something must be going on"…

I smiled…shrugged… but agreed with the "cutie" assessment…and admitted that my strong flirts…had been turned off…when I learned that she was married…I told them…I learned that from the older lady…named Blanche…who usually ran the checkout cash register… What I did not tell my buddies…that evening…was that even though…I knew JoAnn was married…I had continued to flirt with her…and liked her a lot… In fact I liked her so much…a couple of times a week…I had started hanging around the restaurant …until it closed…just so I could walk JoAnn to her car… During those walks…I had also learned… that JoAnn was 17 or 18…and that she was also a senior in high school…what I would have been…if I had not dropped out… I also learned that she was a drum majorette… that led the Douglas High School band …at parades and Friday night football games… I likewise did not mention…that I had an invitation to attend…one of those games any time I could get there…That night…I kept all of that…to myself…

In the passing weeks…it was my roommate…Curtis…who finally blew my cover…when one evening…he read a copy of a poem…I had written… and left on my bunk…when I went to take a shower… When he confronted me…about the poem…I hemmed and hawed…but finally admitted that it was about JoAnn…and yes…I cared a lot for her… He insisted that I should show it to her… but I resisted…I gave him all kinds of excuses… and he finally gave up the notion… Curtis… from Fremont… Michigan… was one of my closest and favorite buddies… He was also the hippest white boy…I had ever met… For example… after a few months in Ardmore… I learned that it was Curtis…who had requested a black roommate…in the barracks…where we lived… Whenever a couple of we blacks…got together to harmonize some doo-op songs…it was Curtis who would join in…

It was also Curtis and I…who often went into Ardmore together…to see if we could integrate some place…where black people…weren't allowed or weren't welcome … We would always wear our uniforms…so that the rednecks knew… we were from the Base… One evening…we tried to integrate the lower level…of the movie theater in downtown Ardmore… There was a long standing… rigidly enforced custom… that relegated black customers to the balcony… and whites to the lower level… After buying our tickets to the show...we both tried to sit together...either up in the balcony...or down on the orchestra level... The ushers and a manager forbid it...and called the cops on us...The cops were firm but polite... and ultimately put us on the military bus...that constantly ran back and forth... between Ardmore and the Base...

On other occasions...we tried to integrate a couple of red-neck-bar hangouts...in downtown Ardmore...At a couple...we were told I couldn't come in...period... Neither of us went in...if we couldn't go together... At one bar...which also contained a few other... white...uniformed airmen drinking...and carousing...I was told I could have one drink...but thereafter...I had to leave... We skipped going in...On those provoking... forays...in red neck land...we were always...made aware that we...I... in particular ...were not very welcome... We never got into any serious scuffles...but there were some close calls...when we were threatened by a person...or persons...objecting to our presence...

Given our close friendship...it was therefore...hard to get angry with Curtis... when he took a copy of my "JoAnn poem"...and gave it to JoAnn at the BX... I was...however...a bit embarrassed to know that she had read it...and I passed up invitations for BX...late night snacks...for a few days... When I saw JoAnn again...I was relieved to learn that she was not angry...or disturbed about the poem... In fact...she smiled and said she thought it was "touching"... Whenever I would see her after that...she would always ask me about my writing...or other rumors she had heard about...the "Rico Kid"... My presence at a couple of off-Base parties...and mention of my nickname...by her female schoolmates...became subjects of inquiry and laughter between us... I denied a few accusations of romantic liaisons ...but was pleased to learn of her interest...or what I thought ...was a little bit of concern ... about my nocturnal ramblings...

One Friday evening I talked a buddy...named Humphrey...into driving into Ardmore... for a Douglas High School football game...Humphrey...a couple of years older than me...was from St. Louis... He owned a snazzy... green...1953 Mercury Coupe...and he and I paled around occasionally... It was Humphrey...who had talked me into carrying a weapon...when we went on liquor runs to Texas... He was also known for his..."take no prisoners" attitude...if there was a dispute or scuffle...with airmen...or civilians...On our way to the game...we stopped for a couple of beers...since we knew we could not get beer...at the game... When we finally got there...sure enough...there was JoAnn...leading the band...first on the field...then in the stands...while the game was being played...I thought she looked terrific... in her blue band uniform... So did Humphrey and he...big brother- like... warned me to "be cool"...I answered back..."Look who's talking"...

Humphrey and I separated... he to flirt with some young girls...I to catch JoAnn's eye... I felt the best way to do that...was to go sit with the band... So a couple of rows from the end of the band section...I found a seat in the very middle of a row... I was not sure JoAnn had seen me...so when the band played...I flailed my arms...and pretended to be directing the music... just like JoAnn... I knew she couldn't miss me then...Some of the band members...did not think very much of my presence... but they went along with my shenanigans... I suppose in deference to my uniform... What I was to learn later...however ...was that a couple of non-band members...did not think...my silly behavior was funny at all...

After the game...two or three of the "local yokels"...as we airmen called them... followed Humphrey and me...back to the car... A few steps from the car...a couple of them made threatening comments to us... This was a typical attitude...we airmen had come to expect...from the locals...At parties and certain civilian gatherings...we servicemen...from the Base... were often accused of trying to hog the girls...or lording it over the locals... with money...cars...or uniform status... Some of the young civilian guys... did not like it...and sometimes things came to blows... Alone... one night... at a local hang-out called...The Hill...I had had a scuffle...with someone who objected to my presence...or something about me... My fist...and a no-nonsense bartender... got me out of that one...but I swore that night... that if I ever came back...to The Hill again...I would be armed...

As Humphrey and I turned to confront the yokels...I was happy that Humphrey was there...If there was anybody on the Base...you wanted with you in a fight...it was Humphrey...He was domino dark...flashed a gold covered front tooth...and a mean disposition... Before I knew what was happening...Humphrey pulled a snub-nosed .38 from his pocket... and scared the very hell out of those young guys...They backed away in a hurry... On the way back to the Base...I laughingly asked my friend...if he really would have shot one of those guys...He said...only if they had tried to hurt us... I was glad to hear him say that...because those would-be tough guys…who had stupidly…confronted us…were really just a bunch of kids…trying to prove something…to themselves…or to each other… Later when we stopped at the Last Chance Saloon…just outside of the Base…I learned that Humphrey had been transferred… and was not going to France…with the rest of us… "Damn"…I said to him… "I'm sure going to miss the hell out of you"…

Young Man in Love

(JoAnn's Poem)

I remember the first night I saw her.
She was busily working away.
She said something to me that ended with Sir.
But my mind was wandering and far astray.

I was looking in her eyes, so dark, so deep,
That seemed to penetrate my very soul.
Slowly my thoughts began to creep,
Around this beauty as if a caressing stole.

I sat down for awhile and began to watch.
To myself, I tried to explain the sensation I felt.
But my anxiety went up one more notch.
Gradually, slowly my heart began to melt.

Here was a being as pictured in my dreams,
With a face and eyes that bore holes in me.
She reminded me of oceans and winding streams,
Of an innocent little rose or a powerful, soaring tree.

I soon left, but my thoughts were behind,
Left with someone whose name I did not know.
Someone who had unknowingly captured my mind.
And sent my heart racing with a brand new glow.

In the weeks that followed I saw her often.
As you might guess and to no surprise at all,
I slowly fell in love, just like most young men,
When the negatives and resistance began to fall.

Soon her precious friendship I won.
However, much to my sad regret,
I learned what a fool I had become,
And through eyes that soon were wet,

I was told that I had come along too late.
My secret love was already wed.
That she could never be my mate.
Painful was the blow, straight to my head.

Then one day, overcome by weakness,
I said to her, please hear my plea.
For I have something I have to confess,
And when I have said it, please forgive me.

I love you with an uncontrollable desire,
That stabs and eats at my very heart.
It is a flicker that grew into a roaring fire,
A flame I wish never had a start.

I turned away from her, realizing the truth,
That I must walk alone and resist the fear,
Accept this as the first challenge of my youth.
For to her and me, I had to be sincere.

That long night I decided to try hard,
To forget this love that haunts me nightly.
This one-sided love I said, I must discard.
No matter how hard, how difficult for me.

Day after day oh, how I tried and I tried!
For months my nights were comfortless,

Amid dreams of her, I woke up and cried,
For her tender kiss and burning caress.

I thought of leaving and running away.
But my destiny then was not my own.
I was compelled and I just had to stay.
My duty was one I could not disown.

Even now as I write this line,
Still caught in the dark web of love,
And still wishing that she were mine,
I search for the answer from heaven above.

For surely in some blessed book,
Is the precious, elusive, answer I seek.
Maybe if I have patience, learn and just look,
This aching will become just a forgotten antique.

The Kid Falls in Love

It wasn't too long…after the Douglas High School band stunt…that my after-work... fun walks…with JoAnn…became a little more serious… It started with her agreeing to let me ride with her…to the Last Chance Saloon…just outside of the entrance to the Base… She had to go by the small…airmen's hangout… on her way home…and I loved having a quick beer …before turning in for the night…Those little…short rides… soon became slightly longer rides…through the small…sleepy towns surrounding the Base… The rides…mostly listening to music… not more than 20 or 30 minutes long...were just friendly…innocent times…when we shared jokes… laughed or kidded each other…the way teenagers do… everywhere… During those polite… peck-on-the-cheek rides…I learned a few more things… about JoAnn…

I learned about her schoolmates…her band-leading escapades…some of her work and family histories… but the most shocking revelation…I learned…was that she really wasn't married! The married "tale" was partly a defensive ploy…used mainly…to keep Base flirts… (like me)…away…

However…she was in a very close relationship…with an older boyfriend… who was also in the Air Force…and in fact…worked in the Motor Pool… on the Base…The big…fancy…late model car she drove sometimes… belonged to him… I was flabbergasted… the night she told me that… I was also elated…in a way…like a third or fourth place runner… who thinks he still has a chance to win the race…

In subsequent walks… and rides…I gently pressed her for more of the story…The more she told me…the more in love and obsessed I became with her…I was struck mostly …by her air of responsibility…toward her siblings and her vulnerableness…It was not easy…for JoAnn to talk much about herself…and her family… In fact…we both…timidly struggled to be honest…but not completely forthcoming …about our histories… At first… neither of us…for example… was completely honest about our ages… At the time…I believed she was 17 years old…and I lied and said…I was 20… In fact…we both were 18… In sharing our romantic histories… mine was easy to spill…since I didn't consider it to be significant…at all… Back then… I considered myself…friendly with two… young… neighborhood ladies… back home…in Buffalo… Sheila Sutton and Beverly Callahan… had been either schoolmates…or girl-next-door…casual dating interests… However…I did not call or write to either…that much…and I did not consider either relationship very serious… Up until then…my interest in the opposite sex…was always hindered by my ever present need to work… or to go to school… My many relationships…with girls… were always shallow… fleeting… and guarded…

As for JoAnn's romantic liaisons…it seemed painful for her to discuss the subject…or talk too much about her romantic interests…in any detail… She told me…between taking care of her younger sisters…and working after school…she never had much time for high school types…or many boys her age… She said her current romantic relationship…was more than casual…but not a deeply committed one… When I continued to prod her about her boyfriend and her future…she seemed somewhat confused… and ambivalent …even embarrassed… She kept repeating that she…very much wanted to finish her last year of high school…then perhaps go on to some college…and move on with her life… She said to me…she felt trapped in both family concerns… and her own personal circumstances… Without her saying it…I also sensed…that she felt alone…somewhat indecisive...and unsure of what would happen next...in her life...After hearing her...I decided that I would ...quietly...on my own...see what I could find out about her boyfriend...

JoAnn...like me...came from a poor...largely...off and on...up and down...single-mother family...Her family had its roots...in the state of Arkansas...Hugo...Ardmore...and Pauls Valley... Oklahoma... Her mother...Faye Jackson...had died a year or so before we met... After her death... her younger female siblings...Ramona ...Menyon... and Gladys... were taken to Texas...to live with her older sister Jerri... Jerri had left home years before... and two older brothers... Ted and Emslie... were in the Navy and Army... respectively ... JoAnn's father...Mitchell Wright...was a hotel chef...who lived in Paul's Valley... Oklahoma... JoAnn...who carried the name Jackson... like her siblings...had only recently learned that Mitchell Wright...was her father...She said ...learning who her natural father was...was quite a jolt for her...and everyone else around her...

Needless to say...JoAnn was reluctant to talk much...about her tangled...and sometimes confusing story...of a divulsive...and struggling family...that had never enjoyed much lasting stability...during her life... Because of her mother's apparent waywardness...down through the years... she had early and often been burdened...with caring for her younger sisters... and assuming a role...that should have fallen...to a much more mature person... When her mother died... JoAnn was reluctant to go along with her siblings to Texas... because she mostly wanted to finish high school in Ardmore...She accepted the offer of her long time friend and employer...Blanche Abrams...to move in with her family... Since she was a young teen...JoAnn had worked in the Abrams' small restaurant... in Ardmore...and now she and Blanche...worked together in the BX cafeteria on the Base... It seemed the more I learned about her...the more vulnerable...and fragile she seemed...and the more I wanted to reach out to her...to protect her...

My thoughts of You

(A Song)

My Dearest, as I sit here listening to
the strains, of a beautiful and lonely song,

I think of the tight and binding chains
that hold and stress me all day long.

For to be near you each and every day,
is the wish that I constantly dream.

For far too often my mind goes astray
loving you Dearest in a way that's extreme.

Whenever you come within my sight,
I feel as though I have come out of a storm.

Everything around you suddenly seems so
bright, as if to keep the world uniform.

You've stored in my lonely heart, a place,
that will always belong to you.

Wherever I go, none will ever replace,
this love that only my death can undo.

If your heart and your love I never win,
I only ask that you remember one thing.

I cherish you with love that is truly genuine.
My fate, heaven or hell, your name I will sing!

Where Clouds Go

Love!...What do you know about love...
that it's more than infatuation...or whatever...
the feeling is?...Folly!...Foolishness!...That's
what it is...Why you're just a kid...a babe!...
What would you know about love...about heart
pulls...desert-like thirst...or near drowning?...
Your heart never skipped a beat...You never felt
like stripping...then running wildly...through
green grass...falling snow...drenching rain...
You never had short breath...felt near faint or
embarrassed to even smile...You never wanted
a cloud to wrap you up...swallow you...and take
you where clouds go...Huh?...Love is serious
stuff!...You don't muddle with it lightly...Be very...
very careful...where you tread fool!...You'll be forever
changed...You will never...ever...be the same...

Love Is On Hold for You

(A song)

A short while...not too long ago...
When I was lonely and hurting real bad...
You held out your hand of friendship...
It was more than I'd ever had...

I swore...right then and there...
To make you my special friend...
To be concerned for all your being...
To stay honest and never pretend...

Now that we're here all alone...
Give me an instant of your time...
I have a vow I'd like to make...
It will be my pledge...for a lifetime...

For love is just waiting for you...
Yes...all my Love... is on hold for you...

Look closely...deep into my eyes...
Just stop...and hear me breathe...
Feel my trembling...shaking hand...
Reaching from my folded sleeve...

Take my every loving wish...
Wrap them up...all around you...
Enjoy the hope they warmly bring...
Claim all the honor you're surely due...

If you are finally...ready to choose...
You don't have to look too far...
For I am here...awaiting your praise...
Ready to be your shining star...

For love is just waiting for you...
Yes...all my Love... is on hold for you...

Can One Become Two

My time in Ardmore was rapidly coming to an end... All of my work duties were now furiously focused on the upcoming deployment to France...Air crews...from the three squadrons... making up the 309th Troop Carrier Group...would fly the Group's assigned aircraft...and related maintenance crewmen...to Dreux Air Force Base...in France... The accompanying administrative personnel...would follow by commercial airplane or military transport ships...from New York City... It was felt that by the end of June...or mid-July... 1956...we would have completed the deployment... My workdays were feverishly filled with duties... related to individual personnel deployment and transportation issues... related to leaving...Personally I grew more short of breath...more anxious...about leaving Ardmore...about leaving JoAnn...

Because I was single...this assignment would be for three years... which would take me to the end of my four-year...active Air Force commitment... Three years apart and a long distance romance was not very appealing to JoAnn and me... Certain personnel (usually officers)... could take families...at government expense...on this deployment... The Air Force would not pay for the relocation...of married...enlisted personnel...but on this assignment...they would only have to be deployed for 18 months... I explained that to JoAnn ...one evening...on one of our after-work rides through the countryside... Earlier I had told her...I had casually talked... to people who worked with her boyfriend... and that it was their understanding that he...was indeed married... and had a family... either there in Ardmore...or in Birmingham... Alabama... his home town... They told me he lived off-base ...most of the time...and had spent a lot of time off-duty...because of some kind of injury ... JoAnn seemed surprised upon hearing this... and grew quiet and pensive... As I tried to reassure her...she cried and said she was afraid... I told her not to be afraid...and that she could count on my friendship...and protection...Before I left her that night...I had asked her to marry me...

Within a few days and just weeks before I was to depart for France... JoAnn and I went to the Ardmore City/County Hall and applied for a marriage license....Neither of us knew what was involved.... We were told it was very simple...no waiting...no blood tests... nothing but a small fee ($35.00)... a couple of witnesses and a sworn oath...before the County Clerk...and you walk out of there married... We weren't even asked for proof of the ages...21 and 17...we put on the application for marriage... On April 25, 1956...JoAnn ...wearing a neat...light blue dress...and I... wearing a hard pressed...summer khaki uniform...with two friendly employees of Carter County...Oklahoma...acting as witnesses... repeated the vows of marriage...and walked out of the building as man and wife... We were both just 18 years young ...and legally able to marry...under then...existing Oklahoma law...

After a short walk in the bright sunshine...and a ride to Lake Murray Park... we looked into each other's eyes and vowed our love again. With only a few days left...before I had to leave...I promised JoAnn that I would hurry back to Ardmore... take her to Buffalo to meet my family...and get on with our lives together... We spent that night...and the few remaining nights I had...at Blanche Abrams' home... It was Mr. and Mrs. Abrams... and their two young daughters...who helped us celebrate our first night as man and wife... The Abrams...had promised JoAnn...that she could continue to live...and work with them for as long as she cared to...I was comfortable with this arrangement...since JoAnn had lived and worked with the Abrams for years... I was happy that they seemed...so pleased and delighted with our marriage...I felt...in some ways...that the Abrams were a substitute family for JoAnn...and that she would be safe...and satisfied living with them...

The day after getting married...I went back to the Base...I officially changed my dependent status...and applied for and was granted...a 21-day leave of absence...before reporting to my next assignment....I routed my travel voucher through Buffalo...so that I could spend some time at home...before going on to France...That evening I called my mother to tell her the "good news"...I had never...before that moment...heard my mother scream so loudly at me..."You did what?...With whom?.... Where?...she demanded... I did the best I could to calm her down...and told her that I would be home in a few days...to further explain...

The gravity of what I had done finally hit me...It had just never occurred to me...that out of respect...I should have pre-warned my family of my marriage plans... I was so convinced of my love for JoAnn ...and the rightness of what I did...that I just did it...without discussing it... or talking to anyone about my plans... Later...thinking about my mother... and how hurt she seemed...I regretted not having...at least...talked to her... before taking such a momentous step...I was nevertheless... convinced that talking to anyone I knew...would not have changed a single thing...

Before I finally left the Base in Ardmore...I decided that I would once more...go and see if I could talk to JoAnn's former boyfriend... I went to his work place and assigned living quarters...but he was not there... I did however...talk to one of his work colleagues...whom I had come to know...I told him that I had married JoAnn...whom he also knew casually ... I told him I would appreciate him passing that word along to Mr. Ex...He promised that he would... I also told him how to contact me...if he or Mr. Ex...cared to discuss anything more with JoAnn or me... I felt I needed to do that...since JoAnn...without saying it...seemed a little shaken about her new status... especially after the reception she received...from certain acquaintances and one of her teachers at school... When she revealed her new status... some seemed shocked and unapproving... This hurt JoAnn...so I tried to encourage and shore up her confidence...since she faced a few more months of school...before senior graduation...

Becoming Two

Can one become two...two become three...and on...and on?...
What makes two...or is there no such thing?...Will we...I...
always be one...no matter what we...or I ...do?...Is it ever
possible to come out of...who you are?...Words...a vow...
they cannot make you two...or three...or more...It has to
get ...and be...deeper...I think...I hope...I imagine...That's
it!...Imagination!...That comes first!...You imagine two...
or three...before you see...before you become...or change...
I saw me throw...before I threw...I heard me sing...before
I sung...I saw the image...before I made it...I imagined...
and then saw me become two...Am I still imagining...still
seeing...just one...or have I now...truly become two?...

There must be a Way

(A song)

Joy floats and swells the air.

Happiness is breaking out everywhere.
I hope the day will be double long.
I want everyone to sing this song.

Today there will be no crying tears.
Only sweet sounds will touch our ears.

This day not a single babe will cry.
Not one, living life will die.

This moment will
Always be with me
There must be a way
to make it last forever.

This day is what the world was waiting for.
From every ocean, river and shore.
Every mouth will fly open and joyfully shout,
As despair and sadness are all driven out

Oh, why isn't this always to be?
This happiness, this joy, this glee.
By what magic did this grand day occur?
There must be a way to make it last forever.

This moment will
Always be with me
There must be a way
to make it last forever.

My Going Vow

(A song)

Well it looks like the train is here...
The long ride is about to begin...
Instead of where I'm about to appear...
I'd rather stay where I have been...

No sense crying...tears won't help me...
to go...where I have to...hate to go...
They just make me...have to carry...
A wounded heart that's very hollow...

Instead of lovely you in my arms…
My dreams will be all I keep…
I'll have to live without your charms…
And learn to find peace in my sleep…

So I bite my lip…keep my eyes dry…
It won't be long… I'll be back again…
Be brave… stay strong…I'll be nearby…
Ready to be where we've always been…

Billy Comes Home Again

The train ride home from Ardmore…was uneventful… For the first time though…I began to feel the "JoAnn knot"…The JoAnn knot was just a little tug of concern…that I would learn to live with everyday…It was a reminder… a daily thought about the well-being …and safety of my new partner… In the coming months…that knot would become my constant companion …At home I was greeted as I expected… Everyone was very glad to see me…I had a thousand questions put to me…in rapid fire order…and I tried to be honest with every one of them… The family now lived on Eaton Street and I was eager to hear how Gwen and James were doing in school… and in the rest of their lives… Theirs was a mixed bag of joy…and restlessness…Neither had learned to care very much more for Louis… our new stepfather… Of course…after our prior phone conversations…from Ardmore…my mother's attitude now was my greatest dread… While I was determined to be resolute…and firm about my life choices… I still loved my mother…and as always wanted the best for her… The very first day back home…after a hot bath and food…I found myself sitting quietly on the front steps…with Dimple…

Dimple

So tell me again…Billy…Why didn't you trust me enough to...just discuss it with me before you did it?

Billy

I meant no disrespect by not letting you know…To be honest… everything was coming at me so fast…I didn't think…I didn't think it mattered that much…to anybody but me…and JoAnn…

Dimple

That's something to say to me…Don't you believe that I…we… care about you…what happens to you? After all you are still my son… Whether you know it or not…I still consider you…just a boy…Billy! You're still just a boy to me!

Billy

But I am not a boy!…I may not be a grown man yet…in your eyes…but I am not a boy!…In my mind…I haven't been a boy since Daddy left…You…you said that yourself!….

Dimple

Yes I did… but I never considered you…anything but my boy…I meant you had to be responsible…help out…do things in a grown-up way…

Billy

And I did that…I always tried to do that… Didn't I do that?…I felt that I did…

Dimple

You did… I'll give you credit…You never caused me any heartache… I never had to worry about you….I always felt I could count on you…That is until now…I mean…..

Billy

You can still count on me…Nothing has changed!…What has changed?…

Dimple

It has!…If you tell me you can go out and marry somebody…a stranger…nobody knows anything about…and that nothing has changed!….I don't get it….

Billy

I mean I still feel the same way about you…Gwen and James…I still care about you…Want to do the best I can for you…You know…like I always tried to do before now….

Dimple

This JoAnn!…What do you know about her?… How did you meet her?…What kind of family she from?

Billy

I love her…She loves me…She's like us…from a struggling family…I met her on the Base… She worked there…She's a nice person…You'll see when you meet her… She's very likeable….

Dimple

And you say she's not pregnant?…Tell the truth now…

Billy

That's right… She's not pregnant… I told you that on the phone… I wasn't forced to do what I did…I hardly touched her before we married…I do love her…and I just know how I feel…

Dimple

Feel!…love!… What do you know about love?… How could you? … You're so young.…You couldn't!….

Billy

Look…you taught me almost everything I know… I know about love because of you… I am not a little boy anymore…I saw her…I fell in love…She needed me… She was almost alone…She…

Dimple

But she's all your responsibility now… I don't get it!…Why would you want so much responsibility now? …Why would you want the burden…and what makes you think you can keep up with a young woman…while you're hundreds…no thousands of miles away?…

Billy

Trust me…I don't know all the answers…but I believe she is good for me…We care a lot for each other… When you get to know her…you'll like her too… I'll be gone just 18 months… Then I'll bring her up here…We'll be in touch almost every day… I ain't saying it will be easy… I just know I have to try… I have to do this…. You always taught me to do what I thought was right…You always said…be strong…take care of things… help people when you see wrong…I got that from you!….

Dimple

I suppose I won't be getting any more money from you now?

Billy

That's right… I had to change my dependent status… JoAnn will have to get some support…She works…but she does need some help… When I make more money…I'll start up your allotment again… That'll happen…That'll happen…

Dimple

I ain't counting on it… You just do what you have to do… Don't worry about us…

Billy

Maybe Louis…will get lucky and finally find a steady…a good paying job…

Dimple

I aint't holding my breath… but if he don't do something soon… he'll be outta here!…

And so it went…It was a good conversation between Dimple and me…I think she got most things off her chest…but I knew she still remained uneasy… Before we parted that night… she held my hand… and ignoring my unease…and skepticism about religion…she insisted on saying a short prayer to Jehovah…I had to promise her that I would be faithful to JoAnn …and try to find a place for Jehovah in my life… In the coming days…I had separate … little private conversations with both James and Gwen… They were just immensely interested in what it was like to be married… Gwen questioned me closely…about JoAnn… James talked mostly about the Air Force and France….All my friends and relatives questioned me about everything…After a few days at home…I did what I always did…when I was trying to mollify my mother…and make her feel better…I baked a big chocolate covered cake…and bought some vanilla ice cream…

During the next weeks of leave…I visited as many of my old friends… and kept in touch with JoAnn as much as I could…My old girl friends were all surprised…curious and very disappointed in my new status…

With any...and all apologies necessary...I tried to explain my actions... swore lasting friendships and promised to keep in touch... As always...I did not have much conversation with Louis...my stepfather...Try as hard as I might...I just could not get serious with him...or easily overcome my dislike for him... I suspect the feeling was mutual...but he never showed it... My plan was to leave Buffalo...with enough time to spend a few days...with relatives and Air Force buddies in New York... Ultimately...I was to go on by troop carrier ship...from the Port of Brooklyn...New York...to Bremerhaven... Germany ... From there I would take a train... down to Paris...and finally go on to Dreux... France...

A Mother's Pain

A mother's pain is special...
It is perhaps
the most genuine
of all pains...since it creates
and
reaches...indeed...seeks to visit it
upon the heart...

Mothers forever give birth...
remember its agony...
hug its oneness...its
uniqueness...

The way it intoxicates you...the
first time... can never be found
again...but they grasp for it...
eyes closed...unseeing...but
forever addicted to the ecstasy...
of giving birth...the first time...

Reflections

Reflections shimmer in a pool of
collected rain...They swim in a
mere by the curb...My urge is to
jump through its presence...sail
the swift winds of transformation...
on the way to not here...But will
all win then?...Will there be only
a mark...from a truck...a cab...a
shoe that will take it away...wipe
all notion of leaving...Set me free
if I can imagine freedom... I will
leave goodwill... your best wish...
your promise...will be mine too...

Crossing the Atlantic

After spending a night in the Bronx...with my mother's brother Julius...and his family...and an evening in Harlem with old Air Force buddy....Aaron Cannon...Julius dropped me off at the Brooklyn Pier... in Brooklyn...New York...It was there that I had my first look at the troop carrier ship...where I would spend the next 10 days crossing the Atlantic Ocean...The United States Naval Ship...General R. E. Callan... was one of a globe-circling fleet of naval and commercial ships...operated by the Military Sea Transport Service... When I boarded her...May 23, 1956...the ship was packed with U. S. military servicemen... mostly brigades of army and marine "ground ponders"...as we called them... There were very few fellow airmen...like me... on board... As the big tugs nudged the Callan away from the pier...out into the harbor...past soaring skyscrapers...and finally into the vast Atlantic... I felt very small... empty ...alone and lonely... I couldn't stop thinking about home...about JoAnn... and what lay ahead for me...

Because they were traveling in units...most of the servicemen on board the Callan...had drills or some kind of work assigned to them... Traveling alone...out of unit... I had nothing to do except explore the ship...and try to learn to sleep in a swinging hammock about 3 decks below ship... I struck up a few friendships...but after a few days...of riding bouncing waves... hearing strange thumps...on the side of the ship...and watching sliding trays in the mess hall...I was one sick young man... I just could not keep food down very long... and my legs just did not seem strong enough...to climb up and down...the narrow ladders and metal walkways...of the ship...

Finally I went to sick bay...where they gave me some kind of medication... That helped some...but I still felt miserable...On the third day out...I went to the ship's mess and asked a cook if they needed any help... Food service was run by...mostly quick acting...no nonsense... Filipino cooks...The shift leader eagerly accepted my help...and put me to work washing silverware...and metal cups and trays... When he heard that I wasn't eating...he gave me saltine crackers and oranges... It seemed to help...but it took a full day of sloshing trays...and silverware...to clear my head up...and finally keep some food in my stomach...

As the days went by...I thoroughly explored the old...well-worn... but cleanly painted ship...I stood in a long line for a haircut...and even relieved a tired soldier-barber... who was almost dead on his feet... For 3 or 4 days...I cut the hair...of dozens of black soldiers... I earned over $180.00 and later lost most of it...in pickup dice and card games below deck... After about the sixth day out... boredom began to seep in... A highlight the seventh day...was being up on deck...watching a tiny black speck...on the sea horizon...grow larger and larger...until someone said it was the luxury liner...the RMS Queen Elizabeth... With our speed of only about 10-12 knots...the big ship...moving at about 26 knots...still took hours...to overtake... pass us...and completely disappear again... We were all very thrilled to see another vessel...and other human beings...out there with us on that vast Ocean... I was very disappointed that we were traveling so slowly... I wanted a race...but eventually contented myself to just waving back at the tiny people...on the great...gliding ship...steadily leaving us behind...

After ten exhausting days at sea...we finally arrived at Bremerhaven... Germany... After processing and picking up my duffel bag...I soon found myself on a sleek...fast moving train...cutting through the German... Netherlands...and Belgian country sides...There were many US servicemen on the train...but the majority of our fellow passengers...were Europeans... Nearly all of them smiled silently...when they looked at we Yanks...so I smiled back... For the first time in my life...it felt strange to be moving about...in the midst of people...and not understanding what they were saying... or just what the various signs you saw...said...Hundreds of miles...and several hours later...we were in Paris...France...A quick change of trains...at the Gare du Nord station...and an hour and twenty minutes later...I was at Dreux Air Force Base...in Dreux...France....

Can People Change?

Oceans...to an innocent mind...are vast...frighteningly
alien places...where the intrinsic darkness...and depth
of its being...conjures up the most vivid fears... a mind
can imagine...This is especially so...for a naked visitor...
on its edge...whose progenitors...long ago...in the virgin
of evolution...gave up highly efficient gills...for lungs
more suited ...for the airiness of oxygen...and hard earth
walking... If only we could reverse the eons...and instantly...
return to the tadpole existence...we once knew...before
innocence...and survive even there...in that vast ocean...at
its cruelest depths... It is true we have happily evolved...
built tolerant machines...boldly challenged creation...yes...
even soared to impudent heights...But have we really?...Are
we that much better than what we were?...We are no longer
welcome...where we once thrived...and there are no signs
that we have found new lungs...for the next atmosphere...we
thoughtlessly insist on creating... Where are we to go next...
minus limbs... or the succor...to take us there...especially
since we know of...and believe in the next coming...whether
biblically...scientifically...or on imperfect wings of reason?...

Remembrance

(A Song)

My Darling, do you remember oh so well,
Those tender, passionate moments of love?
Love that would cast us in a magic spell,
And love as pure as a snow white dove.

Here alone I remember all of these,
And though I am very far from you,
They are the jewels that help to ease,
The pangs of loneliness I can't subdue.

When alone and in a feeling of despair,
There is a little place I love to go,
There the grass is greener and sweet is the air,
And the sky seems bluer than any I know.

Here I bring back those moments divine,
And caress an imaginable form of you.
Here beautiful words I try to combine,
Into poems of beauty just for you.

My Darling, Oh my love, heaven only knows
The longing and impatience my soul holds for you.
But daily and hourly this love waits and grows,
For the day when I can once again hold you.

Darling, just be strong and await my return,
Keep your love pure and deep as the sea.
And just as in my heart, JoAnn blessedly burns,
Let "Rico" in yours, be a yearning just for me.

Dreux AB, France
July 8, 1956

Dreux Air Force Base

The city of Dreux...France...about 45 miles...almost due west of Paris...was not far from the famous Normandy coastline...It was dark when I finally ended the long...and exhausting... train and bus ride... from Bremerhaven...Germany...to Dreux... Dreux Air Base was about 18 miles from the city... In addition to my 309th Group...my new base also housed the 60th Troop Carrier Wing...a unit of the 322d Air Division...They flew older C-119's... on a similar tactical mission as we had... The 309th Group was located a few miles from the main part of the base...in what appeared to be a semi-rural area ...When the Air Force shuttle bus dropped me off...in front of my assigned barracks... I was thoroughly exhausted from the long day's journey...and was not much good for more then a hot shower...and a long night's sleep...on a friendly military cot...

The next day...I began to see and greet familiar...friendly faces from Ardmore...and a few new faces...that had come to Dreux from other locations... They were men with last names like:Miller... Lewis... Connor...Shanklin...Moyer...Stengle... Wiggins...McKissic... Blount...Dingle...Thomas...Shepherd...Joy...and dozens more...I can't remember today...The three squadrons...making up the 309th Group... were housed near dispersed... concrete margarites (circular parking pads for the planes)...along a perimeter road... They were all in close proximity to each other... Outside of the perimeter road was a barbed wire fence ... beyond which...there was open farmland...About 12 to 18 of the familiar C-123b's ...were parked on circular pads...around each marguerite... Each squadron had a barracks for enlisted men... and there was a single building ...that housed officer aircrews and commanders ... There was also a dining hall... and maintenance and storage hangers nearby...

Living quarters for enlisted men were primitive...compared to the comfort of Ardmore...In two-story...open bays... we slept on iron cots...divided into sections...by rows of large... metal...double lockers... We had stall latrines...but open showers... My quarters ... and administration workstation...were conveniently next to each other...on the second floor of the 377th barracks... A ton of processing work...

complaints...and normal bitching about pay... (which now consisted of military script...instead of cash) and mail service... awaited me... After a week or two...I began to hit my old stride... and things seemed to get back under control...

Getting around the Base was hampered somewhat ...since we were located away from the main part of the Base... We had to depend on private cars...a periodic shuttle bus...or a couple of jeeps to go back and forth... We went to the main part of the Base...for shared services like medical attention...central payroll...BX shopping... or to go to free... theater movies...shown nightly...in an old... converted Quonset hut... Food from the "chow hall" was decent...but typically Air Force ... For fancier fare ...which was rare for us... we had to go to a couple of small...country restaurants... in the City of Dreux... or to one of the fascinating eateries... in mighty Paris... an hour and a half away...

My workdays soon found a familiar rhythm... In the beginning... after work...I spent evenings and weekends...writing letters or poetry... usually dedicated to JoAnn...With prompting from my buddies...I soon began to spend 2 or 3 weekends a month in Paris... Unlike those buddies... I successfully remained chaste... but flirtatious...on those boredom... breaking weekends...Upon the urging of some of our pilots and commanders...I was also commissioned to paint a mural... consisting of the 3 squadron logos...and a couple of C-123b's...on the entire dining room wall...behind the food service line... I really enjoyed this honor...and it earned me some extra privileges ...like access to the dining hall...almost at will... and a promotion to Airman First Class...in December...1956...a few months after completing the 50 foot mural... Painting soon competed with my interest and love of writing ... and I soon started to spend some weekends... with the numerous...and always friendly street painters... I found sprinkled throughout the cities...of Dreux and Paris... As busy as I was...I still missed JoAnn...and being home... very much...

My Inspiration

(A Song)

The night here is lonely, dark and cold.
Even the stars have refused us their beauty.
The day is forgotten and asleep are the bold,
But here stands one soul symbolizing the lonely.

For I am the humble remembering my love,
Who cannot stand by my side this night.
Yet I have a defense sent to me from above,
That will ease all the loneliness and restore my sight.

The weapon I have, is the memories in my heart,
Of the dear, precious moments I left behind.
And the tangible hope of returning to start,
A life of beauty that will challenge even time.

You see, I already have my lasting inspirations,
In the entire world there has been none greater.
For waiting for me is a love for generations,
Even in cold darkness, my life couldn't be brighter.

Dreux AB, France
July 14, 1956

Overseas Becomes Adventurous

Approximately four months…after arriving at Dreux…a job opening came up in the Operations section of my Squadron… Operations was the flight management function of the Squadron… It dealt with flight crew scheduling…aircraft maintenance…training and mission assignments …the very heart of our purpose…With all the things I was interested in…my Orderly Room administration assignment…had become too boring…and confining for me…so I applied for and won the new job assignment... This new job freed me up for periodic...accompanying flights...on mission assignments to European and various Mediterrean bases...that the United States maintained...as a part of NATO... At that time...we flew supplies and took part in a few practice...troop-drop exercises in support of Army...paratroop units...strategically stationed around Europe... Partly...as a reward for my dining hall murals...I would occasionally get myself designated as an assistant...aircraft crew chief...on various short delivery missions...to bases at...Chateauroux ...in France... Bitburg ...Ramstein... and Munich... in Germany... We also flew logistics missions out of Athens... Greece...that took our crews to countries like... Italy...Pakistan... Morocco... Libya ...and Saudi Arabia... I did not get to go to all of those places...but I did mange to get to a few of them...On one of those trips...I was able to visit my cousin Wilbert...who was stationed at Furstenfeldbruck...a joint-use airbase... with the Germans...located not far from Munich... Germany...

In addition to seeing all of those...for me ...exotic places... the friendly young pilots...who flew our planes... didn't hesitate to let me occasionally sit...in the co-pilot seat...on some flights... It was a thrill to take the controls...and make simple aircraft movements...and radio position calls to air controllers... The best thing about those times though...was the fact that we were never in any hostile moments... The only time I carried a weapon...in France...or had any real concerns...was on an all U.S. forces alert...during the Suez Canal crisis in October... 1956...Through out that alert...I was impressed to stand guard...around our aircraft...for two nights...carrying a rifle...and wearing heavy Arctic gear... I spent those nights writing poetry ...songs...and giving thanks ...that I never had to serve in any hostile environment...like so many had done...in real wartime... a dozen...or so years...before I arrived...

On another occasion...I drove a six by six truck... loaded with fellow airmen...as a part of a rescue mission...when two KB-29's collided over Normandy...Those revered... mighty...World War II... flying machines ...now converted into...fighter aircraft re-fuelers ...had collided and crashed...as they returned from a training flight... Dreux was the nearest U.S. base to the crash site...and we were drafted into the rescue team...Needless to say...it was not pleasant duty...since we lost eleven...U. S....KB-29 flight crewmen ...and spent two days...recovering body…and aircraft parts…for transport back to the base…I will never forget what I saw…and how I was affected by that experience…

As exciting as my Airforce duties and trips had become…I continued to spend time in Paris …usually on weekends… or holiday passes…I loved to explore the jazz clubs…taverns … museums…and parks around the City… Dressed in civilian clothes… and Cuban-heel shoes …I loved to explore Paris…with others…or just alone…picking my way through the Metro… and the fascinating French language… I spent many Saturdays…learning from street painters …how to paint scenes…and interesting faces…on the artsy Left Bank of the City…

I was always amazed at the friendly acceptance…and the eagerness to help…the street artists… and Metro riders showed me…Without knowing it…they…like some of the young pilots…in my squadron… helped to round out…the many sharp edges…I had learned to hone… for white men …I felt undeserving of my trust…Once again…like a few times before…in my life… they too… became the redeeming spirits… that taught me to always focus…on the essence of the individual…before you…for more precise judgements of human character…They helped me to learn how to see through other eyes…when a discussion point had more than one view…

While roaming Paris…if I could afford it… I loved to eat in restaurants… or just wander in and out of pastisseries… fromageries …any establishment or bistro that looked interesting …A favorite of we airmen…was Gabby's…back then…the only "soul food" restaurant we knew of in Paris… Gabby's… started by…black…U.S. Army vet…Leroy "Roughhouse" Haynes…and his French wife…Gabrielle…was originally located in the Ninth Arrondissement…at 1949 rue Manuel…just off rue de Martyrs…Gabby's was the place…for corn bread…greens …beans …fried chicken and ham hocks…

Gabby's was also a favorite hangout for many well-known…writers… musicians and athletes from back home…I remember conversing there briefly…with Richard Wright…a bulging-eyed…Jimmy Baldwin…and Aaron Bridges…a jazz pianist…who introduced me to a terrific jazz bar…called the Mars Club… The famed Mars … was off rue Marbeuf…not far from the Champs-Elysees… Back then…in Gabby's and the Mars…I have a feeling that I shook the hands…and nodded at more famous…or soon-to-be famous… persons than…I had even a clue about…It was…indeed…a fascinating… and exciting place and time…for an impressionable …youngster … from faraway…Hutch Tech High School…in Buffalo…New York…

Eleven Souls

They slammed together…in a fiery ball…
ten thousand feet…over rolling Normandy…
Eleven souls…who sang "America"…when
they were eleven…instantly became burned
pieces…of flesh…racing to the ground…to
be declared dead…We had to find them…and
the now…machine fragments…they came in…
leave a tiny white…or yellow…or red flag…
for the medic pickers…dragging morgue
sacks…The smell of charred flesh…through
flimsy masks…fainted some of us…The eager
…curious farmers…some very young…pale…
wearing light …wooden Dutch clogs…had to
be kept at bay…behind surviving parachutes…
I kept asking myself…was it like this 13-years
before…when other…keen young singers of
"America"…in gray-green helmets…and wide
…frightened eyes…stormed beaches…scaled
the cliffs…and reddened the cold…Atlantic
shore…with their bodies… Death then…couldn't
have been more vivid…than now…I said…
Surely life is still the same…just as precious…
just as unworthy…to be ended…so ignobly…in
an orgy of blood spilling…to satiate male egos…
strutting their clashing theories…while lessening
the worth of young lives…to prove them…Are
we never to learn…that you only get one chance
at life… and that we might as well… keep it our
own…before handing it…foolishly to lying con
men…selling freedom…love…God…or some other…
God damned …conjured-up…stupidly wasteful…idea…

Gabby's Greens

It was like eating Mama's greens…fatback..
Ham hocks…and corn bread…I hoped they
had washed them well…in the back…like I
used to…three…four times…or more… My
Mama always said…"I don't eat just any
old body's greens…or chitlins… I got to
know where they come from"…she said…
And everybody…can't cook macaroni
and cheese…or know what to do…with
neck bones…dumplings…or pot liquor…
I doubt if Gabby knew… but old Kentucky-
raised Leroy did… It's our heritage…like
smoked herring…to Norwegians…or thin
pasta…to Italians…That's why Gabby's
passed the test…and the taste…for me…
and the brown-skin… culinary…refugees
who streamed to Gabby's… to remember
smells…and the down home…belly love…

It Was Paris

It should have been…like any other meander…through a patch
of green grass…shrubs…flowers and trees…in the midriff…of

a bustling…exciting city…but it was not…The benches…birds…
macadam…etched stone paths…adults with scooting children

…strollers and buggies…most showing damp…from an earlier
shower…were there…Further in…there were fountains…ornate

pavilions…statues…a careful plan…Unless you were close…it
wasn't easy to hear the voices…drowned almost to mime…by the

squawk and beep…of vehicles…from teeming nearby streets…and
the ever present…blue hum…of the Champs-Elysees…This first

stroll in this park…had views…as familiar…as they should be…but
no…they were curiously different…almost impressionistic …with

soft colors…seeping eerily through…a now sunny…high noonday
haze…such as one might see in a Monet…No…this was not…red

dirt Oklahoma…yellow sky Wyoming…or Buffalo's tiny…rustic
Delaware Park…It was Paris…that famed city…only fleetingly

read about …in dry…history essays…meant for America's school
children…This was Paris…a city of beauty…of tradition…of

guileful tales of conquest…from smug…young soldiers…and fellow
airmen…sharing space on an old…transatlantic…troop carrier…

repeating stories…that surely stretched back to…the first marchers….
after Versailles…Without fully knowing it…this first…of many solo

trips…to Paris…and the broad…alluring Champs…with all of it's
inebriating sounds…sights…smells and risks…would become…so

infectious…so life altering…and yes… unexpectedly inspirational…
for one lonely teenager…pinning for his…young mate…five thousand

miles away…On some of those future tours…not always alone…he
would bring pen and note paper…On others…materials…palette and

paint…to mix with itinerant sketchers…of the *jardins* or the *Seine*…
He would learn from the gypsies…the freedom fighters from Algeria…

the cool jazz men…writers and ex-patriots…unshackled from the same
mind fear…felt by the frightened…black thousands…who gazed in

wonder…in the 1745 streets of Nantes…now luxuriating in black welcome…
in a new found…paradise of freedom…It would become…a priceless

education…for the street-tough…precocious dropout…who dared… like so many others… to dream of writing…painting…living fleetingly…

on duty-free…weekends…in this…*la Ville de Lumiere*…the City of Light…It would…with its underground Metro…alluring jazz caves and

convenient *Vespasiennes*…become his first big city… where he would search for welcome…in the eyes of strangers…where his body no longer

tensed…at the sight of *un gendarme*…He would be there…less than two years…but that would be…long enough…for this short…life experience…

to absorb…to drink…to shine as brightly…and as intently…as the first gas lamps…that lit up Concorde and the Champs…a long…long time ago…

Colors

Colors…sounds and shapes…
Come at us…in constant streams…
thanks to consciousness…and our awareness…
But we can order them…appreciate them…or
sometimes…just ignore them…
The magic begins…when we reach out…capture them…
and make them our own…
Rich is the musician…the poet…or
the artist…who wins…our praise and admiration…
Yet they are no greater…nor higher…
than we…who validate them…

Spreader of Colors

I gazed upon the work...pronounced to be filled with human greatness... The colors flowed...from tubes...onto a river of human dreams...not all of them happy or gay...many were hues of blue...some even dark blended too...I would like to always...be the artist who chooses...what colors go with the feelings of everyday people...who can then collate what they see ...with what they feel...My palette would have few...if any dark...dim...or shadowed feelings...which people shun...or frightened... throw away;... just bright... high...soaring colors...that open spirits...wed sweetness... happiness and joy...with love...and life...all the things...that every prayer knows... Maybe the giver of genius ...will let me be...the warmth-artist-of-life...who glimpses...even captures infinity...and brings it to the strokes of my brush...since I want to banish sorrow...pain... and even death...Nothing will be given...if you are affected...since my brush will carry no shades...for dwellers...still in shadows...no relief for destroyers...or disrespecters...of the pricelessness...of the human spirit... Only the worthy...will see the sun...from this spreader of colors...

The Mars Club

The odor of linseed...and Old Overholt...was a fitting reward...after a long afternoon...trying to capture...on canvas...the sky behind the roof

line...and the flying buttresses...of a famous...old church...the people loved...The freelancing Corsican...Henri...had coached me well...but

refused...my Gabby's food offer of appreciation...Now after finding my way to the Mars...I was happy to rest weary legs...and wait for the usual

masters of sound...to play into my eager ears...I loved the Mars...It had a sheen...a lively presence...that made young eyes dance...and my heart

fly...with the fast screech...or the low...mellow...sound-rain...at this stop ...on the Zodiac...As is custom...bodies were close...color to color...lips

sipping...toes tapping ...or just faces...hiding behind...unneeded shades...
sailing off on a far constellation...out there...somewhere...It was never

soundless...in the Mars...Between names and brilliance...the smoky din...
there was always Aaron...tinkling or telling stories of the latest...from his

Billy...whom I always wanted to meet...but never did...I loved Roy's bass...
since it went with...and was always needed...by every player...especially

Al...the limber acrobat...who also painted...I was told...that worldwide
famous...had been to...or also came...to the Mars...I didn't know enough

to be impressed...and I told few...that I was just a teenage airman...from
Buffalo...New York...who was learning...how to paint the welcoming...

cultured *jardins*...streets of *Montmartre*...or the storied banks of the
Seine...
by talented...willing strangers...There were other...jazz hideouts...from

Hitler's devotees...like Tabou...Saint Germaine...Storeyville...or the
Latin Quarter...that I...and one or more buddies...often scoured for lovers...

or just sound...from back home...We enjoyed being mistaken for musicians...
athletes...or just exotics...on such eager soirées...Still...I loved most...to

find the Mars...alone...after painting a view...and Gabby's greens and corn
bread...I told few that I rode the train...back to sleep on an iron...military

cot...on a United States airbase...every Sunday evening... a masculine
Cinderella...in a world...where the magic slippers had Cuban heels...and

to lose one...was just to lose one...nothing more...nothing less ...It
was that way for me...quixotically...back then...in *la ville de merveille*...

Dear John Letter

As busy as my days were...at Dreux...I still found time to expand my mind...by reading and taking an English correspondence course...offered by the University of Maryland...I also read a lot of history and political theory books... I read about the Enlightenment...the Russian Revolution... Karl Marx...and books by Richard Wright... and Ralph Ellison... I was determined to continue learning...since I planned to attend college...once I returned to the States...Early in 1957...as a member of the Base basketball team...I traveled around France...Germany and Belgium ...playing local village teams...as a goodwill gesture...from the United States...

Given that we played a largely American game...that the Europeans were just learning...we never really lost a game... We often sloughed off...and deliberately let teams...make the game closer than they really were... At every game...we exchanged small gift or tokens...with local opponents ...This act of gift-exchange...was especially appreciated...when the gift we received...was a ribbon-adorned bottle of wine or calvados... the village or region was known for... On one trip to Belgium...I twisted an ankle in a game...that forced me to use a crutch...for a few weeks...I recovered without lasting effects...

After returning from one such game trip...I received a jolting...searing letter from JoAnn... She wrote to say...she thought it would be best if we ended our marriage... since I would not be returning for another 9 or 10 months... Her letter literally...forced me to instantly...sit down and gather myself... I was completely overwhelmed...by this bolt from the blue... and immediately wrote back... pleading for further explanation ... Within a few agonizing days... she wrote back to tell me...that while living with her father in Pauls Valley ...on a holiday visit to Ardmore... she had stupidly let herself be alone...with a friend of the couple ... she had previously lived with...in Ardmore... She said the man had forced himself upon her...and that she was now pregnant... She begged for my forgiveness... and hoped that I could go on with my life...happily...without her... As I read her letter...between my own heartbeats...I could imagine and feel the tears...that she must had shed... while writing the letter...After those aching moments...I became dazed... and unable to concentrate ... for days...days that unfortunately ... stretched into...many confusing weeks...of mental pain and anguish...

After...the letter...I veered back and forth between... a scalding hatred...and pitiful... loving sorrow...for JoAnn...For weeks...I suffered alone...telling no one what had happened to me...Me...the great Rico... had received the dreaded..."Dear John Letter"...and I was too embarrassed to say a word to my buddies...or to write home...to my Mother...with the bad news... I spiritually drifted...unable to do much...except what I had to do...on my job... I stopped playing cards...with my friends... and spent more time alone...drinking a potent mixture...of Old Overholt rye whiskey and beer... I had a brief fist fight...with a burly... white Alabaman...when he tried to turn off the music...a young Mexican airman was playing on our floor...

I could not concentrate long enough to paint...but I did scribble...a few self-serving words...that I couldn't bear to read more then once...or even keep... I stopped writing two or three letters... a week to JoAnn... I wrote her a letter demanding that she send...at least half of the money...she had been saving ...while she lived with her father...I stopped thinking of myself as "two"...I became a lonely "one"...The hardest thing to do...was to keep it all to myself... Only one of my friends... Willie Wiggins...from North Carolina...sensed that I was troubled ...but I told him nothing ...I told no one...of my pain...and just smiled away my sorrow...

After a few weeks of numbness...a few painful...expensive...phone calls... and lonely walks wherever I found myself...I began to write again... I stopped the self-flagellation... and mentally prepared to end my marriage... Increasingly I found it hard to communicate...with my family...about my plans... My tour in France was set to end in November of 1957... After returning...I would have another year...before ending my...4-year...in-service...Air Force commitment ...I decided I would do nothing... about my now failed marriage...until I returned to the States... However... I no longer felt the same loyalty to JoAnn...and tossed away any restraints ...when it came to attractive women... Whenever I saw beauty...I flirted with a vengeance ...My buddies noticed the change in attitude...and asked me what had happened... I flipped them off... but said nothing...to them...about the real reason...for my new demeanor ...my new attitude...

Just Let Me Die

It comes like creeping serpents low...
sometimes high...brown and green...
with flecking tongues of hard hurt...
Resting never...it knows when your
breath is thin...short...when you
thought yesterday was enough...But
no!...Here it comes again...this time
yellow...dark...black...low...like a
thief to rob me of my soul...Don't you
ever come in blue?...skip a grave or
two?...Have mercy...you bastard of
the ages...you scourge of all things
living...you robber of love...hope..
smiles...One day!...One day I'll find
a way!...I have to believe!...I have to
hope!...There must be some kind of
usual day...a new birthday of just
clear...free air...open eyes that can
take energy and see desire...once more...
No?...If this isn't so...isn't possible...
Then just let me die...right now!

Don't Tell Me Not to Love You

(A Song)

Don't tell me not to love you.
You can't command me anymore.
You can't tell a heart that's true,
To get up and walk out the door.

Don't tell me not to love you,
Just because you've found another.
You say, forget about all we ever knew,
And have no feelings for what we were.

Don't tell me not to love you
Just because you can't be true

Don't tell me not to love you.
You say you're concerned just for me.
Well you can't shun me like an old shoe.
And say we're not what we used to be.

Don't tell me not to love you.
As if you're going to die tomorrow.
Don't say you've done all you can do,
And leave me here in all this sorrow.

Don't tell me not to love you
Just because you can't be true

Don't tell me not to love you.
I intend to hold on to my feelings.
I'll just suffer like all fools do,
And hope I can go on to other things.

Don't tell me not to love you.
I'll just have to be what I can be.
I'll try hard to keep my skies blue.
For I know one day I'll be free.

Don't tell me not to love you
Just because you can't be true.

Antidote

The antidote for sadness is
joy...
Joy is contagious...I am told...
If so...I'll be looking for it
today...I want to be infected...
For if there is some joy
somewhere...coming here
this day...
I hope it comes with a sturdy crane...
to lift the heavy hearts...of an
endless line...of fools like me...

yellow stripe

there was a day...you'd
scream your pain and shout
it to the heavens...you strutted
and gutted and danced in the
sun...or under the full moon...
not the least bit afraid...of
anyone...now you hide the pain...
and hope it's still there in others...
because like you...they are playing
the deception and hold back game
too...to try to fool the fools...but
you can't hide your soul...and the
yellow stripe...running from the
top of your head...to your last
toe...what you can feel but can't
see...I can feel...smell...and see too!...

The Down Winds

A weed of the Cosmos...bends toward down...
It's season is ending...Gone are the hours...

when energy from sun rays...joined minute
ions ...invading its feet...to help it find the

sustenance...to maintain...and keep...the gift
of life...What has changed from yesterday?...

Why are there seasons?...Why does light
dim in the middle of an eternally lit journey?...

Should open eyes despair... or lift lids in
anticipation... deny the season it's planned

halting ...and for a twinkling...be the true
usher for the ending?... What difference does

it make... who finds the river shoals first...
when we know they are there?...Willfulness

may be a choice... but also a usurper of
the ultimate truth... Who can know...if it is

there to be undone?...Who are we...to change
the plan...to be divine?... The season is not

ours to metamorph...So ride the down winds...
you weeds of the scheme...Ease is not yours...

Just stop...and go where they go...Sureness
cannot...for all that ever existed...be ours...

Le Petite Coquette

It was a sport ...we self anointed...airmen slicks...from Uncle Sam...
played on the streets of Paris...Bordeaux...Nantes or wherever we

were...It was a simple metier of ...street courtship...learned from
young Frenchmen...who created and perfected it...If you...alone...

spotted young beauty...walking alone...or in pairs...you simply...
without threatening...followed them quietly...safely...along streets

...in stores...parks or wherever ...pretending no interest...with no
eye to eye at first...just gradually coming in view...until they noticed...

without alarm...your presence...During such rituals...I imagined
being a proud peacock...with a splendid array of tail feathers...so

irresistibly beautiful...she dared not let them go by...without at least
a touch....a smell...even a huff...The game ended if they felt danger...

but if they boldly...sophisticatedly...caught a floating feather...joined
in...and cautiously welcomed...the voiceless coquette...an initial attempt

at pickup...the first precious points were earned...Many enchantments
began...just as this...with as much curiosity...and delight... as such

innocent...human encounters go...Such can only exist...on the streets
of a trusting place...with beauty...and a level of life...where first real

notions of acquaintance...is always confident...A place...without the
spoilage of tales about...Eve and Eden...darkness and light...years of

original sin and fear...A place without the soil...of immediate rejection...
before the heart...had a chance to speak...before value was made...or

was even known at all...To me...this was different...Yet it was further validation of the laments...the dirges...of the home critics...the alienated...

who believed that humans...need not wear disguises...for acceptance...or love...because light...a molecule...an atom was late...or arrived too soon...

This was a delectable...refreshing freedom of spirit...that was liberating... Just one more...of the many reasons...to love a place more than home...

The Photograph

To meet a request from home...I had a formal portrait...in my Air Force uniform... reproduced by a photographer...who had a small... studio-store...in Dreux...It was his custom...to place copies of his work...in a street window display... He hoped that others would see it... admire the work... and come in... When I went to pick up my set of pictures... the photographer asked if he could continue...to keep a copy of my portrait...in the window ...a little longer... He said...the picture had won him more work...I agreed...to his request ...since it cost me nothing...Before I left...he off-handedly said... a beautiful young girl... had stopped and admired the portrait... two or three times a week... He said he knew little of her...but believed she was a music student... since she always had a violin case with her... He said she usually rode a bicycle... and always came by in mid-afternoons... He welcomed my expressed eagerness to meet her...and invited me to come back to meet her...some afternoon...

In the next week...I twice rented a bicycle on Base...and with a little assist from the base bus...pedaled into Dreux... On the second trip... sure enough ...I saw the young lady...the photographer mentioned...He was right...She was very young...and very attractive...Not wanting to startle her...I pedaled to a spot...across the narrow street...from her... and just sat and watched her... When she noticed me...she quickly mounted her bike ...and pedaled away... I followed her...from a non-threatening distance... She soon stopped...parked her bike in a rack... outside of a store front... She glanced back at me...just before she entered a door…leading to an upstairs apartment… As I pedaled by the door…I noticed a sign that read: *Des lecons de musique- a l'etage…Music Lessons – Upstairs* … I pedaled back to the photo shop…and told the photographer what had happened… He suggested that I write a note… and he would see that she got it…I said…no …help me write the note… and I will get it to her…He agreed…

With the note we crafted…on my way back to the store front for music lessons…I stopped and bought a shiny…red apple…placed it and the note in a small bag…and tied it to the young lady's bicycle handlebars… The note read: *Hello…Don't be afraid…I am the man in the photograph…I just wanted to say hello…and tell you my name…You are very beautiful* …I pedaled away…vowing to return the next day… For two consecutive days…I visited the photo shop…but did not see the young girl…

It was in the next week…after another weekend had passed…that I finally saw her again… Just as before…I chose to wait across the street… from the photo shop…As she pedaled up…I am sure she noticed me… but as she had the last time…she stopped briefly …glanced in the shop's window…then pedaled off again… Once more… keeping some distance…I decided to follow her… This time she did not pedal to the storefront…but instead stopped at a small corner park… When she dismounted her bike…and sat on an iron bench…I pedaled up to her… sat on the bench…and in my broken French/English… said:

Hello…Mademoiselle…Please…may I join you for a moment?

She

You are the one in the photograph…yes? …The one who left the apple…

Me

Yes…My name is Rico…Do you speak English?

She

A little…very little… I see you speak French…

Me

I speak very little French…but I always try…I am learning…

She

And I am learning English… I started learning in school…

Me

You are very beautiful…What is your name?…

She

Marie-Letizia!… Most…in my family…call me Letizia….

Thus…was the beginning of a new flirtation…a new relationship with someone…who would once more…briefly become special in my life… It happened at a time…when I was trying to heal… when I was searching for the emotional balance… I couldn't seem to find in the… routine of military life… and my other…off-base activities… Before too long…after that meeting …I began to share lunches …dinners…long walks and biking adventures…in and around Dreux with my new friend…

Letizia had completed the equivalent of high school …and was studying the violin… while she decided whether or not… to go on to a university …in Rouen or Paris… I learned that vying for her affection… and my competition for her time…was a long-time friend and former classmate …named Amande…In coming conversations …Letizia would reveal that Amande…had always told her…that he wanted her to be his wife… Another potential chink …in my desired relationship with Letizia… was her beloved father …Joseph …who disliked black people… and would…if he knew of me… disapprove of her seeing me… None of this discouraged me...or made me less interested...in our growing friendship ...Once again...I was being challenged for a friendship...I wanted very much...

Marie-Letizia

Her pulchritude...feigned
fragile...fine...
Limoges porcelain...She delighted with
a face...
pale...delicate...perfectly
punctuated...
with marble brown eyes...against
a wisp of dark bang...on her
forehead... She wore a single
schoolgirl's...stranded braid...that
gently touched her hips... Her smile...
broke slowly...dryly...but like her voice...
sweetly... Surely it would...be
a sin...to touch her...
I almost...hated myself...
when I finally did...

French is Like Jazz

French...to me...is a beautiful language...
It is not merely spoken...but breathed...

sucked...wheezed and hummed...It
reminds me of jazz...when it is cool...

full of expression...unfit for lazy tongues...
or the untrained on an instrument...

I swore that French would be mine…
                    when…lying head to head…Letizia

breathed…the soft passion of a pleading
                    Verlaine…into my ears…with the same

delicate pause…beauty and inflection…
                    of one of her Mozart… concertos…

Mesmerized…and full of gratitude…I said to Letizia:
                    "Que vous merci pour ce moment"…

Confessions and Healing

I met Letizia…almost four months…before my tour in France… was set to end…In those remaining months…I became obsessed with trying to spend…as much time as I could…with her… mainly because she inspired me to write… and paint again… However …despite my new infatuation …my pain and thoughts of JoAnn…continued… I kept remembering…the all too brief…but warm time…we shared…In my head… I also kept hearing…and remembering my Mother's words: *"what makes you think you can keep up with a young woman…while you're hundreds…no thousands of miles away?"*… Her words haunted me…almost as much…as the love I still had for JoAnn… I must have called myself "stupid"…at least a thousand times…More and more…I ached for someone to share my torment with… someone to confirm…or rebuke me…for my mistake…I just wanted to open up…to someone…about what really kept tearing … at my heart…every day… On a bright picnic afternoon…sitting in the grass of a lovely meadow …I found that someone in Letizia…

Letizia…was the 20 year-old daughter…of a former farmer…who now made a living repairing small tools…and leather goods… He gave up farming…when he injured his back… about 5 years…before I met her…Her mother…Hortense…slender and poised…an older version of her daughter… was from a farm family… in central Normandy… Letizia also had an older brother…Lucien… who attended a university…in Rouen… She had great hopes that...she too...unlike her parents...would also attend a university... She hoped to become a musician... in a grand orchestra...one day... I would never get to personally meet... a single one of Letizia's family...although... one weekend...I did see her mother... from a distance ...when she and Letizia... shopped for vegetables...at the market in Dreux... Whenever we were together ...Letizia and I spent hours...telling each other... about the people in our lives... our countries ...families...our ambitions...I took her to the Air Base...to show her my dining hall murals... and she was fascinated with my painting and writing... I was just fascinated with everything about her...especially her quiet maturity...and sense of strength...

In the beginning...I was hesitant to be completely honest with Letizia... especially to tell her the complete story of JoAnn...in my life...However... one Saturday afternoon... in a park ...while we shared...sandwiches and white wine...I opened up...completely about JoAnn...It was the first time...I had told anyone...other than my mother...of the dreaded letter I had received from JoAnn...

It was cathartic...almost purgative...to tell my story...and hear the judgement of someone I trusted...Letizia was patient...and understanding of my anguish... She bravely tried to comfort and assure me...and to my surprise...reminded me of my own youthfulness... how it is easy to make mistakes...when you love someone...when you are so young... I was impressed with the wisdom...of this 20 year-old... this lovely daughter of a French farmer... who had met me...just weeks before... In appreciation...I wanted to write a poem...and express my gratitude to our friendship...but I hesitated...remembering the last time I wrote a poem...to a young girl...I was convinced I loved...Instead...I promised her I would let her help me... paint a scene...when we visited...the beach at Deauville...the following week...

A Single Violin

Setting sun...sand...her smooth
silhouette...the soft surf...and
smell of the Atlantic...that the
odor...and touch of her body
challenged...the dance...and

wail...of a single violin...all
wove silky mind spells...gentle
affection...faint teeth breathing...
and healing...I would joyously
keep...the far too short...far too
rich moments...close...and never...
ever...be the same person again...

Deauville

So even villains...and assassins...can love beautiful places...
that calm the spirit...soothe the mind...nourish character...

It's not enough...that they killed bodies...brought pain...destroyed
spirits...They also...wallowed...like animals...marking scents...

as if...all beauty...belonged to just them...as if their presence...
would be the first...the last...the only...that we better humans...

deserved to know...We and the people before us...and all those after us...
reject the notion...the folly...the twisted brain...of the would-be

conquerors...who lost their purpose...and this place...after they
came...like bold thieves...with no invitation...Our return will sweep

their odor...reclaim the prize...and curse the fools who had to run...
to save themselves...from the righteous...wrath of the people...

The Croix de Guerre

As she sat...I rushed out of the surf...as if having just
stormed from a gaping...Higgins...wielding a tree limb...

instead of a carbine...I announced that I had come...to
free her...from the dreaded...northern slime...gripping

her beloved land…little more than…a dozen years before…
She said…"*Who are you dear hero?…Is your name Henry*

Johnson?"…Startled…I affirmed my own presence…and
asked who was this Johnson…she seemed to know… Then

there…on the beach…at Deauville…a slender…beautiful
young daughter…of a French farmer…gave me a lesson…

in American history…that my own Country…perceived to
be…unimportant for me…and all the children of America…

She then told me of Johnson…and a companion…Needham
Roberts…black American fighters…in the first great war…

who…alone…in the trenches…of the Argonne Forest…killed
or fought off…more than a dozen…invaders from the north …

Deemed unworthy…by their own Nation's military…fighting
in French helmets…under French command…they fought…

for a land that appreciated…wanted them…They fought to show
valor…they never doubted… They fought to be more…than

menial laborers…in a land where they could still be…unjustly
lynched…For such…France bestowed upon them… the Croix de

Guerre…its highest honor…and first ever given …to American
soldiers…Sheepishly humbled by my ignorance…the narrowness

of my American education…I thanked Letizia for giving me this
tale…and I swore that I would make it my story…and never forget…

It would be more than a few years…before I unraveled the story…
of the diminutive Black American hero…Henry Johnson… In my

pursuit…I would learn a great deal more…about the character of the
land I called home… and how it treated…its brave…black defenders….

The Hell Fighters

He was a small man…just over five feet…but hard and able….from
lifting thousands of bags…boxes…and carries of people…who called

him Red Cap… Virginia born…Carolina raised…he was as American…
as you could be…But he was black…a curse in his own Country…like

others before…and after him…As a part of an all-black Regiment…
called the "Black Rattlers"…they…to preserve whiteness…were given

to the French…to fight under French command…rather than be mixed…
with white U.S. soldiers… He and the Rattlers fast proved their worth…

as solid fighters… He and a comrade routed more than 30 of the enemy…
killing or wounding nearly half…one May night…in 1918…in the

defensive trenches…of the Argonne Forest…On that heroic night…
he joined Crispus Attucks…at Faneuil Hall…the fearless chargers…

of the 54th Massachusetts…at Fort Wagner… the Buffalo Soldiers…
from Fort Russell…and the Red Tail…air fighters…from Tuskegee…

all whose blood…courage and labor…wrote as many pages of what
we call…American history…as any brave defender…of the land…Yet

their rich stories…for years went unheard of… unspoken to the children…
deliberately ignored…and missing from the legacy of America…It was…

as if they were invisible moments…that did not matter…When the grateful
French…awarded Johnson…the Croix de Guerre…with Palm…and Star…

the French…like the Germans…now called Johnson…and his unit…
"Hell Fighters"…a testament to their ferocious bravery…to their final

acceptance… Later…ashamedly…America found him…worthy of a
lesser medal… and a Roosevelt would acclaim…him… and his unit's…

proud military accomplishments…Johnson…the fighting hero…would return home…to modest parade recognition…that was not specific to his

deeds…But with wounds…that left him unable to lift bags…as a Red Cap… unemployed…and homeless…lifted from a cold Albany street…he called

home…he died silently…It was 1929…and he was just 32 years old… Sadly the school children…of America…like me…and most others…unlike the

school children of France…would seldom hear the stories…of the too often scorned…and unjustly rejected…black fighters of America…Once more…

the false notion of superiority…the stain of the sin of slavery…as always… took precedence in white American character…It was not the first time…It

will not be the last time…Sadly …such is the enduring burden…of all black people…and white people too…who live in…and love the promise of America…

This Land Is Ours Too

Their covenant didn't include us…Like many there…we were
faceless…unworthy to be…a high part of…this thing of theirs…

this land…this place…Their god was not our god…their solemn
invocations…came only from them… Yet at every step…we too

served and earned the land…not just with toil…but with blood to
leaven the loaf too…from Attucks…and the Rhode Island Proud…

before even the Declaration…we went…we came…We helped
old Hickory…in the Delta…climbed the mast and fought on Erie…

killed children of former masters…wearing the blue of the 54th…
and the little Colonel…wouldn't have won San Juan and Kettle

without us...We helped expand... throughout the wild west...and swallowed dirt in the Argonne Forrest...After escorting bombers

to Germany... we...the fearless Red Tails...had to sit behind the krauts with blond hair...in our own homeland... The medals...if

they came at all...were late...unwritten in history books...Such is our journey...our burden... to earn what is ours...as much as any...

So we will sing our songs to our own children...tell them to be proud... stand straight...before any man...any foe...This land is ours too...

The Cathedral

There before me...straight out of my...*Architecture of Western Civilizations*...reading assignment...from Buffalo Technical High School...soared the mighty Cathedral at Chartres...Sitting up high... with unequal spires...it rose upon high ground...above all around it... With its...famed "flying buttresses"...a nave and transepts...that filled the cruciform plan...like that more famous edifice...on the island of the first Paris...my thoughts flew back...through a few short years...that seemed like dozens...to high school...to a sleepy morning lecture...about the excellence of European design...So this is the grand...ancient place of worship & commerce...that has marched through...so much of French history...a testament to the egos...of self appointed emissaries from God...a crypt for holy bones to rot...like Egypt's pyramids...a statement of stratified...human intelligence...& labor...From days of peasantry...when the church sold vegetables...from its arches...through the Revolution...when the wild atheists...wanted to burn it down...to just little more than a dozen years before...when men of the American force...I now represented...wanted to bomb it to the low ground...at its base... Each time it was saved for the worshipers...for the faithful...for the selves ...who used it then...& continue to hold sway... Surely their God...had its arms around its magnificence...Still...like all things human...all things earthly...it cannot last forever...But I hope those arms never tire...& stay strong for us...& it...for a thousand years more...

The Silent Scream

Thank you for freeing me...from a cage of wonder...

doubt...and unknowing...This feeling is explosively

liberating...delightfully pleasing ...in a cellular titillation

that pulls breath from the top of me...My flesh never felt

such softness...such wetness...Is there a grander feeling...

a more purely selfish...silent scream...so absorbingly

indulgent?... I think not!...Never have I been so instantly

addicted...so captured....for I now will be lost forever to

myself...as I reach... over and over again...searching

for a return...to this joy...to this sweet...trusting ecstasy....

A Painful Parting

After meeting Letizia...the weeks...and my remaining months...in France...now seemed to fly by... Unlike my first months...in this new land...when I ached to return home...I now dreaded going home... I faced the unpleasant prospect...of unwinding...what was a brief... failed marriage... but I now wanted to...somehow...make Letizia...a part of my future... That...I concluded would be difficult...since I had another full year...in the Air Force ... and I lacked the financial ability...to do what I wanted to do:...I wanted to take Letizia with me... or some how... remain in France ...I had been reassigned to...a staff position...in the Operations Directorate...of the Eastern Air Defense Force (EDAF) ...at Stewart Air Force Base...in upstate New York... I was scheduled to report to Stewart...in December...1957 ....after a 30-day leave of absence... My inquiries about remaining in France... went nowhere...My orders were firm...Sadly...I prepared myself mentally...for my inevitable departure from France...

In my last weeks in France... I tried to spend...as much time as I could...with my new friend... We both...had kept our relationship a secret to all but a few of my buddies...We did our usual...borrowed car adventures...around the nearby towns and Countryside...and spent a final 3-day...weekend in Paris.... I wanted Letizia to show me what she loved about Paris... and I took her to my favorite hangouts...and the places I adored...She loved to explore museums...parks...and ride excursion boats on the Seine...I loved visiting Gabby's ...the Mars Club...and other jazz haunts...up and down the Left Bank...

Although we both... had short-time lumps...in our throats...we both thoroughly enjoyed being with each other ...Riding the train back...to Dreux...we vowed to somehow ...be together again...On my last day in Dreux... Letizia met me at the train station...I wrote my next assignment's address ...and my mother's phone number...on a slip of paper...and shoved it...and a short poem... into her coat pocket... I promised her... that I would write to her... at the address of the apartment in Dreux... where she took music lessons...We bravely embraced ... swore love... and fidelity...and for the second time...in less than two years...I climbed aboard a train... with eyes moist...and a huge lump in my throat...I did not know it then...but it would be the last time...I would ever see...dear... lovely...Marie-Letizia...

From Me

(A Song)

If you ever see a flower that you like...

That flower will be me...

If you ever taste a taste that you enjoy...

That taste will be me...

If you ever radiate in a snug warmth...

That warmth will be me...

If you ever enjoy a cool...hugging breeze...

That breeze will be me...

If you ever hear an irresistible melody...

That melody will be me...

If you ever speak another...single word...

That word too...will be...

and come...happily...from me...

Merci

(Thank You)

Merci d'etre venu dans ma vie...
(Thank you for appearing in my life...)

Je vous remercie de votre amitie...
(Thank you for your friendship...)

Je vous remercie pour votre amour de guerison...
(Thank you for your healing love...)

Je vous remercie de me faire mieux...
(Thank you for making me better...)

Je vous remercie de me montrer comment pardonner...
(Thank you for showing me how to forgive...)

A Sip of French Wine

France...through the eyes...of a young tough...
from the streets of Buffalo...was a singular...

wonder...pace...aroma...and air of life... The
wonder...was a proud history...the scent was fine

wine...and the air of French life...like its wine...
was sipped...and savored...unhurriedly ...and...

certainly...as satisfying...as any I had ever seen... I
stepped upon its ground...and left changed forever...

not solely because of a wounded spirit... but with
a fresh... heightened gratitude...a new sense of the

world... a new imagination...that I doubt...I could
have found at home... in the churn... and turmoil of

black America...1957...While young...bold...confident...
when I came...real poise ...arrived for me... in France...

Back in Buffalo Again

When I left Dreux...in November...1957...my orders called for me to fly home...via Turbo Prop...airliner...from Orly Airport...to New York City...with a brief stop at Shannon Airport...Ireland... The flight... my first in civilian aircraft...seemed long and boring... After arriving at Idlewild Airport...New York...I spent the night...with my Uncle Julius' family...in the Bronx... In appreciation...I gave Julius' wife Ellenore...a small bottle of Channel No. 5...I had purchased in Paris...Now on leave for 30 days...before my next assignment...the next day...I caught the New York Central train for Buffalo...

On the way...I wondered what my duties would be...at Stewart Air Force Base...which was a few miles from Newburg... New York...I was now assigned to the Plans and Programs Unit of the Operations Directorate ...of the Eastern Air Defense Force... (EDAF)... EADF was a part of...the North American Air Defense (NORAD) system... which was charged with overseeing ...the installation of an automated surveillance...and response method...to intercept enemy bombers or missiles... Stewart was also the home of the 330th ...and 331st ...Fighter Interceptor Squadrons ...They flew F-86L Sabre fighter aircraft... as a part of the Nation's eastern air defense... My duties would be purely administrative...and unconnected to flight operations...

The train ride to Buffalo...back to my mother Dimple's home...was largely uneventful l... Before I left New York...I sent a card to Letizia... back in Dreux...and I kept thinking about what I would say to Dimple... about Letizia...about JoAnn...and what had happened... to my aborted marriage... The family now lived...in an upstairs flat...above an Italian family...at 201 Sycamore Street... In addition to my mother ...and her husband Louis...my siblings... Gwen and James...still struggling in high school ...also lived there... My mother's brother ...Frank ...and his wife... Etta...also lived in the three and a half bedroom flat... William ...the oldest of my mother's brothers...lived with his family...in a lower flat... next door to 201 Sycamore... The brown...heavy air of poverty... and need...as always...still prevailed ...I soon learned that...both Gwen and James...were dispirited ... bored...and tired of how life was unfolding for them...Within a period of months ...both would become...like me... dropouts ...and leave home...

My mother had insisted that I come stay with them... when I returned from France...I dreaded the cramming ...but I hoped there was still a friendly couch ... that I could borrow ...for a few weeks... until I left again...for Stewart...When I arrived...not much had changed... Money and jobs were scarce... Dimple was not working...and Louis worked... only part-time... as a security guard... My Uncle Frank... and his brother... William...were seasonal stevedores ... on the steel loading docks...of Bethlehem Steel... They worked... mostly during the warm months...loading steel on ships plying the Great Lakes...My first few days back...were filled with story telling...and answering questions about my future... my brother James...of course...was thinking about also joining the Air Force...and Gwen just wanted to leave... period... I wished...so much that I could have helped them…somehow…But like them…I too… was wounded…and broken of more than spirit…

At first…I put off calling JoAnn… who had given birth to a baby boy…in September… I dreaded the painful conversation…about our future…that we had to have… sooner or later… As usual …Dimple waited for the right time… for our inevitable conversation… about what had happened to my marriage… Finally…after a couple of days …when we had just finished supper…sitting alone at the kitchen table…we had that painful conversation …

Dimple

All right…tell me what happened… What happened to JoAnn?

Billy

All I know is what she told me… I was eager…doing my duty… trying to get through
my 18-month assignment in France…and get back here… get on with our lives… Then out of the blue…she writes to me and tells me she's pregnant…

Dimple

Pregnant with another man's baby…not yours?

Billy

That's right… She says she went visiting…or to a party at the lady's family she previously lived with…before moving to Paul's Valley…to live with her Father… While there…she says she was put upon…I guess…raped…by one of their family friends… She swears she never intended for such to happen…but it did…

Dimple

And you believed her?

Billy

Look…I don't know what to believe… All I know is…I married a girl…went off
to France for 18-24 months…expecting to come back…and make a life with someone
I cared for very much… and she writes to me…and tells me she's pregnant…

Dimple

Look…you two were just 18…just barely grown…You were a couple of kids…
Now…do you understand what I was trying to say to you…before you left…You
can't expect young girls…to sit and wait for you…for long periods…without temptation … or something happening…
that's not in your best interest…There is no such thing as…a long distance romance…Do you understand that now?…

Billy

Yes…Before I left France…I met someone else…a beautiful… caring person…who….

Dimple

Wait a minute…wait a minute; One woman at a time!…You already have one long distance…failed marriage… So now you want two?… Did you marry her too?

Billy

Of course not… She was someone who helped me through…the hurt and tough pain… She stabilized my spirit…restored my confidence… I'll never forget that…

Dimple

Good…I am glad you met her…But let's forget about France right now… Let's talk about where you are now…You're married to this young girl…with a baby…that's somebody else's…what do you want to do now?…

Billy

Divorce her!… Find someone else…to live my life with… What else can I do?

Dimple

Yup!…That would be the right thing to do…if she was unfaithful…if she is lying
about what happened… But what if she is telling the truth!… Suppose she was raped…Suppose she was trying to be faithful… to a dummy…5,000 miles away…who thought he could marry a young girl…and leave her exposed to her surroundings for two years…

Billy

Getting raped is one thing…but having the baby…

Dimple

What would you expect her to do…try to get rid of it?… That's a lot easier said
then done…for a small-town…country girl…besides it's against Jehovah's will to abort children… Lord…I wish I could get you kids…to understand Jehovah's will…how we are not in control… and it is his will…that will be done…

Billy

That may be...but I have to decide what I want in life...It's my life!...I make the decisions...about what happens in my own life...

Dimple

Nope!...You make choices!...The decision is up to Jehovah... Sometimes you make the right choice...sometimes you choose wrong...but you never can overcome Jehovah's will... You chose to marry that girl...but you left her exposed... Both of you didn't know what you were doing...There is always evil...out there...lurking to disrupt and change...interrupt our choices... destroy our dreams... Lord...do I know about destroyed dreams... poor choices... But I also know how to let his will be done...Tell me now...what's in your heart right now?... Do you hate JoAnn?...Do you still love her?...What?...

Billy

I don't know... I just don't know...One minute I can't stand to hear her name... The next...I just melt...remembering how much I cared about her...how much I wanted to get her out of Oklahoma...and make her my wife...But now...it's hard...I just want out...Get it over with...

Dimple

You still care about that girl...don't you?

Billy

I guess so...but she's different...She's not the same... She's.... she's...

Dimple

She's what?... She's not a virgin!... She wasn't when you married her!... The only thing that's changed...is the baby... Suppose she'd had the baby...before you married her?... She very well could have…you know… Lot's of women have babies… before they're married… Marriage is just a legal thing… It has nothing to do with the experience of the people who get married… It just says…from now on…you two have a legal chance to be with each other…to be faithful…live your life together… You two weren't really married…before you left… You cared about each other and slept together… But that's not a marriage!

Billy

But what about vows…and faithfulness…Don't that count?

Dimple

Sure…but so does being there for each other…nourishing and building a relationship … You can't feed a woman's body and soul…writing her poems and love songs!… My advice to you is to look deep in your heart…just like you did before you…so-call… got married… If you still care for that girl…then go to her… If you don't care for her…forget about her…and get somebody else… Don't let a rapist…and a baby steal what's in your heart…and keep you from what you really want to do…

That's how the conversation went…how my pride was laid bare… and how my Mother's words…forced me to examine what was in my heart… whether I really cared for JoAnn…and what I really wanted to do… I stopped thinking about…and wishing for Letizia…as much… as I had been… and once again…JoAnn began to dominate my thoughts… I thought about what Dimple had said to me… and I called JoAnn… to show interest in her well being… and to try to determine her current attitude… toward me… I wanted to show her…that I was…at least interested in her well being …She told me that she had given her baby my name…and that she still loved…and wanted to be with me… Rather then talk about a divorce…an annulment…I promised that I would continue to call… until I decided what our next steps would be… I encouraged her to be sure of what she also wanted to do…

Dry Rivers of Desire

Not every river is a wet one…Some rivers are dry…unseen
spiritual conveyors…of countless human emotions…They are

dispositions…that reflect the spirit…wishes and desires…
of every mortal whoever strove…to live…create…help…

win…lose…destroy… find some meaning…or higher
understanding…of this forced obsession…this consciousness…

that we call life…Not a single one…of human kind…chose to
be so…Yet all…but the imperfect…make contributions...to

the running…perpetual dry rivers of desire…that swim resolutely…
with every human yearning there ever was…or ever will be…

They are rivers…where yesterdays and tomorrows…crisscross
and meander…some with bright endings…that find the calm

of smooth currents…Others that are buffeted…by rocks…high…
dropping waterfalls…whirlpools that kill hope…or get caught up…

and lost forever…on the wings of dying winds…So goes the
way …of dry…flowing rivers…bearing human wishes…and

cravings…I think that they…though full of precious trust…
will suffer the same fate…that awaits all rivers…wet or dry…

The Must Do

The swirling wetness murmurs…gurgles…
gushes…and foams…In an instant…it can
go from a caressing…trade wind ripple…a

benevolent carrier of your spirit…to a violent…
snuffing…churning…destroyer of your life…
The ocean can do this…Air can do this too…

with soft…warm…friendly…or hard swirling
viciousness…Even a human like you…can do
this…to a soul wanting…trying…to just live…

The ocean…the air…the land…can't change
what it is…what it must do…what it has to do…
Can you…dear human…change what you

think…you must do?…Or are you just as
immutable…unchangeable…as the ocean…the
air…the land…the inevitable…the must do?….

The Cool Prince of Darkness

Like so many…when Miles kicked in…he was just an eager kid…
looking for help…inspiration…how to deal with urges…his

own plan…to be great… Natural flair…earned him training…a
grudging respect…and silent certainty…from fellow travelers…

like Parker…Birks…Stitt…Hawkins…Trane…Evans…dozens…
Soon a masterful mute…in a familiar horn…took it…and him…

beyond the spectrum…the flavor…and the thym side of rhythm…
to a new height of cool… Mere genius didn't fit…Others alleged

that… On this journey…alone…he flew back to the bowels of
the sun…where we all came from…then reported again…what

all of us… had long forgotten…that hot comes before cool…and
that even bitches…can be made to dance… to a cold brew…round

midnight...if you will it so... You can beat devils...throwing long shafts of evil...and even turn malice...pain and addiction...into sounds

of glory...redemption and love...just by being...a pure human being... Such was the light...that came from...the cool Prince of Darkness...

Reconciliation

During this time at home...my cousin Wilbert...who was also in the Air Force...was home on leave too... He was on his way to his next assignment...in Bangkok...Thailand... Just before I arrived on leave... he had recently met...and decided to marry a young lady... who was a church friend of his sister... He asked me to be his best man...and I... of course ...accepted... While growing up... Wilbert and I were almost like brothers... I trusted him and freely shared my status...my anguish... and my marriage situation with him... One evening...while downing beers...and reminiscencing about my visit with him...a little more than a year earlier...in Germany...I told him the story of JoAnn...what had happened...and the dilemma I faced... He patiently sympathized with me...but he too...tossed the ball back to me...and encouraged me to look into my heart...and don't be afraid to admit a mistake...or to be upset about people...who do not understand or like your choices ... He said to me... *"Hell ...in this Air Force business... we never know...what happens next...I am about to marry a woman...I have known less than a month... We think it's the right thing...Maybe it is...Maybe it ain't... But if it isn't... I'll just dump her and start all over... Nothing is cut in stone...That's the way I see it"....*

They were simple words...that I'd heard before...believed in...but somehow...they rang new with me...Wilbert and Dimple both...were saying the same thing:... don't be fearful of your feelings...your steps in one direction or the other... If they turn out to be mistakes... they are correctable...Thinking back...that was what Letizia...in her quiet... soft manner... also said to me... Those words...in spite of my back and forth feelings...about Letizia... helped me to decide...that I would let JoAnn's will be done... I called and told her that if she still wanted to be with me...I would accept full responsibility...for naively leaving her in

Oklahoma… I told her I was ready to forgive both of us…and try to make the marriage work…

It was not easy…for me to come to such a decision… I was still wounded … and occasionally thought of Letizia…in my quiet moments… I knew if there wasn't an ocean… and economic realities …between us… my decision may have been a very different one… I told Dimple… Gwen and James…my Uncle Frank and Etta…what I had decided to do… I let Dimple tell Louis… A few weeks after that… ignoring the pleadings of her father not to go… JoAnn and her baby …bravely …arrived at 201 Sycamore…It was a strange…and nervous night…when she arrived… with lightly falling snow flurries… and a ton of uncertainty…and awkwardness …ahead for both of us… I knew I had done the right thing when JoAnn said to me…"Despite what has happened…I just had to be with you"….

Curse of Dependence

Why do…what we do…with…or for…each other?…
Why do we even need each other?…Could it be that

permanent …re-living of the helpless dependence
we all have…when we are born?…Are we doomed…

by a silent instinct…to be…forever in need… both
physically and mentally…of someone…something…

somewhere …no matter what?…Is it possible for a
human…to be born…and not ever…need another

single soul again?…Can we ever be freed…of this hard
addiction to dependence?…When a bird…pushed from

the nest…learns to fly…does it still need to keep the
pusher…the nest… the reliance?…Or can it fly off…

free of hinge...free of all claims...free to soar heaven?...
Dependence...it seems comes in shades...degrees that

suit our penury...internal or carnal...Is it timings that
match our weaknesses...our penchant to always be human...

no matter what...we do...or what we think?...Perhaps
such is the curse... none can change...or control...ever!...

Mighty Trane

Mighty John William...could dance up
on rails....and run between ties...while
picking up red hot coals...He could make
you giddy...lace up your feelings...then
snatch tiny strings from your shoes...He
struggled so...with all kinds of voodoo...
tempos...rhythms...always ready...looking
for transition...and rare space...to blow...to
strut...run a gig...even march to Souza...while
playing dirges with pallbearers...He imagined
infinity and tried to touch it... He ran with
giants...who stole a whiff...geniuses...friends...
every one...But John William!...John William!...
Man...you something else!...Something else!...

A New Start

After JoAnn's arrival...and a cautious...delicate...reconciliation...we decided to start all over again...We both probed each other...for assurances that we were doing the right thing...for both of us...Because of how we decided to live...it was not only an adjustment for us...but for everyone in the crowded little flat...at 201 Sycamore...Personally...I now had to try to be a husband...and an ill-equipped father...as well... I had to both recall…and forget…good and bad feelings…I had spent months trying to understand… More importantly…I had to finish my last year…on active duty in the Air Force… As my leave of absence wound to a close…I decided that I would report for duty…but leave JoAnn…and my new son…Stuart…(whom I later nicknamed Ricky)…in Buffalo… I decided that whenever I could…I would come home on weekends… since the trip from Stewart Air Force Base…near Newburgh…New York…was just six hours…a train…a ferry…and a cab ride away… With luck…I thought…it wouldn't be much of a burden…to be a weekend commuter…

When I arrived at Stewart…my very first day…the Duty Sergeant… in my assigned Orderly Room…after routine information…said…"I hear you play basketball…We can use you on the EDAF team…We got a game tomorrow night…You interested?"…I answered yes…if it did not disrupt my weekends too much… Soon after signing in…I explored my new quarters to see what life would be like at Stewart… My barracks were sturdy…two story buildings with open bays…sectioned off…with lockers…We had privacy in latrines…and showers…Surprisingly… although filled with other airmen…the bays were quiet and orderly…I didn't know a single soul…so I spent a lot of time making new friends… and trying to learn my way around…My work assignment…was basically serving as the administrative assistant to a stiff-neck…Major…from Connecticut…named Conrad… When I reported to him in the EDAF Programs building…he told me to take the rest of the day off…since notice of my Security Clearance…wouldn't arrive until the next day… That was the first time I learned…that my job required…a "Secret" Security Clearance…

My new assignment…consisted mainly of routine order creation and response…and the physical upkeep of a large presentation room…It was filled with the latest audio-visual equipment…and dozens of classified cans of 9 millimeter film…on the latest developments in defensive… or offensive missile and aircraft technology… The Major and I…were responsible for two or three film presentations a week…for a dozen or so… officers and senior airmen…working on air defense/offense issues… While other officers and technicians handled most of the actual presentations… the Major and I…were the facilitators…the "go-for's"…who made sure the equipment worked…and that necessary accommodations were provided…

Our audiences usually consisted of the top brass on base…an occasional visitor from the Pentagon…or civilian military contractors… I found the new job fascinating…the first few months…However…I soon grew bored and restless…especially when it became apparent that my superior… Conrad….and I…really didn't like each other…

One Monday morning…after returning from Buffalo…the mail clerk…from the Orderly Room…called me and said he had some mail for me… That surprised me…since I almost never received any mail…other than official notices…When I stopped by to pick up the mail…the clerk told me…he had three letters for me…that had been sitting around since before I arrived… He said he had forgotten to give them to me…when I arrived…because he didn't go through "old holding mail" that often…He sheepishly mumbled that at first he couldn't make out who the letters were for… After calling him a "dumb-ass" to myself…I took the letters…and immediately knew they were from Letizia…

My initial reaction…when opening the letters…was guilt…since I had not written to Letizia since arriving back in Buffalo…months ago…I had thought about Letizia…often…but the pull of reconciliation with JoAnn…dominated my thoughts and concerns…Letizia's letters dated back to a few days after I left France… She expressed love and yearning… and always ended the letters with vows…we used to utter to each other… or with a one or two line poem… The last letter warned me …that I would not be able to write to her at the address I had…She said…thanks to help from her brother…Lucien…she had finally been accepted at the university in Rouen…and that she would let me know how to write to her later…I was happy that she was now at the university…but shamefully… with a lump in my throat…I numbly hoped…that she would move on with her life…and forget about me…I felt helpless to do anything about the promises…I had made to her…

After a few months…I began to count the weeks…and days to my discharge…Conrad grew more and more chilly…toward me…especially when he learned that I was not interested…in re-enlisting… In the meantime…I faithfully commuted to Buffalo…on at least three weekends a month… On those weekends when I didn't go home…I hung around the base…playing basketball…writing…or took bus or car trips to nearby sights… I began to pal around…with one of my basketball teammates…

Jim Drake...who owned a small English convertible... We would take short trips to the surrounding towns...or sites...listen to jazz...or put our pennies together...to buy beer or wine... We enjoyed each other's company...got drunk on beer and wine...and played basketball...It wasn't until the last day I saw Jim...that I concluded that he probably was gay... Despite his completely normal...never suspect masculinity...his goodbye was a little surprising...when he hugged me...a little too tightly...and cried...

Moment to Moment

In deep moments of despair
it is absolutely amazing to me
how it seems so easy to feel
that the worst only happens to you...
It is enough...the despair...the anguish...
to cause self sorrow and make
you curse your god...and your existence...
When it happens...and it does
over and over again...if you keep breathing...
I have learned to just pause...stop the
self-serving pity...think about and look at what
really could be worse than that moment...
and acknowledge that you don't know what
the next moment...the next day...the future
will bring...If you see great joy in the future
rejoice in its coming...if you think there is
sadness on the horizon...give thanks for today..
For...if it is coming...it has not darkened
your presence yet...and today...this day...
this moment...there really is no
reason yet...for your distress...

You Still Own My Heart

(A Song)

Now I've messed up; can you forgive me?
What can I say, I don't deserve sympathy.
I couldn't blame you if you walked away,
And ignored me no matter what I say, *but*

Wherever you go, what ever you do,
You'll still own my heart and I'll still love you.
I'll still love you.

I know you were faithful and did your part.
One couldn't ask for a bigger heart.
You gave me your precious, precious love.
I felt it was sent from heaven above, *but*

Wherever you go, what ever you do,
You'll still own my heart and I'll still love you.
I'll still love you.

I wish there was something I could say or do,
To change your mind; somehow convince you.
I thought I was clever, that I was being cool.
Now I know I was just being a fool, *but*

Wherever you go, what ever you do,
You'll still own my heart and I'll still love you.
I'll still love you.

I'm not asking you to accept the blame.
I'm the one who is filled up with shame.
You deserve someone better than thankless me.
No matter how desperate I make this plea, *but*

Wherever you go, what ever you do,

You'll still own my heart and I'll still love you.
I'll still love you.

Losing you will be very hard to take.
I dread to think of the coming heartache.
With lonely nights and numbing blues,
I guess I'll just have to learn to lose, *but*

Wherever you go, what ever you do,
You'll still own my heart and I'll still love you.
I'll still love you.

Accepting award from John Hettrick

As President of First Independenc

As VP at Marine Midland

Author's Brother James

Author's Father Richard

Author's Mother Corine

Author's Sister Gwendolyn

In the Air Force

Painting murals in the Air Force

With the Carters in the White House

the balance scorekeeper

wouldn't it be just wonderful,

if there was a great scorekeeper somewhere,

that kept count of all the days of despair,

and all the days of joy, we have had, and then

made sure that the days, all balance out in the end.

if there was a great scorekeeper somewhere, what kind of

days, and how many would still be ahead for you, before the end?

Looking Beyond the Air Force

During most of the last months of my active Air Force duty…I became less and less interested in the Air Force…I thought more and more… about what my life would be like… after my discharge in November… Of course I had to find work…since I now had a ton of responsibility…I also thought constantly…about how I would continue pursuing an education … During my stay in France…I had taken two correspondence courses in English literature… and creative writing… from the University of Maryland…Since I had dropped out of high school…and earned a GED diploma…while attending Air Force Tech School in Wyoming…I knew if I wanted to go further…I had to find out if this qualified me… to attend the University …In August…1958…I wrote to the Registrar of the University of Buffalo …Their response referred me to the possibility of attending Millard Fillmore College …the University's night school…for part-time students… I learned that if you were an armed forces veteran… you could also receive a few credit hours for that service…

It was also in July…1958…that I learned that I would be separated… two months before my official separation date in November…It was never explained to me…why I qualified for early discharge…I suspect it had something to do with me declining to re-enlist...Whatever the reason...I was grateful to move on... to get on with the next chapter in my life... In the first week of September...1958...I was officially "separated" from active duty...My eight year obligation... however...continued in an inactive status...subject to re-call at any time...While I was never again called to active duty...I was not finally discharged ...from the Air Force... until November...1962...exactly eight years after my 1954 enlistment...

When I arrived back in Buffalo...I immediately started looking for work... My only income was a modest...but very welcome...unemployment check...During her first months in Buffalo...thanks to babysitting help...from my mother and sister Gwen...JoAnn had found work as a receptionist ...She...and especially the baby...had melded into life at 201 Sycamore without too many complications...Frank and Etta...especially delighted in having a young baby around...and our contribution to the monthly rent was very welcome...During this time ...I also made inquiries about my education qualifications under the GI Bill...but because of the skimpy education...and living allowance offered...I concluded that I had to put off school plans...until we had more income...

While collecting unemployment insurance...to make extra money...I would do any odd job I could find... During most of the summer and fall of 1959...I worked as a part-time stevedore on the Bethlehem Steel loading docks...My uncles...Frank and Bill...had been working on the steel docks for years...and it was...with their help that I got hired... The job required that I belong to a small...mostly black...Chapter of the Long Shoreman's Union... At the first Union meeting I attended...I was immediately elected Secretary of the Chapter... My uncles later... laughingly explained...that I was elected because I was the only member there...with a high school diploma...and no one else wanted to...or could write the minutes of the meetings...

One early evening...in October...my mother called me to the telephone...She said there was a long distance caller...asking for me... She said she had accepted the call...but I had to pay for it...Puzzled...I took the call and was totally...and completely...surprised to hear Letizia's voice...After exchanging greetings...Letizia said to me...in fractured ...but surprisingly good English:...

Letizia

I hope I am not disturbing you…but I still had your number….and…

Me

Oh…no…You're not disturbing me…It is good to hear your voice…Your English is excellent….

Letizia

As you encouraged me…I have been studying English hard… almost as much as my music…I am at university now…

Me

Yes…I got your letters…I received them late…but I did get them…I apologize for not writing back…I have been…

Letizia

Yes…yes…I understand…busy… Did you return to your wife?…

Me

Yes…I hope you understand that….I…

Letizia

I do…I do understand… There is no need to explain…It is good…since I have some news for you also…After many years of friendship…Amande and I were married …earlier this year…We had a beautiful… curly haired…baby boy…this past August….

Me

(Surprised but relieved)

Oh…I am so happy for you!… I am very happy that you have someone to love and care for…It is very good…this news…And a mother as well…This is indeed good news…

Letizia

I do not want to go on wasting money…on the call…but I had to hear your voice once more…and wish you the best…I will keep your poems…always…

Me

And I will never forget you…Thank you for being in my life…

Letizia

Be well forever…Goodbye…and *bonne chance!*

A quiet sadness came over me…after we ended the call…I was both sad and happy that Letizia had also moved on with her life…and that she had married someone she knew well…Still I couldn't stop cursing…and mentally berating myself…I couldn't stop feeling awful…about not being able to keep a heartfelt promise…It wasn't until days later…as I replayed her call in my mind…that it hit me…I remembered that she said…she had .."had a curly haired baby boy"…in August…A dread came over me!…I began to sweat…Could that baby…no!…I said …almost in panic…to myself…It couldn't be that worst of thoughts… Surely…I said to myself… she would have told me…But she didn't…and mental flashbacks… images and questions…dogged me… mercilessly… The worst was:…the thought that Letizia and Amande were raising a child…that could be mine? … I have been haunted by that unconfirmed thought…and the tragic irony of such a possibility…from that day…right up to this very moment… The thought haunts me pitilessly…

If it is so

If it is so…then I send

this blessing…
May you always be

safe….and strong…
able…and loving…

more honorable…acute…
and respectful…than

your provenance…Be taller than your
natural height…defeat any dark inclinations…

you cannot change…Take the
tiny…inherited kernels…and prayers…all

that I can give now…Grow them…Stay
faithful… and please do…what

I was…sadly…unable to do…

The Young Eagle

A young eagle flies…free
and soaring…even though
one wing is broken…Despite
its wound…it still must find
the valley…where the reward
is lush…nourishing and worthy…
But there are no soft…light winds…
cool sun rays…or warm nights…
to help his flight…just dust and

foreboding...in his sharp gaze...
untrue strikes...by his keen claws...
binding wetness...for his feathers...
Yet...fly on he must...It is in his
sinews...the only promise...for
all of his kind...There is nothing
else to do...but fly...and search on...

The Grind Begins

In December...1959...I got hired at the Chevrolet Engine Plant... in Tonawanda ...New York...a suburb north of Buffalo...Soon after receiving my first check...from Chevrolet... ($96)...JoAnn...the baby and I...moved to an upstairs flat...at 93 Mulberry Street...in an area of Buffalo ...called the Fruit Belt...Months prior to the move...both James and Gwen... discouraged...by the spirit-killing poverty...and mimicking my own earlier feelings...had left home ...James went into the Air Force... and Gwen moved to Detroit... Michigan... where she lived with relatives and friends...

It was also in Detroit where Gwen... also re-established contact with our...long departed...father... At the urging of his brothers and sisters... he had moved to Detroit from Washington ...D.C...Although still unable to work...he had taken up with another woman ...called Martha Bailey...Mostly dependent upon Martha's income... they had been living together...as man and wife for years...Because of my current financial circumstances ...and remembering all the hard scrabble years...and how he had abandoned us...I was not very anxious to see my father...Richard... any time soon...

On Mulberry Street...I settled into the rhythm...of marriage and fatherhood...The hardest task was moving around without an automobile... At work...which I got to riding with others...after a few miscellaneous tasks...I finally became a permanent machine operator ...grinding crankshafts or camshafts to go into GM vehicles... At home... my thirst for education...was pursued by reading and writing...It was during this time...that I wrote...and copyrighted two short screen plays...I also honed my sketching ...and painting skills...when I could afford it... I exhibited and sold...a few of my sketches and paintings...in the early years...of the Allentown Art Festival...In 1960...after my mother and Louis moved to New York City... JoAnn became pregnant...and Carmen...our first child was born in October...of that year... The next year...with savings ...and an income tax-return check ...I spent $500 on my first automobile...a used 1955...blue Chevrolet sedan...

That same year...in the fall of 1960...my sister Gwen...who now lived in Detroit...married an Army veteran...named Howard Glenn... I rode to Detroit...with an aunt and her family... to attend Gwen's wedding... While there...I unavoidably...reconciled with my father... Richard ...It had been 17 years...since I had last spoken to him...and he was extremely moved to see me... He and his wife...Martha...insisted that I spend... one of the two nights...I would be there...with them... I accepted their invitation and...they were very gracious...and welcoming...That night... while Martha was away at her job...as a cook and dishwasher...at a Greek restaurant...in downtown Detroit...Richard and I exchanged stories... sorrows and regrets...

My father...born in North Carolina...was the youngest...of six sons... in a family of thirteen children...Ten of his siblings...and he...shared the same parents: Tom and Eliza Bailey...His two youngest sisters...born after Tom died...were the offspring of Eliza and her long-time employer...a white...North Carolina dairy farmer...Richard's father...Tom...was a sharecropper...sawmill worker and laborer...whom Richard believed was born in South Carolina... Eliza (Williams) was also born in South Carolina...Richard knew little of his father...since he died when Richard was very young...Grandfather Tom...died soon after returning from a six year prison sentence...for shooting a man...in a fit of anger...at a Sunday afternoon picnic...

Richard married my mother...Corine Elizabeth Stewart...when she was eighteen years old...two years before I was born... Nearly all of Richard's life...he had suffered from an epilepsy-like illness ... he is believed to have acquired...after suffering from spinal meningitis...when he was seven years old...Despite his illness...Richard had worked as a laborer...carpenter...painter...and railroad checker... However ...he was constantly plagued by long periods...when he could not work ...because of seizures…and bouts of depression… His illness is what ultimately… destroyed his marriage to my mother…Corine… He abandoned his wife… and their three children … when I was six years old… I had not seen him since that time…until that night in Detroit…in 1960…

Listening to him talk about his life…nervously explain his sickness… it was not hard to forgive him… and I was glad that I did that night… It was liberating to renounce all the curses…and bitter regrets…for not having a father…for all those years…before that night…I didn't know it then…but that time would be the last time I would ever see him…He died …from pneumonia…slightly more than two years after that night… on October 1 1962…He was just 48 years old… and never had a chance to see his grand children…Because of financial hardship…regrettably…I was unable to attend his funeral…

My Son Billy

I kept looking at him…when his eyes were
away…trying to see some trait…hear some
inflection…or tendency….that we shared…
I saw none…He was just one tired…older
than his age…victim of circumstances…he
could not control…he was a victim…of a
devastating illness…I hoped was not inheritable…
I avoided the temptation…to tell him how much I
missed him…

…when I baked my first coconut cake…
…when in the 8th grade…I made a game
winning jump shot…in basketball…
…when I made the 8th grade…valedictorian
speech and won the Jessie Ketchum Medal…
…when I first came home…in my Air Force
dress blues…ram rod tall…a leader of men…
…when I brought his first grandchild home…
from the hospital…

and I left un-asked…the most important…of all…

but knew the answer...the next day...when I was
awaken...by him...and three squealing young...
neighborhood women...ogling a half naked me...
lying in his bed...Richard said..."He's my son...
Billy...Isn't he beautiful?...I love him so very much!"

Collector of Bread

I watched him grow older...I
heard him as he grew wiser...
each day of our parallel lives...
My fleeting curiosity in him...
in his words...in his appearance...
slowed...steadied...matured...
Like a mellowing French wine...
that is unmistakably French...he
became his own one-of mankind...
I looked for little lessons in
everything he said...or did...
in my presence or not...He
showered me with mind jewels...
as numerous as the twinkles
in a clear night sky...Like him...
I too became a collector of bread...
to feed the hungry observer...with
time enough to watch...to hear...
to listen...to sprinkle...jewels too....

The Beat Goes On

With two babies on our hands...my respect...love and affection for JoAnn...continued to grow...She became a very careful...nurturing mother...who tried very hard to please and take care of her family...She worked very hard...to keep our little flat clean...orderly and livable ...We lived frugally...but with great optimism...In September...1961...I finally registered... and was accepted into Millard Fillmore College...at the University of Buffalo ...With the initial financial help of the GI Bill... ($70 to $80 a month) I started out taking a few night courses a semester... including summers... It was a year round choice...that required a lot of energy... focus and luck...It was also a tough way to get an education... but if it is the only way...and you really want it...as I did...then I felt it had to be done...

While working a full eight hour shift...at the plant...I developed ways to study while I worked...On weekends...I would read assigned book chapters...then write questions and the answers on 3 by 5 index cards... that fit in my shirt pocket... The next week...I would read and study the cards...while a camshaft ground away... in my machine...I repeated this method all during my time at Chevrolet... It proved effective enough... to earn an overall B- average in my courses...An exception...would be the only F... I ever received...when I walked out of a Physics lab class...in a bitter dispute with a young lab instructor...

I almost universally liked...and respected my professors and instructors...at UB...Among the dozens...that I had...I remember: Myers...Ahmad...Tam...Mason and Ertell in Economics; ...Boddy... Stadler...Thiesen....and Labaki in Math and Statistics; ...Macdonald in French; ...and Barnes...in English Literature...While a few would welcome me...for late night or afternoon exchanges...most were...like me...busy and unavailable most of the time... Because of time limits with professors...and a lack of genuine friendships...I felt I left much on the table at UB... However...I am glad I had the benefit...of four years in the military ... before attending college...I also appreciated my prior experience ...with the French language ...The latter made me...a star pronouncer...in that class...

In the early 1960's...the grinding task of going to school...working and raising a couple of kids...should have been enough to think about... to do... But other things...mostly political... were also happening in Buffalo...and other places around the Country...Those happenings caused concern and pause... for a young man with a dream...The Civil Rights Movement was picking up steam locally and nationally... Racial tensions arose...when the black population of Buffalo exploded...Whites began fleeing Buffalo…and critical businesses…and industries … (steel… chemicals…flour milling…aircraft…etc.)…also began to leave the City… By 1970…the population in Buffalo…shrunk to 375,000… from its height of 532,000 in 1950…

Looking back…a hugely important occurrence…the opening of the St. Lawrence Seaway …helped to begin a kind of…near-death spiral for Buffalo …that would affect the City's economic…and political spirit in profound ways…for years to come… I believe…the opening of the Seaway …and the political fear of its new…growing black population… killed too much of the civic pride…and spirit of renewal…the City of Buffalo…desperately needed back then…The political shunning…of the core City of Buffalo…would be repeated again and again…when later decisions were made about the design…and location of the professional football stadium … the State University…and the ill-fated…Light Rail Transit System… All…were investment opportunities missed…and poor decisions that…in my opinion …stripped Buffalo …of population… momentum…and a chance for vitality…

A Queen's Tears

The President…and a Queen came…to open a
new way to the sea…Two nations…plus…gladly
celebrated…but another proud Queen dolefully cried…
after feeling the acute pain… when the long ships…
showed only their wake… It was…as if…someone
stole all the grand garments…the Canal had long
bestowed… and left the Queen to scour…for whole
new ways…to dress for the ball… Soon the door fell
down…the wind stayed cold…and an august people
lost its old love for a lake…that had been so kind…
Open prairies…became the new home…for far too
many of its grand places…its new generations…its
kernels for planting today…for tomorrow's city…Sadly…
the old Queen will struggle long…to stand high again…

Death Penalty Days

Don't kill someone for me,
claiming you represent the State.
Don't make me a party to a felony,
and force me to be a helpmate.

Sure, people do some horrible things,
sometimes even to people I dearly love.
My problem is, I don't trust killing schemes,
that are flawed with mistakes, not unheard of.

The system is as fault-ridden as humans are,
filled with economic, religious and race prejudice.
And until it can be made absolutely without mar,
I'll oppose it as just mish, mash, hit-and-miss.

For to take one life in a flawed mistake,
is just not worth ten million guilty.
To get to chemicals from a burning stake,
compensates no one, it seems to me.

Execution supporters, the most religious among us,
are the most eager to kill, to righteously avenge.
Despite professed commandments and denials of lust,
they soil their souls with certainty and revenge.

As a soldier I came to bitterly realize,
that I too, could become a killer.
It was hard for me to rationalize,
to avoid what could be forced on a dissenter.

My comfort came in finally deciding,
that I always have the right to self defend.
That if ever confronted with death overriding,
I'd do whatever I could to avoid my own end.

But that does not mean I will ever give in,
to the fear-filled madness of the avengers.
They believe their righteousness has no end.
They've reconciled their faith and see no dangers.

They are the true conservatives, who eagerly take us,
back to where we were...long, long ago.
Back to the caves, the stakes and blood lust,
blunting, slowing virtue and good places we can still go.

1963 – A Profound Year

In 1963...we moved to another rented flat at 629 Woodlawn Avenue... in Cold Springs... That year I upgraded my automobile to a used 1958 Chevrolet sedan... Moved ...and excited...by the rhetoric...and spirit of civil rights...I...and two of my work mates ...from the Chevy plant... Jimmy Bumpers...and Elmore James...drove that light blue Chevy ...to the 1963 March on Washington...It was a moving experience for all of us...At the March...what amazed me most...was the shear number of mostly black people...all with a single purpose... to make a statement for fairness...from their government...I was profoundly moved by the unity of purpose...determination...and fearlessness of so many thousands of both white and black people... petitioning their government for fairness...I was forever changed...by the experience...

When I returned some years later...I wrote a screen play called... *Sweet Corn in The Morning*...that I felt captured the essence of that experience ...The play was about the continuance of black peonage in the South...and how right up to the March on Washington... southern whites in America...were still brutalizing innocent...black people...with impunity ...I also wrote a number of poems...that I felt captured the spirit...and meaning of the March to me...Back home...increasingly... it became harder for me to stay focused on work...and learning ...rather than demonstrations and civil disobedience ...Again...I expressed those frustrations...by writing cutting-edge songs...poems... and plays... Unfortunately ... sometimes ...my writing took on bitter tones...that was too descriptive of my disgust with events...that terrible year...1963...

In so many ways...1963 was a trying...and momentous year...Especially affecting was...the boycott campaigns around the Country...the church bombings in Birmingham ...Alabama... the dozens of bitter lynchings and racial incidents...all over the North and the South... I was especially affected by the brutal assassinations of a very brave...and exemplary... Civil Rights leader...Medgar Evers... and the young President ...John F. Kennedy... It was a time when I found it hard to forgive some whites... and the system of justice in America... In my life...so far...I have not found another year... that matched my loathing for the tragic...ugly racial events... that happened...all throughout my Country...back in 1963... However...as ugly and politically obnoxious as 1963 was...I believe the atmosphere created that year helped President Johnson and the Congress to pass the momentous Civil Rights...and Voting Rights Acts...in 1964 and 1965...These Acts were almost...exactly 100 years late...and was really the beginning of meaningful emancipation for black people in America...

Schwerner, Goodman and Chaney

The task was simple...register black people to vote...
in their Country...a democracy...a land of the free...
where the people...supposedly...get to choose their
rule makers...to share in governance...to be fully...
members of a mortal tribe...Of course...it was a noble
goal... for a long excluded people...worthy of any of
the soaring commandments ...that exemplify the lofty
American creed... But lurking in the dark shadows...
of the land...hatred...ignorance... bitter losers...decided
to become cannibals again... Three young sons...then bled
the soil red....suffered the pain... the fatal end ...some of us...
have to pay... to be included... to purge the Nation of the
unenlightened... the un-evolved... the sub-humans...who
stay among us...even up to this very day...God help us!...

Mr. Evers

I could never be as courageous as you Mr. Evers…
I know I could never grow so tall….Who ever saw

a man grow that high?…Its way too tall to grow to…
Why it's unheard of…for just an ordinary man…

to rise up in the human family…and be so doggedly
courageous…so singularly unafraid of white evil…

Most of us grow to just over five feet tall…Who
would have ever thought…that a proud…fearless

man…from Mississippi…could grow up to…twice five
feet!…and he would cast a shadow across every black

soul in sight…all across a whole nation and its people…
You did Mr. Evers…You did grow tall…mighty tall!

Brave Brother

What did you do today…brave bother of the resistance?…
What act of courage did you ferment…on our behalf?…

"We showed them Niggers… We showed 'em we ain't
taking their disrespect…They done gone too far…They
have forgot who runs this here Country…They done forgot
who their masters are… It's white people…who own
and built this Country…We showed 'em!"…

But what did you do to show them?… Did you lynch
somebody?…Did you beat up somebody?…

"No…we planted a bomb…at a place we knew where
they would be…We went to a church last Sunday and
left our dynamite calling card!"…

And what did your dynamite do for you and us?

"We killed some of them...four little girls...they say...
That'll show 'em we whites mean business...all business!"...

I Hate White People

I hate *white people* who keep me from hating white people...*They* get in the way of my rage...and my sometimes wish to kill them all...*They* challenge the rationale for my hatred...*They* startle my insistence... my conviction...and remind me to remember...that *they* are like me...that *they* are my cousins...*They* force me to wonder if the whites...who hate me...are just paying us back...for ravishing them...and driving them out of paradise...long...long ago... It cannot be as simple...as what I look like...what threat I bring...just by my very presence...Can we break the cycle cousin?...Is there a way to be reconciled...to settle it?... Is it possible for all the different...colored birds...to be just birds...for all the different...colored humans...to be just humans?... Maybe so... maybe not...not without help...from the far outside...like oxygen being denied to all birds...to all humans...Then at last...perhaps...we can once again...be one...just birds...just humans...all of us...without oxygen...

I Hate Black People

I hate black people who...in the pitiful
tradition...of empty humans...when offered...
a piece of bread...or a special place...at
the table...or in the line...of reward...would
sacrifice...the souls of ancestors...the souls of
their children...their very own souls...to fill their

bellies...with less than food...to soothe tired feet...
with legs open... soles in the air...to stroke the
mirage of a moment in the sun...They are the true
slaves...They are the real lovers... of the slave
master...They are the lovers of rapist...and
hangmen...They are the soul-less...who...like
pitiful Jews in German camps...during the ugly
unspeakable...would strut...in pieces...of prison
guard uniforms...lording it over fellow Jews...
in a pathetic attempt to...salve the pain...of their
own insanity...You know who they are...They
know who they are...The old people...used to
call them "toms"..."handkerchief heads"...
"rope holders"..."grave diggers"...I cringe
for their colorless souls...I cry for their dry
ignorance...I reach for the memories...they
lost...or have forgotten they ever had...I walk
away...forever...from even a hint of their very
existence...Only they can stop my steps...
reconcile with me...for I can never...ever
...reconcile with them...the soul-less...

Too Soon to Say

We were there...in a collective of humans...
Blacks...browns...whites...celebrities...athletes...

leaders...Randolph...Rustin...and Romare Bearden...
All of us...petitioning a government...we thought

cared little for our cause... The crowd was familiar...
festive...overwhelming....united...determined...

It was a day...when the sun was broiling....so
unyieldingly...but also welcomed...I kept asking...

will all this make a difference...Will the killing
and brutality...finally end?...Will a nation that

promises so much to its citizens...and the human spirit
...redefine the word citizen...to finally include us?...

Will our nation...at last...know that we too belong...
It is too soon to say...too soon to say...I am afraid!...

Lena Horne

Just after I shook Wilt's and Harry's

hand...I hugged Lena Horne at the

March On Washington...I just...walked

up...said my name...and:

"Miss Horne...
I just can't let you
go by...without
telling you...that
you are the brightest jewel
in my own treasure chest
of wonder and beauty"

She smiled and responded:

"Oh my!...You dear
boy... you!...Why...
thank you!"

That hug and her smell

made enough days for me ...

to get me deep into 1964...

The Beatles

Talk about sneaking up on you!...Few things have ever...
on a pure skeptic...with credentials...I never for a moment

got serious about little...white...tow-headed Fauntleroy's...
in English smocks...yelling and being yelled back at...by

screaming banshees...all out of breath...even fainting...So
what's the big deal?...I said...Hell...what do they know

about rhythm...melody...truth?...What do they know about
sweat...the sun...the whip...the blues?...Let me out of here!

But on the way out...it took me years...their sound caught
my ear... & slow walked the mock...I disarmed to listen...&

slowly...slowly began to hear...I came to see...that their reach...
for their own sound expression...was not that far from blues...

from Delta slide...or Memphis bump... It was just the same old
style...now pushed through the sieve...of a Liverpool pub...with

its own twang...hop & rhythm...Their young star edge... their
amped up search for purity...was...in its own way...the essence...

of English gold...& for sure...a kind of compliment...to an art
form...& genius...we all know well...So now I yield to their flair...

without a single scream...or even one tear...but with solid respect...
& a smile that says....Damn!...They don't need me...after all!...

As I neared graduation from the University...I continued to release my pent up emotions... about the violence and civil disturbances...by aggrieved black people... by penning letters to newspapers... My opportunities for debate and exchanges with others were very limited... so writing letters...

to me...was one way to express my eagerness to debate...to challenge...The following letter to the Buffalo Courier Express was a typical example...I am not sure the letter was ever published.....

629 Woodlawn Avenue
Buffalo 14211 New York

January 2, 1966

Editor
The Morning Mail
Buffalo Courier Express
Buffalo 40, New York

Sir:

I read with interest the moving article in Sunday's paper by Anne Matthews. Justice Hamilton Ward's denouncements of crime and anarchy and his grave warnings were correct and timely. I deeply respect his opinion but feel perhaps some things were left unsaid.

I think it would be a tragic mistake to just condemn crime, punish the criminal and feel we are preserving order and protecting society without being concerned with causes. I can think of one in-stance where we would not be protecting society but just putting off the day of reckoning. I am referring to those misguided souls of the Watts area of Los Angeles mentioned in the article. The significance of the Watts riots was not just simply a mass violation of the law by criminals that need condemning. The Watts riot was a signal. A signal to our great land that within its midst, smoldering with hate, insanity and depravity, there exists a growing element of society whose blind rage can wreak havoc on this land greater than any it has ever imagined.

Text books tell us that criminal behavior is "nonconformity to the official values of a society." Surely we cannot expect the inhab-itants of a Watts area to believe in those values if the rewards of society, that reinforce those beliefs are never forthcoming. We in America stress competition, achievement, success and we believe no one should be denied a chance to show what he can do. Yet the Watts areas in America are denied. The number of losers are growing. Contempt is wide spread and television conveys the dazzling success of the winners.

The Honorable Justice condemned the philosophy of excuse but I think, without realizing it perhaps he condemned the philosophy of guilt. The Nation and its values have been laid bare to the bone and we all have taken a new look at ourselves. Many of us do not like what we see.

We know we would not think of robbing a bank, committing a murder or burning down a city block, but we smugly go our way evading taxes, twisting laws for profits or political power, breaking traffic regulations designed to protect all and I might add, even though it is not statutorily wrong, flubbing an indifferent nose at the spreading squalor of slums and growing corruption of those trusted with responsibility.

I am not trying to purge anyone of responsibility for criminal acts and I am not saying that decent "law abiding" citizens should feel guilty. I am saying that we all should become "more law-abiding." We should preach the rewards of a society that lives up to its Constitution, its state and local laws, and its proclaimed belief in a fair chance for all. We should punish the criminal and give our enforcers the tools they need to get the job done. On the other hand we should not lose sight of causes. For I am afraid if we start at the top of a tree bearing rotten fruit and strike at each blossom with the sword of condemnation, we may never get at the roots sunk deep in the midst of fertile ground.

William R. Bailey

The Prize Looms

The school and work years of the 1960's…in spite of their difficulty… were weighty times for my growth and maturation…I also increasingly appreciated JoAnn…for her strength…. and her assistance …in my efforts…to better our lives… However…I missed not being able to spend more time socially…with interesting people…on and off campus…I especially regretted…not being able to participate in sports…and debates…For entertainment …JoAnn and I… spent time with family… close friends…and an occasional movie…I immensely enjoyed playing whisk…and penny-ante poker…with my uncles… and friends …Bill and Johnnie Middleton… and their two daughters… who lived across from us on Woodlawn Avenue ...In school...I took elective courses in French... and music...and of course continued to read ...write...and paint...

After nearly four tough years...of work and night school...year around... if I wanted to graduate from the University...I would have to quit the Chevy plant...and take courses offered only during the day... When I gave notice that I would be leaving the Chevy plant... my foreman and a couple of plant superintendents...approached me...and offered me a promotion to foreman...or some other administrative positions...My plant supervisors had long watched...and taken an interest in my efforts to go to school...and even kept me on the day shift...and in the kind of work...that assisted my schooling efforts...I appreciated their efforts...on my behalf... and their offer for promotion... However...I had decided that my hoped-for...degree in Economics...would better serve me in a different kind of work...so I turned down their offers...This...of course...now meant that I had to find a new way to support my family...while I finished my studies...

In the fall of 1965...with graduation in sight...I quit Chevy...to take my final University courses during the day... Before leaving...I had found a night job...as a janitor with a contract firm...cleaning the Mall on Niagara Falls Boulevard... Within a few weeks...because I came to work almost every night...I soon found myself the leader of five or six men of that cleaning crew...Early in 1966...I quit the janitor job...to better accommodate...my school schedule...and to make more money as a cashier and bagger...at Twin Fair Super Market...

All during that time...when we had baby sitters...JoAnn would work as a secretary...for a small accounting and insurance business...on East Ferry Street... Finally in June...1966...after nearly five years...of year-around work and study...in a ceremony at Memorial Auditorium...I was awarded a Bachelor of Arts Degree in Economics...from the University... As far as I knew...it was the first time...someone in my family...had completed college...I had some proud family members...and a beaming JoAnn...standing with me...that afternoon... It was a long... hard slog to get there... and I couldn't help but feel gratitude...to the University and everyone else who helped me get there...especially JoAnn...

Will They Come With Me

Now I feel the energy…the power…
the essence of being…of knowing how
to be content…with what I know…
I don't need any more assurance…I have
enough to know my place…to be fulfilled
with what I have been…or will ever be…
The journey to here…from wherever I
came…brought me so…in spite of my
ignorance…my glorious shortcomings…
my many failures…and missed chances…

Now *they* feel the energy…the power…
the essence of being…of knowing how
to be content…with what *they* know…They
don't need any more assurance…*They* have
enough to know *their* place…to be fulfilled
with what *they* have been…or will ever be…
The journey to here…from wherever *they*
came…brought *them* so…in spite of *their*
ignorance…*their* glorious shortcomings…
their many failures…and missed chances…

Is It Just Me

Where are the bright …young white people?…
on whatever side of the argument…Where
are you?…It's a school…a university!…It's
where you learn…teach…I thought!… But
no …no one breathes a word…Their eyes
dart away…on banner headlines days…only
the book…is raised… not like Berkeley…or
Kent State… No one dare read my poems…
or really wants to know…what I believe…
what I feel…Are they all dead?…Or is it
just me…my own days…of run & rush…to
get on with it…to sleep & get back to work?…

A Bagger Becomes a Banker

A few months...before I graduated...I had begun to think about my next job...Inspired by the nomination of Andrew Brimmer...to be the first black man...on the Federal Reserve Bank Board of Governors...I had hopes for a good job with a federal agency...like the Federal Reserve Bank...or some other government agency that would offer a decent living...and an opportunity to continue pursuing a higher degree in economics... I made a few inquiries... and in late June...I also followed up on a potential offer for local employment...that I received from my mother's employer... My mother... now separated from her husband...and returned to Buffalo... from living in New York City...was now employed as a housekeeper...for Betty and Adam Cornelius Jr...Mr. Cornelius...CEO of the American Steamship Company...was a director of the Marine Midland Trust Company... Aware of my struggles for an education...Cornelius had said to my mother...Corine...if I wished...he would be glad to..."put in a good word"...for me at Marine...The bank...he said...was anxiously looking to hire qualified minorities...for the bank's Officer Training Program...

Having nothing to lose... I agreed to accept Adam's offer for an interview at the bank...soon after graduation...Within a very few weeks... after graduating...I received a call from the bank... and the interview was arranged...I was invited to come to the bank by the...then head of the bank's personnel department:...Miss Allalee Babbidge... During my very friendly...interview with Babbidge...she asked if it was O.K. with me...if we had our picture taken by a photographer...from the local newspaper... Though somewhat surprised...I agreed...and I...along with another young candidate for a trainee position...had our picture taken with Babbidge... The picture appeared in the newspaper...the next day...

Seven days later...I received a formal offer for employment...into the bank's 2-year...officer training program...at a starting salary of $5,800...I was told that during the training period...my salary would be reviewed every 6 months... My mother...and the Cornelius'...were thrilled with the bank's offer...JoAnn...was slow to express strong approval...until she knew that the offer was acceptable to me...and that it was what I really wanted to do... I took my time deciding on the offer...and discussed it with a placement counselor at the University...The counselor was highly enthused about the offer...and said it was a rare occurrence...for big U.S. banks...to hire minorities like me...right into their training programs... Sensing a challenge...and an opportunity to "break some ground"...a few days after that meeting...I accepted the Marine offer...A week later I reported for work...

Not East, but Wes

When some took you to the stars...roamed high
clouds...of gases...space dust...and cool chill...

he...alone...learned to fuse heaven and earth...
water and air...while skipping it through your

hair...at breakneck speed...still keeping you
warm all along...On his strings...which made

souls dance...there were two before him...but
with his block...and doubles...he startled at first...

then reeled us into...his set table of greatness...
His was a new way...pristine...unused before...

like musical commandments...etched on Gibsons
...brought down from mountain tops...Here was

a young black Moses...His melodies... could help
you cross...an ice coated Indiana road...or skip

down a hot...dusty path to find water...in a field of
tall Mississippi cotton...Thousands have chased

his magic thumb...A young student...I know...
picked up the tool...went to school...practiced...

tried to play...until he heard John Leslie's way...
He decided that day...that where he wanted to go

was already taken...so he moved on...in search
of a new lane...to unchallenged human perfection...

Such was the singular greatness...of the giant from
Naptown...There will never...ever...be another...

The Promise of the Covenant

The fabric...the white male tapestry...imperfectly
cobbled...was straining...tearing...threatening to

disintegrate...Property tenants...who owns what &
who...long worshiped as a white man's right...was on

the block of judgement...Abe's leaky canoe...found
by him...but pushed into the dark water...by growing

winds...& hands that were avid...wobbled...&
swayed... It made him so desperate...To only stay

dry...just to keep the cloth...he would sell his very
soul...The slaughter was intense...Then with abating

breezes...sure fingers from Guanyin...& the guiding
oath...the blood letting ended...The soft threads...

though torn...& tattered...survived...unlike Abe...
who fell in the chaos... It would take a slick son...

of the Perdernales...100 years from then...to stop...
& borrow the dreams of two martyrs...find the old

canoe again...& push on...That he did...with more
firmness...& guile...against long delays... upon rights

& suspended hopes...with even more meaning...&
effect than Abe...or the many oarsmen...before him...

Yes he was corrupt...maybe even racist...in his own
way...but he knew hard living...& he needed salvation...

That is what the promise...of the covenant must be...
must live...must keep growing...for each...and all...

Senses

When we see...there is more to see...than what we see...

When we cannot hear...sound is still there...or is it?...

Do all who feel...feel the same touch...that you feel?...

Is the taste of a blackberry...the same to all who taste it?...

Do all smell what you smell...when they smell a rose?....

We are all more than our thoughts...more than what we see...

what we hear... what we feel......We are also there...

for the long... leaden...silence...between our thoughts...

The Marine Midland Trust Company

When I parked my car...in a lot at Washington and Swan streets... and made my way to 241 Main Street...the Administration Building of the Marine Midland Trust Company...I could not help but remember my childhood...and the many times before that day...when I eagerly turned the corner of Main and Swan Streets... Back then...I and my siblings...or neighborhood buddies...Eddie Lawrence or Eugene Brown...were headed to one...or all three of the movie theaters...lining that block of lower Main

Street... Looking back...those movie houses...the Little Hippodrome... the Keith...and the Academy...were physically smelly and dismal ...but delightful places...for we kids...to watch...Errol Flynn...Little Beaver... or dozens of quick ...gun-drawing cowboys...slay badmen or Indians by the dozens...

As I walked into the bank building...I kept asking myself...am I doing the right thing...What lies ahead for me...a bunch of badmen and hostile Indians...or friendly people with open arms...The Country was still churning with incidents of black civil disobedience...like race riots in Los Angeles...Rochester...Chicago...and Omaha... There were "Black Power" demonstrations by the young firebrand...Stokely Carmichael... and Buffalo's own race riot...by a crowded...exploding black population... was just a year or so away... It was also a time when Muhammed Ali was destroying black and white..."palookas" in the ring...and Willie Mays was cracking home runs...over stadium fences... I wasn't completely discouraged...

As worldly as I was in 1966...I really did not have any close white friends...at that time... As an adult...I was never as completely comfortable around whites...in my own Country...as I had been with whites in Europe... My poems and plays...still had a bitter cut to them... in 1966...and in some ways...I felt guilty about not being in the streets... demonstrating with the brothers...against "the Man"... Instead...here I was joining the "buttoned-down" ...white shirt crowd...in the pinnacle of the establishment...to try to learn what banking was all about... It was an odd feeling...that would stay with me for months...

That feeling...however ...was not initially fed by the employment reception I received at the bank... Almost without exception...I was treated courteously by almost everyone I met at the bank...I later learned that I was the only minority in a group of 14 in that year's officer training group...There had been only one other black person...a former professional football player named...George Scott...that preceded me in Marine's officer training program...At that time...Scott was about six months from completing his training and was still...technically assigned to the bank's Credit Department...where all trainees were officially housed... Scott would eventually become a branch manager...after an extended training period...

After processing and orientation...I eagerly soaked up as much as I could about the company...Marine Midland... Marine was started as a state-chartered...commercial bank in 1850...by eight businessmen... from around New York State...Based in Buffalo...its early focus was on the city's thriving lake...and riverfront grain and milling industries... By the early 20th century...the now nationally chartered bank...was part of a multi-bank holding company...with banks scattered throughout New York State...The holding company...headquartered in Buffalo...was then Chaired by...J. Frederick Schoellkopf... After dozens of acquisitions of commercial banks and trust companies...and almost as many name changes...when I arrived ...the Buffalo bank was called the Marine Midland Trust Company...

That bank was then run by a board of directors...with John Galvin as CEO and Robert Scheu...as President...Galvin was a cherubic...back-slapping Irishman with close ties to...the Democratic Party-dominated City Hall... Scheu...descended from a prominent German family... was a quiet...country-club type...He had most of the operating departments reporting to him... Under them were an assortment of very competitive... executive...and senior vice presidents...that actually ran the banking departments...An executive vice president named Haddon Smith...was the chief credit officer...at that time... The Credit Department...where grunt trainees like me were housed...reported to Smith...

Marine's business focus was primarily commercial lending...which included an active portfolio of commercial and real estate loans...It's retail lending business...sourced primarily through an extensive branching system... was driven mostly by direct personal and auto secured loans... The latter tended to be cyclical...along with auto dealer financing... In a limited way...Marine was also one of the earliest banks to market credit cards...Back then the credit approval process was quite formal...personal... and less automated...Commercial customers were closely nurtured...wined and dined...in a very formal bank dining room...or at one of the many private clubs...the bank's officers belonged to... Most of those clubs had tightly controlled membership policies... which...I was to learn later... would be a bit problematic for my career...The bank's reputation was solid though...and up until then...it had consistently performed profitably...It was "the" bank in Western New York...

Damn Road

Damn! What am I doing out here?

Shit! I should quit this stuff.

This is the pits,

the real blues.

All people are fools. I'm a fool too.

They've all been tricked and so have I.

Somebody's laughing and counting,

and I am rushing and puffing, just getting by

You'd think that I

would know by now,

that the best way to do this, is to learn to talk.

Stand up and talk! Sit down and talk!

Have a meeting......Have two meetings!...

Sell the bastards your kind of truth,

and get off this God damned road!

joann's children

it's tough...this man's world...you

run hard...or you fall behind and lose...

home...work...street and ghetto calls...

not much left...for tiny feet...smooth

behinds...eyes that sparkle...sweet milk

and sugar...for joann's children...it is

the curse of ambition...and ego...a

cocksureness...that has to be shortened...

before it wounds...or destroys...the reason

for it all...it is not so easy....for me....it is good

...and i am lucky... joann...loves being a mother...

The Training Program

Marine's training program...which was officially two years long...was typical of banks at that time...Most training was done on-the-job...for periods of one to five weeks...in various departments or business areas... depending upon progress... In-house training was supplemented with skills development courses given by industry experts...offering certifications in commercial...retail...real estate...and general banking... Marine also paid for outside...weekly counseling sessions on grooming...bank etiquette... and speech making... I later learned about...and also took part...in off-site...industry and university-offered training...in advance banking and management skills... It was a very comprehensive and effective training process that...if successfully completed...generated a valuable core of capable...young bank executives...

I soon learned that...in the 1960's...there weren't more than a handful of blacks...receiving that type of training... at major banks...in the entire Country... It wasn't long before I came to know nearly all of them... personally...Also at that time...as they still do today...companies in greater Buffalo...also participated in a United Way...loaned executive program... To supplement the staff of the United Way...companies would pay the salaries...of their junior executives...trainees...or soon-to-retire officers...and loan them to the charity's fund raising efforts every year... I and a couple of my fellow trainees...were selected for the program in 1966... Initially I was disappointed to be selected...since I was eager to get on with training and learning about banking...

However...by the time I finished the United Way experience...my attitude was very different... The program proved to be an excellent way to understand the philanthropic...community effort...that took place every year...and an excellent way to learn about and understand the many neighborhoods...and non-profit organizations operating in and around Buffalo... I also met some outstanding executives...and public servants... that would prove to be very valuable contacts later in my career...

While working with the United Way...one of the organizations I worked with was the local Red Cross Chapter... I had an especially poignant...very personal experience about what that organization was all about... when in late October...1966...the flat we lived in at 629 Woodlawn Street caught on fire... That evening...the landlady...who owned the house and lived in the upstairs apartment...fell asleep and left a pot burning on her kitchen stove... While having dinner with JoAnn and our two children...Ricky and Carmen...a neighbor rang our bell and told us the house was on fire...

We called the Fire Department...bundled up the kids...and rushed them over to the Middleton's...who lived across the street at 622 Woodlawn... I rushed back to the house...and called out to the landlady... who had now made her way out of the house... In what seemed like just minutes...fire trucks arrived and started streaming water on the house... Luckily...the fire was contained to mostly the upper flat...and our lower quarters suffered mostly smoke and water damage... The firemen...who were very skilled...grouped...covered...and saved most of our belongings... but with the utilities gone...and now reeking of smoke and water...we had to vacate the premises immediately...

Within an hour...after the fire was subdued... the firemen were wrapping up and preparing to leave when a Red Cross representative... named Jim Burns...whom I had been working with... on the United Way drive...arrived on the scene...We heartily greeted each other...with all the irony of my situation.... and he immediately gave us very generous vouchers to find temporary living quarters...and cash for food and clothing...if necessary... This first-hand experience with a United Way agency...was extremely helpful in sharpening my speaking...and fund raising efforts for United Way agencies...from that day on...

The fire incident led us to move...for a few months...to an upstairs flat at 37 Butler Avenue... and later in the summer of 1967...with a Veterans Administration loan...approved by Erie County Savings Bank...I purchase our first house...at 147 Urban Street... After that year's United Way drive was successfully completed... I returned to Marine...to resume my training... When I returned...some members of my training group had moved ahead of me...but I didn't regret...for a moment...my experience as a loaned executive... for the United Way...

Not long after resuming my training...I received very favorable job evaluations and my first 10% salary increase... True to their promise... those raises continued every six months until I completed training... In the months following that raise...I would learn about or receive training in credit analysis...branch operations...trust administration...auditing processes... and spend time in every major department of the bank... I also completed night courses in accounting...commercial...retail...real estate...and asset-based lending...In 1968...after about 20 months at the bank...shortly after the arrival of my second daughter...Donna JoAnn...I was asked to report to the bank's senior credit officer...Executive Vice President Haddon Smith.... I had not had much contact with Haddon...so I didn't know what to expect...when I nervously reported to his office that afternoon... He was very friendly and congratulated me on my progress in the training program... He was especially interested in how I had been received...by customers and employees around the bank...I assured him that...for the most part...I was well treated and had no complaints... I also told him I was eager to continue learning and that I liked what I was doing...

Toward the end of our meeting... he handed me a sheaf of letters...and memos... the senior officers...and even some board members had recently received...Most of the letters were from corporations...foundations...and national civil rights organizations...inquiring about Marine's hiring...and lending efforts in Buffalo's minority communities... He asked me to read the letters...make inquiries or do whatever you can...to learn what other banks were doing for minority communities...around the Country...He said he felt the bank should be doing something...but he didn't exactly know what... He told me that...as of that moment...I was on special project...reporting just to him...that he expected me to get back to him periodically...and to make any recommendations...to the bank...that I could come up with...in response to those letters... As I left his office... he emphatically emphasized that I keep the task quiet...but let him know whatever I needed to complete the work... It didn't hit me until I got on the elevator to return to my desk...but that afternoon...the bank's formal training program... for me...had ended...

Little Things

I said to her...fear not my love...keep faith...
trust me....Don't give in to the storm clouds...

the nay-sayers...and the greedy robbers...who
steal our labor... I will do great things for you

things that will dazzle you...make you proud...
Believe me...You will live in a castle...eat

delicate beef...and steamed vines...and wear
the finest that can be bought...my Queen...

She then firmly...softly...said to me...My
love...begin with the little things...Before

you can do great things...do the mundane...
the small symbols of intent...and character...

Sweep and mop the floor...take out the refuse...
change a diaper...cut the grass...be on time

and show me...you can do great *little* things...
and are willing to give me...*all* that I need...

not just castles and diamonds...steaks...
hot dreams...and fancy limousines....

The True Genius

The most brilliant of brilliance...has to qualify...
be dignified...be accepted...for validation...The

mob...the trend...the smug keepers of yesterdays...
the killers of dreams...will not always let it surface...

be born...grow with enough light...live...As always
one more soul...has to need it...want it...value it...

or it dies...in the dust bin of maybes...want-to-be's...
that huge barrel of lost gifts... The wealthiest man

ever...will be the gatherer...of lights...flickers of
inspirations...spilling's...of lost utterances...from the

ignorant...who were before...or after their time...The
true genius...will not want....or need ...any of them...

Finding the Recommendation

I was eager to get going on my new assignment...When it all sunk in...I realized the enormity of what that assignment meant...Here I was...just a couple of years away from school...and a janitor's mop...

working on a project...to come up with recommendations...for a large... very powerful institution in our community...Those recommendations...I concluded...could have a significant...and lasting impact...on Buffalo's minority community...The more I thought about it...here was my chance to "help the brothers"... Here was my chance to make my contribution to civil rights...to the struggle... I rationalized that...what I had a chance to do...was just as important as marching in a street protest for justice... After all...it made sense that the struggle had to be both inside...and outside...of the establishment...we blacks were petitioning... Buffalo's black community ...like communities everywhere...needed jobs...better schools...housing...business opportunities...and a willing big bank...like Marine...could help in a huge way...

In the 1960's...nearly the entire City of Buffalo was in decline... In addition to other trends...the opening of the St. Lawrence Seaway... in 1960...had an enormous...negative impact on the City... Lake borne traffic now by-passed the City... Grain storage...steel...aerospace... chemicals and flour milling industries began to shut down...Whites were fleeing the City in droves...as Buffalo's black community grew from just over 36,000 in 1950...to more then 100,000 by 1967... Naturally... Buffalo's black community was also in tough shape...

They were hemmed in...in old...crumbling...eastside neighborhoods... where there were no new housing units being built... Buffalo's public schools had been adjudged by the courts...and the U. S. Commission on Civil Rights...as being the 4th most segregated system in the North... Black children's reading scores... were 3 to 5 years behind whites...and the tiny black business community was mostly...a short list of mom and pop service providers... In June 1967...copycat riots...led by mostly black youths...broke out in and around the intersections of Jefferson and Ferry streets... and William and Jefferson streets... There were dozens of injuries...some by gun-shot...and many arrests...by riot-prepared police... But thankfully...no one died... Later in 1968...when Martin Luther King was assassinated...there would be additional...but smaller disturbances... on the east side streets of Buffalo...

The political atmosphere...in the black community...in the 1960-1970's...was also churning feverishly...with new and old political tensions... Black political representation...in Buffalo... by the 1960's...

had traditionally been exemplified...by elected...Democratic Party Councilmen...from the Ellicott and Masten Districts... Politicians like King Peterson...Charlie Black...and George Arthur...had come out of the Ellicott District...Cora Maloney...Billy Johnson...and later...David Collins...were or had been City Hall representatives from the Masten District...The Democratic Mayor...Frank Sedita...dominated City government from 1958 to 1973...

From 1962 to 1965...his long reign was interrupted...for a term...by the Republican administration of Chester Kowal... Sedita had un-elected... black confidents like Jessica Johnson...businessman Herb Bellamy...and others...to solicit advice from...Other prominent and influential black elected...and un-elected politicians...at the time were...Councilman-at-Large...Delmar Mitchell...County Legislators...Roger Blackwell...and Lillian Meadows... Assemblymen Arthur Hartwick...his successor... Arthur Eve...and Ambrose Lane... Lane...who was the first Director of the Community Action Organization...in Erie County...was a lawyer... and ally of Arthur Eve... He also was the first black to run for Mayor...of the City...in 1961... Some believe his run was one reason...Sedita's rule over City Hall was temporarily interrupted...in 1962...

There were other influential...local political action groups...like the well known Buffalo Chapters of the NAACP and the National Urban League...A pesky...new organization...BUILD of Buffalo, Inc...a confederation of many neighborhood groups...was beginning to agitate and lead noisy demonstrations around Buffalo...BUILD grew out of the efforts of Reverend Richard Prosser...a Presbyterian minister... from Chicago...Robert Coles...a prominent...local...black architect... and others...who led fund-raising drives...to help bring community organizer...Saul Alinsky's...Industrial Areas Foundation...to Buffalo... A similar effort had been done...by activists...in Rochester...to create the organization FIGHT...after riots there in 1964...It was felt by many in the community...that Buffalo's black community was poorly represented...by the traditional...quarreling...black political establishment...and needed a vehicle...like BUILD... to sharply voice its dissatisfaction with conditions for Blacks...

I felt it was important for me to know...and understand as much as I could about black community politics... before recommending a program to the bank...that would affect that community... I quickly learned that "black community politics" could not be easily separated from "politics"... generally...and that all politics...lead to the usual centers of power...almost always under the command...of the white power structure...It seemed... at the time...1960's –1970's...that the Nation at every conceivable level... was in political turmoil...

The Johnson Administration's War on Poverty...was creating new tensions...by funding new groups...that ...in some ways...circumvented the usual flow of patronage...and money...into poor neighborhoods... Buffalo was no exception...Like everywhere...aggrieved blacks...the anti-Viet Nam War activists...and opportunist of all kinds...were putting the establishment on the defensive... In some instances the establishment sought accommodation...and reconciliation...At other times...it was defensive...defiant and immovable.. I thought...navigating between the currents would not be easy...for me...or the Bank...The painful... sometimes trying time I spent studying...and trying to understand...just some of those dynamics...were never regretted for a moment...

The Black Diaspora of Buffalo

They were mostly children of the great migration...
fleeing southern apartheid...& soul-less...bitter
white men...losers...of the war to keep slavery...

Due north...east...west...anywhere but south...
they fled...to New York...Chicago...& Buffalo...
many with little but...a string-tied box...& a bag
of cold biscuits & fried chicken...Few would be
welcomed...greeted warmly...

Most were firmly resented...especially so in Buffalo...
where tired feet could walk...to mills & plants...but
wounded...confused psyches...were dry lynched...
nearly every day...

Herded...encircled...yes contained...by the earlier arriving...
German...Irish...Polish...& Italian...the new...
took their turn...in the hoary...wooden neighborhoods...
behind mostly departing Jews...who left a knowing...but
empty smile...& a few temples for the precious Jesus...

Frightened by the black wave...the growing...dark vote...
whites flew the lake...& the rivers...by cutting ruinous
by-ways... & snake trails...to go east...west...north...
dragging all their places...away from *them*...who were...
blacker...poorer...lesser...They left the revered...Doric...
Ionic...& Corinthian symbols...to rust...slowly killing...
the proud old Queen...that had spawned so many before...

The dark wave was not...unlike previous change...when
accommodation...inclusion was viewed as positive...even
necessary...if the beloved Queen's grand reign...was to
continue...to consolidate...to become *us!*...

But a black fear prevailed...especially so...when an ominous
inference of threat...from gleaming eyes...reflecting hated
Birmingham...recalling Memphis...Attica...Watts...unwisely
hinted at revenge...takeover...another grand design...for leafy
Delaware Avenue...

They were unashamed to be graceless...the lowly...&
the high...who smiled thinly...but bore...the oldest sin...
since it was they...who urged...the Johnson Act slights...
of new comers...to this place...stolen from the Seneca...
It was they who placed the strips... the ugly designs in
corn & alfalfa fields... It was they who fanned flight...
and let the illness come...instead of talk & understanding...

In time there would be a reversal...of the dark wave... when
warm lands...they had abandoned...calmed...when white
men...now slyly...hid their ugly...southern ropes...Still

the tired old Queen…coughed …grew feeble…bereft of
opportunity…of civic binding…& suffered even less pity…
less succor…than ever before…

Yes… it will take a miracle…to restore the Queen's grand glory…
The wounds are deep…the dry macadam…dying
neighborhoods…
are still sprawling ugly…pushing to nowhere… But magic…like
change…can always be there… The gathering can be saved… if
the discerning remember… that there was a reason… the ancient
ones came…to the mist…to the call of the water…

It was to stay close…to nourish each…create affinity…to be near
to how they…like all souls…began…So take heed…the siren of
salvation…you who flew… Return to the water's bend…to the
lake…Bring back your places…make a new wonder…It is not
impossible…or too late…to save & keep…an old Queen…

A Stolen People in a Stolen Land

I was struck…by the shortness…of his stature…the

mellow chocolate color…of his smooth skin…the

broad smile…thin mustache…the instant…Baptist-

preacher-baritone…of his voice…He was clearly a

fitting contrast…to the tall…red-bone…broad nose…

commanding tenor voice…of my real hero…Yet…

I was still drawn to him…cheered for his campaigns…

respected the fear he created…in some whites…and

was finally resigned…to accepting him…when he

denounced war mongers...and the destructive selfishness ...of American capitalism... For years...I had studied and compared...his rhetoric...with the cutting recitals...of the reformed pimp...who cut to my soul...who seemed...to speak for me...whom I identified with...whom I admired most...he...who frightened all white people...when he said... like Denmark Vesey..."freedom...by any means necessary" ...Listening to the preacher...that evening...at crowded Kleinhans...filled with rapturous admirers...I kept wondering if...that evening...was similar to the reception...Frederick Douglass received...before a thousand or so...that afternoon ...at Front Park...more than a hundred years before... I wondered if Douglass was as smooth...as adept at conscience pricking...as almighty-God-provoking...as the obsessed... little Birmingham preacher...chosen this time...to ride the wave of change...for a stolen people...in a stolen land... I wondered if a hundred years from then...would there be another...anointed provocateur...once again...riding the wave of change...for the same stolen people...in this same stolen land... I wondered...how many hundreds of years... would there have to be...before a people...before a land...

would be stolen no more...and most of all...who would reclaim them?...Who would you give them back to?...Who would now re-claim...the stolen land...and the stolen people?...

and so they slew the dreamer

and so they slew the dreamer...was it because
he spoke up for the people...was it because he

finally condemned the war...or was it just pure
hatred...from the most dangerous creature on

earth today...a white man...who thinks he is
superior...more worthy...god's chosen...over

all men... i am sure such nonsense is not new
to men...it's just the latest insanity...the latest

act of cannibalism... only fools can believe...
devouring one human can save their own soul...

the dreamer was just a surfer...swept up to
ride a wave seeking justice...the end of brutal

white domination...he was the chosen symbol...
of a people...his killing won't kill the dream...

no...the very opposite will happen...like a hand
in a viper's mouth...the cannibal cannot steal...

from providence...that which it keeps for itself...
every man's fate has the same ending...so be it...

The Community Development Division

After listening to local politicians...and groups...I then set out to find out what the banking industry itself...might be doing...in a special way...to help minority communities... Early on...I contacted various banking associations...around the Country...At the American Bankers Association...I was given the names of a handful of banks...and individuals who were doing... or had done...extraordinary lending...of some type... in minority communities ... I chose two bankers to go visit: Larry Toal... at Chase Manhattan Bank in New York City...and John Williams at First Pennsylvania Bank...in Philadelphia...

Both banks had made modest lending efforts in their minority communities ...mostly in response to community inquiries from local groups... Toal's program was largely centered on making government guaranteed loans...through the U. S. Small Business Administration (SBA)... When I visited him...his efforts were relatively new...and not widely supported in the bank ...The program at First Pennsylvania... supported by it's President...John Bunting... was a little older...larger... and driven by a close working relationship with a local community group... When I went to Philadelphia...I also had an opportunity to meet...John Clay...a black lawyer...who was one of the leaders of the outside group... that worked with Williams ... That connection with Clay...would prove to be of enormous help to me later on...

I concluded that...while both bank's programs were laudable...they were young... modest... and...in the case of Chase...had only tepid support from senior management... I came home from each visit with lots of notes ...brochures...and reams of information about government lending supports ...like the SBA... and other government loan programs... At that time...historically...at Marine...there was very little use of SBA... so I went to the local SBA office to get as much information...as I could... about their programs...After about 6 weeks... I put together a thin presentation...for Haddon Smith...that contained my recommendations for a new Marine Midland Bank... minority lending program...

The recommendation encompassed more than lending... however ...It contained recommendations for lending...hiring...and purchasing products and services ...from the few...minority-owned businesses... in our market...When I completed the presentation... Haddon told me he liked the idea ... and then asked me...who in the bank could run a program like that... I told him I had not thought about that... He paused for a moment and then said...why not the person who came up with the idea!...I paused for a moment...but before I said anything else...he said..."Think about it for a while...Come up with a name for a new unit...or department... that you can run. I'll make you an officer of the bank...at the next Board meeting"...

I was extremely nervous about the proposed task... At that point...I had never made a loan in my life...As part of my training...I had analyzed credits...both retail and commercial ...but then I only made recommendations to others... I explained that to Haddon...and he said... think in terms of a referral function...He said I could source... screen...package and deliver loans to whatever areas of the bank that made sense... The actual loans will be housed and administered in the various departments...He said...you can recommend...track...follow and assist with the loans...as necessary... It won't be long before you'll get the hang of it...and then you can make your own loan decisions...

As for hiring...and purchasing...he suggested I put together presentations for people...in the appropriate areas...of the bank... He promised that the effort would be strongly supported by senior officials... The longer he talked...the more excited I got...Before I left...I had not only accepted the job...but also suggested that we call it...the Community Development Division (CDD)... Haddon said..."Good...it has a nice ring...and you'll be Marine's first Community Relations Officer"... Later I almost floated out of his office...Pausing at the door...I looked back and said..."And money?"... Haddon... smiled...and said..."Don't worry...I'll take care of you."

I Discovered Music

Music...what joy...what a pleasure...
I wonder when I discovered it?...
Yes...I discovered music!...I invented it...
Think about it...we all did!...We all

heard rhythm before melody...Don't
you remember the dark thump...thump...
thump?... It was always there...night and day...
It never missed a single beat...Sometimes
Melody...gurgling harshly...came...It was
uneven...a disturbance...even frightening...
But give me back my thump...thump...thump...
I will soar with melody...again...when I can see!...

What Makes a Song

*What makes a song...a song?...Is music
just long words...from slow organs?...Or
is there something really...different about
tone...and words?... Song and utterance...
both stir us...and convey...Are they equal...
one above the other?...Which do you prefer...
powerful or soothing words...mighty or
calming songs?...Both connect with us...
greater than a look...more than seeing...
or even feeling...since we can hear a word...
or a song...long before we know...where
they come from...or ultimately...and finally
where they will take us...*

MUSIC

MUSIC ...PLAYED OR SUNG...IS AN EXPRESSION OF WHAT WE FEEL ...AT A MOMENT IN LIFE...GOOD...BAD...HAPPY OR SAD...IT IS A RESPONSE TO WHAT WE SENSE...WHAT WE MUST CREATE...BEYOND WHAT MEER WORDS CAN DO....

Just a Thought

I woke up and slowly discovered me... you...and something called time...Did everything begin with that awakening... or have I and time and everything always been?...Is there such a thing as an existence without a beginning...without an end?...Is it possible to escape the vicissitudes of chemicals ...strings...stacked in complex forms...competing for consumption...and an extension of time?...Is it possible to link...and remember the many cycles ...the many rounds of consciousness...if there are many or any cycles?...Or are we locked forever in a maddening state of unknowing...beyond the uncertain realities...we ourselves...can only perceive...this very...fleeting moment?

The CDD Rollout

It is one thing...to talk about a tailored...special...bank loan program for minorities ...and something entirely different...to actually create one that works...both in...and outside of the bank...It was felt that the program should be sensitive to charges that banks... historically ...had not gone out of their way...to loan in black communities... Whether it was mortgages ...personal loans...or business loans...blacks felt they did not get a fair hearing... with loan requests to banks in our City... Inside of the bank...many senior.... and middle management lenders... disagreed with charges of discrimination... A common comeback to me was... "Hey...a loan is either good or bad...It has nothing to do with color!"... I knew better...and had armed myself with community testimony ...and government statistics...on the bank...and the industry...that indicated otherwise...The subsequent Congressional passage of the Community Reinvestment Act (CRA)...in 1977...would later confirm this belief about U.S. financial institutions...

My campaign in the bank…required meetings…with individuals… lending groups… committees …and even the Board of Directors… I had handouts that described the mission… loan policy…and goals of the new unit…The information spelled out the relationship…and responsibilities…the Community Development Division (CDD)… had to other bank departments …the government programs available… and most importantly…why there was a need for the new effort…At most of the group meetings…I had senior executives with me…to help explain the bank's commitment… At other times…I was on my own…

Internal reception was mixed… While always being received politely…I could tell that many people didn't buy into a so-called "preferential" lending program…for minority communities… and still others warmly welcomed the effort…. I had particularly good support …from managers of branches …and other lending departments that served mainly minorities .... As might be expected…they became a major referral group for the new CDD…

After finding a small office…and space for a secretary…and an assistant…on the first floor of 241 Main Street…the CDD was open for business… At the suggestion of one of the senior officers… I chose as my assistant…Thomas N. Barone…who had real estate appraisal …and loan experience…The secretary for the department…was an old friend …Dorothy Slaughter… who had been working as a teller in a downtown branch…. Both individuals were selected… not only for their technical skills… but for their maturity…and sympathy for the purpose…and goals of the department… Branches and departments were told not to turn down a business loan request…from a minority…before letting us look at it too…

As the word got around about our mission… we began to get a steady flow of applicants…and referrals… For various reasons… we turned down far more applicants…than we approved… But a major part of our frustration was internal resistance …and a reluctance of bank loan officers to approve a recommended loan…from us…Some loans… especially proposed SBA participation loans…required more paper work… and effort… Because the SBA guaranteed as much as 90% of qualified loans…it became a popular way to approve many minority loans…In time our little department would become quite expert at packaging and getting loans approved by the SBA… This bank/SBA loan partnership…would eventually become a growing Marine vehicle…for riskier lending to all borrowers…regardless of the borrowers color…

Still…we turned away far more loan applicants…than we got approved…However …most turn-downs had more to do with loan viability…and applicant qualifications…than internal resistance… As the months rolled by…we steadily built a small portfolio of minority business loans… Some of the loans were government backed…Many were made with no government participation… We referred and made business loans…real estate…and personal loans… 90% of the loans supported businesses selling retail products…or services…Word of our program …was spreading in the community… I began to spend a great deal of time talking to groups… and leaders about our efforts…

To my knowledge…no other bank in the City had a comparable effort… and my little department was stretched…to handle the volume… We also had a major change at the senior level of the bank…Upon the retirement of John Galvin…Bob Scheu became the Chief Executive…and a young…rising star…named John L. Hettrick…was eventually named President… As is common with executive changes… department reporting changed as well…My department was taken from Haddon Smith…and given direct reporting to Hettrick …I later learned that Hettrick had asked for the change to strengthen… and support our internal bank acceptance …He also told me…he knew of the internal problems we were having…and that he felt that what we were doing was very important…to the bank…and the community…

Hettrick was right…The changed reporting did make a huge difference…The difference was mainly because of his strong personal interest…and support… He insisted that I meet with him frequently…He expanded the space we occupied…and approved additional hiring for the department… He assisted our lending efforts in loan committees… and took a personal interest in my development…I was selected for coveted… off-site…executive training at Columbia University…and the industry's… 3-year…Stonier Graduate School of Banking at Rutgers University …

The most important occurrence was the new respect our little department got in the bank… My phone calls were returned a little faster… More people…in and out of the bank …began to take an interest…and assist in our efforts… I was invited to more luncheon meetings…at private …or to Rotary Clubs...where the only black people you saw...worked in the kitchen ...Respected local leaders...like Dean Elton Smith...from St. Paul's Episcopal Cathedral ...in an effort to draw attention to our efforts...invited me to be a noonday speaker ...at the downtown Cathedral...

People interested in helping or learning about our efforts...began to take up more of my time... George F. Goodyear... a Marine Bank Director... from a prominent...local family ...donated more than $300,000...to create a foundation...which I named the Buffalo Equity Foundation... As requested by Mr. Goodyear...its purpose was to promote better race relations in our community... I used the Foundation's funds to help fund a comprehensive ...case study of Buffalo's Inner City businesses...(Alan R. Andreasen...Inner City Business...Praeger Publishers Inc...1971)...I also used the Foundation's funds to purchase real estate for the African American Cultural Center...and bus transportation for the B.U.I.L.D organization...

The Foundation also funded a number of smaller dollar...lower profile projects...all in keeping with Mr. Goodyear's wishes...to quietly... without fanfare...promote better race relations in the community... My fellow Foundation Directors were...Dr. Frank Evans...a well-known... eastside family doctor... Claude Clapp...the first black superintendent of the Buffalo School system...George Nicolas...an engineer with the Bell Company...and Cooper Lord... a well-known local attorney...To this day...very few people knew that the Foundation ...would never have existed without Marine's creation of the CDD...and Mr. Goodyear's generosity...

While the bank did not purposefully seek publicity...nevertheless... local publications and the Wall Street Journal wrote an article...and took an interest in what we were doing... After the Journal article...I received a call from an irate...Marine Midland stockholder...who felt our program was a waste of bank funds...and he opined that I should be ashamed for being associated with it...I politely defended the program... but referred the caller to the bank's Public Relations people...The call was a negative experience...but it helped to prepare me...for such sentiments... at subsequent presentations...

Not long after that call...I was asked to join the Urban Affairs Task Force of the American Bankers Association (ABA)...I traveled with Hettrick...to West Virginia...where we made presentations before senior bankers...at the Green Briar Resort... I also accompanied a senior Marine officer...Arthur Ziegler...when he testified about our bank's efforts... before the Senate Banking and Urban Affairs Committee...The net result of those presentations...was that Marine and the banking industry... generally...at a time of great turmoil in the Country...was beginning to be recognized for positive lending efforts ...in troubled minority communities...around the Nation...

In the second year of our department's creation...I was promoted to Assistant Vice President ...a level no minority had ever held at Marine... As a member of the ABA Task Force...in the next 3 or 4 years...I...along with other Task Force members...developed model minority lending programs for banks...and eventually traveled to more than 14 major cities... to promote bank lending in minority communities... We also advised and assisted the SBA... in the design...and creation of Minority Enterprise Small Business Investment Companies (MESBICs)... and encouraged the industry to establish...a One Billion Dollar loan commitment...to minority business lending...

For more than six years...even after I had long left Marine...I lectured at an ABA sponsored...commercial lending school...on lending to minority businesses...That effort occurred mostly as continuing...banker education...at the University of Oklahoma...My major reference...was a thesis I wrote for graduation...from the Stonier Graduate School of Banking ...The thesis called: A Management Assistance Approach For Banks Making High Risk Loans to Black owned Businesses...was placed in libraries at Harvard...Princeton...and Rutgers universities...

Positive and Negatives

Life...however...wasn't all peaches and cream...Our portfolio of loans was under-performing ...relative to other conventional loans...Our loss... and delinquency rates were 2 or 3 times the bank's conventional loan rates...and the risk reality of lending to minority businesses began to set in... The need for equity injections...accounting and management assistance...for our borrowers... became a high priority...for our efforts...I scrambled to put together groups... and individuals ...who would be willing to contribute their skills...and know-how to assist individual minority businesses... We directed borrowers...and applicants to franchise opportunities... and paired up some of our borrowers with retired executives... from an SBA ...small business counseling program...

All of these efforts proved to be worthy...but Hettrick and I still had to fight off grumbling...and criticism from certain people in the bank... They were dissenters who did not approve of our program...period... Whenever I could...I always explained that a high-risk ...loan program... in minority communities... should be expected to under perform... relative to conventional bank loans...I explained that we should not focus on the 12% to 15% delinquency...and loss rate...but on the 85% to 88% performing rate...for people who had little opportunity...equity or hope... before we assisted them... My appeals had some effect...but I later learned that bank opponents of what we were doing...were very determined...no matter what we said...to undermine our efforts...

Out in the community...things were also bumpy...One private club... the Tuscarora Club...hearing of Marine's minority loan program...called the bank's Public Relations people...and asked if a speaker was available... to come to one of their luncheon meetings...to explain the program ...and answer questions about the bank's commitment... After checking with me...the bank's PR people...arranged for me to make a presentation to the Club's members...at the Club...A week or so...after I agreed to make the presentation...a representative of the Club called the bank and said...they wanted to confirm the luncheon ...but the meeting wasn't going to be held on the Club's premises...but at a local YMCA ...away from the Club...

While I was eager to tell our story...I thought it strange that they moved the meeting...and I mentioned it to John Hettrick...He instantly sensed what was occurring... The next day...he called me and encouraged me to go to the luncheon...on the Club's premises...as originally scheduled...I asked him what had happened..."Why did they change the venue again?"... Hettrick said..."I called and told them if they didn't have you make the presentation...at the Club... Marine would cancel every paid membership...it currently had in the Club"... Then it all became clear to me...On the scheduled date...I went and proudly made the presentation... at the Club...When I arrived for the meeting...every staff member of the Club...including the black cooks...lined up ...at the front door...to greet me when I arrived... In spite of the rocky start ...my presentation was well received...and I was glad to address the august...Tuscarora Club... assemblage...

As I had to justify...and defend our loan program...to interested whites...I also had to defend the program...and sometimes my own safety...in the black community...In one incident while having a beer with a loan client...in a tavern on Jefferson Avenue...another angry black customer threatened me with a semi-automatic pistol... The slightly-inebriated fellow...was angry about a loan turn-down...by one of my assistants...and he felt I had something to do with his failed loan request...

He was right about my involvement...since I reviewed every single loan request... that was made to the department... The angry one called me an "Uncle Tom"...a front for the "white establishment"...who was just... "ripping off the black community"...He insisted that I was just a... "token black"...with no real power...I tried to reason with the fellow...offered to buy him a drink...and to review his loan request a second time...He didn't calm down...and put his pistol in his pocket...until my companion... Jim Bell...a well-respected...local business man in the neighborhood... intervened and promised to also help...the aspiring... would-be business man... I offered to review his request...and was very willing to give the angry one a second look...but I never heard from him again...

Applicant to the Banker

B: So you want to buy a business?

A: Yes...Sir...I know I can do this!...
I've known Mr. Murphy...many years...
He's a good man...and I been a customer
of that place for years...I know what clean
clothes look like!...I know Mrs. Sally...his
right hand person...She said...She'll stay
with me...teach me everything she knows...
Murphy said...he'll stay with me a year...
I've saved up a third of the price...I just
need the bank to loan me the rest...

B: But you made…almost as much as Murphy… In your plant job…last year…

A: I'm tired Mr. Bailey…I got to get out of that plant…This is my great chance…

B: You'll have to work hard in the dry cleaning business too…

A: But not like in that blast furnace…I been in that hell-hole 25 years…I need out now!…

B: Why don't you do this…work in the cleaners… for a year…Learn every job there…Learn how to buy and repair your machines…chemicals… customer servicing…everything about the dry cleaning business you can…I'll get you in a specially designed…basic business accounting course we run…After a year…you'll be better prepared…without risking your money…

A: Huh…I don't know…It sounds like you trying to find a way to turn me down…

B: Nope!…You're wrong…I am trying to help you to have a chance to succeed…It will be the best way to protect your savings…and the bank's investment too…Murphy…or his right hand lady…might quit…get sick…Why don't you….

A: Naw…That's all right…I'll go to another bank… They said I could get some help here…I see that was wrong!…You people…just fronting!… Y'all…just fronting…for the man!…I'm out of here!

Tuscarora Majesty and Curses Too

Their arrogance knew no bounds...They borrowed
the name...without knowing the history...the duty...

Wrapped in the blankets...of whom they admired...in
love with the majesty...of a grand...early people...they

brought European airs...superiority arguments...myths...
theories...All without knowing... the accompanying

spirits...decrees... ancient curses...the war settlements...
energy flows...between a people...especially the lasting

power of the mighty Catawba...With their genes flowing...
I ripped away the mask...and lived a sweet moment...for

my ancient grandmother's spirit...I stood in a room of fools...
smug newcomers...thieves of nobility...with names from the

proud land...heritage...and dowry...They had to now bow
before a sent son of the Catawba...a proud grandson of the

Kituwah...who didn't fully know the oath...or even understand
the terms of the ancient peace...or how a curse survives...But

that day...they heard the message...nodded to the aims...the
path taken...and unknowingly renewed...an age-old sacred truce...

To John

Everyone...need not wear a cool dashiki...
become bait for Bull Connor's vicious dogs...

shout..."Black Power"...or take a racist's
blow...on the Pettus Bridge... Some of us

...can win the war...in board rooms...high
committees...courts trapped by the great covenant...

all the places...the virus dwells...To secure the
oath...we do it with our minds...our reason...our

firm appeals... to sane men...who side with our
long struggle... And there are some... good men

all...Johns'...Charles'...Thaddeus's... Lyndon's...
who believe in fairness...who recall playmates...

nannies...and old...black Joe's...who smiled...
bowed...shielded...and saved their children too...

It takes all...the fierce...the mild...the forever
loving...those who are determined...to let all

of our children...live the promise...and insist that
we all... dance...and drink... the rain drops too...

watchers of dancers

fight for yourself...they'll hand you
a piece of bread... fight for your
children...they'll extol your fatherhood
... grant you another bit of fare...then
scuffling past that...you become a
politician...a fighter for a tribe...a
witch doctor...who sells promises...
dreams...hopes...still you can't avoid
...provoking...or creating more jealous
conjure men...long selling their own
magic potions...to be faithfully consumed
...by the watchers of dancers...they are

hopefully...looking for redemption... salvation...all that any dancer...can bring... but as always...power comes not from the dancers...the cute self-preeners wearing costumes...no...it flows from the hopeful...the watchers themselves...for it is they who pick...the elixir of choice...the winning heal... needed revolutions fail... when neither...the dancers...nor watchers know...or understands...the real essence... of the prince's power... that it comes from the watchers...the people...who give wind to sails...waves to ride upon...toil to build upon...and sweet....long breaths ...to dancers...

Lending Becomes Political

One evening when we were enjoying a few beers...John Hettrick... ever aggressive and charged to go...asked me...why aren't we doing more...What else can we...the bank...do in the community? ...What more is needed out there?...I said...many things... housing... daycare...a shopping center...stores on the east side...you name it... I told him...from what I could see...there just weren't any groups or individuals...in the minority community...able to do large development projects... He said... well let's find a way to do some demonstration projects... bring in other companies... developers...etc.... I promised...I would look into it... and check possibilities...

After our talk...I talked to companies...and other bankers around the Country...I remembered and talked to...John Clay...a lawyer whom I had met in Philadelphia...He was the person I met...when I visited First Pennsylvania Bank...before we initiated Marine's loan program... His advice was that we should let high profile...development projects...to the extent that we can...come from the community... If there are no groups... go out and create them... At that time he promised that he would come to Buffalo to assist us...if needed...

It then occurred to me that...I and Marine...now had enough credibility in the black business community...to loosely pull together a group of our borrowers...and other respected leaders to address some of the larger needs of the community... I met with individuals like Charles Price...a United Auto Worker's representative...businessmen...Lennie Glover...Jim Bell...Carl Mackin...Jessie Jackson...Bob Pippen...Assemblyman Arthur Eve... Ambrose Lane...Bill Gaitor and others...We called for...and held a meeting of black men...one Sunday afternoon...at the John F. Kennedy Recreation Center... I arranged to have Philadelphia's John Clay...come and speak to the meeting... Nearly 50 black men attended...

As you might expect...it was not hard to find speakers that afternoon... but the most important speaker ...was Clay...He...inspirationally...spoke of what had been done in Philadelphia...how community groups had worked with local banks...I reiterated Marine's willingness and interest in helping the community... and told the group what some of the possibilities might be... Out of the meeting...small groups were designated to meet with Attorney Will Gibson...to work on incorporation papers...for a new...non-profit...and a new for-profit corporation... It was proposed that the organizations work together...for the overall betterment of Buffalo's minority community...

Within weeks...two new corporations were formed...We called them... the Black Business Development Corporation (BBDC)...and the Black Development Foundation (BDF)...With an eye toward a lending vehicle... for the bank's loan program...I ...without becoming a director...chose to carefully guide the selection of the BBDC Board of Directors ... Ambrose Lane...and others gravitated toward the non-profit...BDF board... For the BBDC board...I selected respected business men...some of whom were my customers...and Charles Price...a well-known union activist... from the United Auto Workers...as Chairman... I felt that if we were going to develop projects...that required bank loans... businessmen and a for-profit BBDC...was the best vehicle to work with... I offered to become an advisor to the BDF...but because I declined to actually join the BDF board... and other reasons... a slight schism developed between the two organizations... I didn't know it then...but looking back... I believe that schism...later on... unfortunately... would become a virulent hindrance ...to an important development project...in the community...

Mr. Minister

He just seemed on point…more right to me….
The sonorous preciseness of his words…fit

my disposition…Sure…my brain could count…
could nod to the marchers…the singers…the

lamenters…But my soul…my manhood screamed…
mimicked his certainty…Whiskey!…Filth!…Self!

Pride?…Yes!…Race?…Yes!…Yes!…Mr. Minister…
You are right!…Tell 'um truth!…You are right!…

When I finally saw him…touched his hand…I
was struck by his broad nose…penetrating eyes…

easy smile…Was John the Baptist…a reformed
hustler too?…Is this the magic that angers…the

little con man in Chicago?…he with the jealous heart
…and an alleged taste for children…Only minutes

could my ears bear him…but this red-bone could
sting my ear…capture my gaze…hold me all night…

I tried to read…as much as I could…yet there just
wasn't enough…to fill the seething thirst…I searched

him out again…in Harlem…Still not enough…I sought
out local proxies…flirted with the creed…I cursed

and despised his critics…be they indicted white men…
soul-less contemporaries….or sweaty…confused

handkerchief heads…sliding around in brown pews…
hollering…shouting…and begging for salvation…

And oh…I cried a thousand deaths that Sunday…
when the nigger vermin… with their marching orders…

from Chicago…from Washington D.C…from the
very Devil in hell…gunned him down…in a ruthless

crucifixion…with vile bullets…before his children…
before the eyes…and the very face…of the Nation…

White lips curled up…at the way-past Saturday night fight…
Was it our liquor?…our women?…our dope?…they asked…

For weeks my being sneered…and twisted with the loss…
There was venom…for the guilty…seen and unseen…

There were tears…for his children…and prayers that
their nightmares would be brief…short…uncutting…

Mercifully…I cried for me too…felt the bullets…cursed
the white evil…the black fools…but I refused to die too…

There is scant testimony….to refute…the shallow gray
mockers…the cocky enslavers…all those hollow…lifeless

manikins…who say…he saved not a single soul…that no
government decrees…came from him…that no river leaks

his blood…that even his manhood…waivered…showed
its frailty…and worse…no gray marble shines his name…

But hear this you people: …For as long as there freely
breathes…a real black man…in America…his spirit…his

words…his life…will be a signature life…forever recalled
moments…in the epic struggle for dignity…for long dead…

and living slaves…who are still looking…still working….
still singing and watching …over their precious children…

The Man in the Bubble

They wrapped him up in a bubble of Earth's sustaining cords…that
now allowed him to breathe…to exist there…harsh to his form of life…
and hurled him into…a far celestial heaven…long from here…Will

thin life cords…stay together…break away…or will he own them…
keep them…use them wherever he goes?… On this lonely sojourn…
unknowing of his destiny's ultimate greeting…he has to nurse and

stay his life's links…his fixes…keeping them all whole…able and just…
so as to survive and return…if he chooses…For him to fatefully lose
…the service of any…of his vital attachments…would most assuredly

mean his demise…So as wise as…this traveler must be… so must be
those he left behind…for though they roam a wider world… a world
they assume will always be…that world too…is on a fearsome journey…

in momentary welcome…whose cords for life…are just as precious…
just as needed…vibrant and necessary…The choice…for the man…in
the bubble…is no less twin…to the heedless…to the blind…he left behind…

Cradle of Black Pearls

Within a matter of months…with John Hettrick's encouragement…the bank financed major projects …that would be…largely in response to loan requests from the BBDC… At our encouragement…the BBDC had quietly…through agents and lawyers…began to acquire options on parcels of land in the Cold Springs area…One parcel was at the corner of

Michigan and Emerson streets… The BBDC and the bank agreed that it would be an ideal location for a small daycare center… For weeks… my assistant…Tom Barone…had been working with a friendly builder… and other specialists…to design and build a day care center on the site… Tom…proudly…even came up with a suggested name for the center:… Cradle of Black Pearls…

The BBDC board loved the name…and a loan package for nearly 100% financing was approved by the bank… The modest building…with its Mansard-styled roof…soon graced the tiny site…The weekend before it opened…I painted children's…animal cartoons on the interior walls… Soon…40 to 50 families a week…were using the facility…Community praise came to the BBDC…and I…my staff…and John Hettrick…were delighted for the community…

The BBDC was also…secretly buying options on land…to build a block-long strip plaza…on Jefferson Avenue…between East Utica…and Landon streets…The commercial activity… along Jefferson Avenue…was badly deteriorating and we felt that a small plaza…with bright new stores… might halt the slide…and bring life back to the street …Marine had a branch office on the corner of Jefferson and Landon streets… and would agree to be the anchor for the small plaza… The handful of options needed… included commercial property along Jefferson Avenue…and residential properties… behind the needed commercial front… Critical property owners…in the middle of the proposed project site… despite generous offers for their land… began to hold out…The land purchase offers were increased …Still a couple of critical…parcel owners refused to sell…

It soon became apparent that money was not really the issue…for the holdouts… I concluded that something…or somebody…who was aware of what was to be built…was behind the holdouts…The board of the BBDC felt that an unnamed political faction…or individuals… fearful of the BBDC's…growing political prominence… wanted to stop a critical… badly needed ….improvement for the community…The holdouts lasted for more than two years… before the BBDC…at great loss to Jefferson Avenue… eventually abandoned the plaza project altogether…

In the meantime…At our urging…Carl Mackin…a BBDC board member…and a few of his colleagues agreed to pursue co-ownership of a Tops supermarket franchise…from Niagara Frontier Services (NFS)…

Haddon Smith...who originally help start Marine's CDD ...had left the bank and joined NFS...a long time customer of Marine's...Haddon and the bank... encouraged NFS to pursue the establishment of inner city stores...by utilizing our minority loan program...Buffalo's inner city... like many inner cities...was essentially a food desert ...that lacked nearby sources for fresh fruits...and vegetables...

The plan called for a 25,000 square foot store...on Jefferson Avenue ...and a larger...60,000 foot store...in a newly built...City-owned plaza...at the corner of William and Jefferson streets... Mackin...a BBDC board member... who had supermarket management experience...was an ideal candidate for the project...Financing for the projects would come... primarily from both the bank and NFS ...Mackin...and his partners... contributed small amounts of equity...and pledged their homes to secure the loans...When the William and Jefferson...Tops store...triumphantly opened...it earned the BBDC more community praise for their co-development efforts...

American Politician

Breath whistled through...my teeth....
My eyes...bulged
with raw incredulity...
I shook my head...slowly...from side to
side...Believability was
lost yesterday...last night...
before this fool brushed his teeth...
The process cannot...
must not...dare not...be
so low...Is this...the best...the only...
way...for representation...all
we have?...Must his shoes...be
gobbled up so fast...with feet still in
them?...Is there not...a
better...less obvious way...to
lie...to unashamedly belong...
to another...before
even the promise?...

I guess it does not matter...The sheep...
by the tally...of crooked
vote machine numbers...
nodded the wolf on by...oblivious of
the rock...just ahead...
when...as did Judas...
he will duck behind it...before the sun
sets...lie again...and
continue to lick his fat
fingers...after every shit...

The Worst Thing in America

*The worst thing in America...is not
what you think...Ask anyone for an
opinion...and the list will be miles long...
Few that you ask...will know that their
own mirror...every morning...can add to
the list...Most times that mirror...will reflect
a disinterested...hugely misinformed...highly
misguided...easily propagandized...dupel of
human creation... The worst thing in America's
...false democracy...is a dupel...who cannot
keep...the most precious things they own:...their
labor of value... a genuine self-interest...and
the only true religion they need: mutualism!...*

Joe's Milk

She was delightful...almost
like Lula...my grandmother...

As she left...the old Italian's
store...with just a single bag...

I asked her...how did she like
her shiny...new market...over

there...in that very...new place?...
She answered...Yes...I know...

and a black man owns it...Isn't
that a grand thing for us?...Sure!...

We making strides!...Then...do
you shop over there some time?...

Just once... It's real new...Crisp!...
Then why not...go there again?...

I might...again...sometime...The
meat seems fresher...their greens

stay cold...and they got more things...
but I don't know Mister...Joe's milk...

here...just looks...a little whiter!...

The Gren Ki Club

The BBDC...with its community profile growing...now seized upon the idea of creating an organization supported...mainly by black-owned businesses in the City... a kind of black Chamber of Commerce...The organization would be a non-profit...service organization...to promote minority business ownership in the City... give out kids scholarships...etc...I offered to help the Corporation purchase a small...but solid...abandoned... two-story building at Genesee ...and Herman streets...that had previously been a VFW Post...I felt the small building... which had a kitchen... bar...dining and club rooms...could be acquired...and renovated for a very modest investment...Up until then...the BBDC had held their meetings in donated...and borrowed spaces...scattered around the eastside...

The BBDC board members loved the idea of making the location... both a business...and recreation retreat... that they would support by paid memberships...and assessments...They envisioned the building becoming a member's restaurant... bar and meeting place...something never seen before in Buffalo's minority community...I created a loan package... that was approved by Marine... With sweat...and modest equity... within months thereafter...the non-profit... renovated...and restricted membership...Gren Ki Club was created... Members were given "green keys" to enter the building ...and no one else had access to the building... if they were not accompanied by a member ...

After it opened...the Gren Ki Club...instantly...became hugely popular...as a meeting and gathering place... Businessmen ...politicians... women's clubs...and just ordinary people wanted to join...or become active in the club ...In its beginning days... the club served luncheons ...and held fashion shows on weekends...Parties were held at the club...for O. J. Simpson... and the Buffalo Bills football team ...Local and national politicians...and notables of all sorts... visited or wanted to join the club...

The tiny club was our very humble version...of Buffalo's black Saturn or Montefiore clubs...minus the longevity...Board members of the BBDC...beamed with pride...at their new status and respect... However... neither they...nor I...fully anticipated the political implications of what we were doing... Assemblyman Arthur Eve...and other aspiring political types...joined his ally Jim Bell...and others as strong advocates...and supporters of the Club ...City Hall operatives... Councilmen ...and their allies...feeling threatened...began to frequent...and some even joined the Club...It became clear...that eastside Buffalo politics... had begun to flow through the Club's life... The Democratic political establishment... became very uneasy...This had positive...as well as negative political implications...for the BBDC... and the club...

It also had marked implications for my personal career...After running the CDD for three and a half years...Hettrick told me he wanted to promote me to a Vice President position...He said in order to do that...I needed to get direct...line lending experience... instead of remaining in...essentially...a staff position...He said he felt it would be difficult to place me in a line position...without branch operations...and direct... conventional lending experience ...

He told me if I agreed to run a branch office for two years... he would promote me to Vice President...and see that I move on... to a more important lending position in the bank... He asked if I thought my assistant... Tom Barone...was ready to run the CDD...I said I did...but I felt that I needed to stay engaged externally...since Tom...as loyal and committed as one could hope for...did not know the target community...as well as I did... By accepting the branch manager position... we quieted a lot of the internal...bank critics...who had always argued that I really had no "real" lending or line management experience...

Hettrick said it was always understood...that it would be necessary for me to continue to be the face of the CDD...even from a branch location... With some mild trepidation...about dropping four management levels... below Hettrick...soon after I accepted...I was named the Manager of Marine's Main-High branch office...Not long after that move...I was also...asked to become a member of...the Board of Directors of the Buffalo General Hospital... It would be the very first time that a minority member...in the City of Buffalo...would be asked to join that prestigious Board...of powerful civic leaders...

When I accepted the invitation...I could not help but remember ...when I was a just a kid...riding a bike on High Street...when the Buffalo General Hospital...had finally agreed to accept black patients...onto its august... healing wards...I later learned that my invitation to join the Hospital Board...perhaps had something to do ...with the Hospital's Federal approval ...to build and manage a new Community Mental Health Center...Very soon after becoming a Board member...I was asked to be the Board's advisor...and liaison to that new Center...

At home...things were also changing... In February...1971... our third daughter... Angela ...was born...In that same year...we also moved to a newly built house...at 50 Fieldstone Drive... Grand Island... New York... It was a time of rapid change and many late arriving meals for me...My activities...as a board member of the General Hospital... chairman...or president of the Narcotics Guidance Council...the Gren Ki Club...the African American Cultural Center ...along with my national travels for the ABA...all placed a heavy burden on JoAnn...as she... heroically ...shouldered the lion's share of caring for the children...

Still…she too…found time to become a member of the Junior Board… of the Buffalo General Hospital… Her membership was a suggestion of Marcia Hettrick…John's wife… whom we both quickly grew very fond of…While on the hospital Junior Board…JoAnn volunteered my services to meet and escort the famous singer…Ella Fitzgerald…who had agreed to come to Buffalo…and perform in a concert to help raise funds for the Board's charitable activities… Delightfully…I spent a couple of days chauffeuring…and helping the famous lady… before and after…a singing concert at Kleinhans Music Hall…

All of this activity continued to raised my community profile…and requests from community groups… for volunteer assistance soared… To the detriment of my family time…I became a very busy young man… Most of those personal commitments…came from my own inability to say "no,"…but I could also feel the huge dearth of so-called "respectable"… black business leaders…that would be acceptable to the needs…of so many local…representational boards …and committees…

While I have always… personally leaned toward democrats…I also responded to requests from Republican politicians like…local Judge Joseph Mattina… who asked me to serve on the Erie County Narcotics Guidance Council… Congressman Jack Kemp…who asked me to serve on his Military Academy Selection Committee…and Governor Nelson Rockefeller… whom I successfully petitioned for a small grant from the State Council on the Arts…for the African-American Cultural Center…I could not help but feel that there was clearly more at play…in my career… than the silent hand of John Hettrick…guiding my growth as a banker… However …as I continued to collect community awards…and citations… I also attracted some unwanted attention that I…unfortunately … became increasingly wary of…

The Tisket Lady

It was just like a spoiled…
Junior Board…strutting its
stuff…doing its own thing…

A white Rolls Royce…for the
lady…It was the Committee's
choice…And oh…there was me…

to meet the Tisket Lady too…with
white chauffeur….and wide eyes…
at the airport…and the Statler Hotel…

So what did I know?….She was the…
famed…singing…Tisket Lady…and
I was to be her escort…her body guard…

Pity me…I never knew…how rare…
the rehearsal…the short concert days…
her presence…the wonder…reverence…

She could have…been my mother…
just three months older….They would
later die…only one month apart…

Still…for three quick days…I was
a young man…sharing a splendid life…
that went… up and down…around…

Long…before the Rolls…the awe…
the Statler Hotel…Kleinhans Hall…
the nervousness…the joyous music…

I had heard the Tisket Lady sing…
Then I knew her breast…her throat…
the salty sweat on her brow…then

a long appreciation kiss…and hug…So
sing on…sing on…Tisket Lady…and
bring your Yellow basket…next time…

The Beggar

I slipped past the begging beggar/...without the
slightest taint of guilt/...After all/...I had nothing
to do with his rags/...nor did I want...to be burdened/
with his ugly pain/...whether it was the misfortune
of his birth/...or the foolishness of his life-steps/
...Whatever/...Besides I had nothing to give that
day/...Perhaps the day before/...but not that day/...
So I walked straight ahead/...with head held high/...
and eyes focused/...only turning slightly/...when I
heard him say/..."Hey...have a good day...my dear
friend/...A good day wish/...is worth more than...
anything I know/ or own/...and a wish for you/...is
all that I can give"/...I stopped/...I thought/...turned
back to him/...and thanked him for his gift to me/...
me!...his fellow beggar!/...

Treachery Raises its Head

One bright sunny day...while managing the Main-High branch office...John Hettrick called...and asked me to come to his office...It was an unexpected call...so I asked my very able...and loyal assistant... Richard Shanley...to take my appointments...and I went immediately to John's office... When I arrived at his office...John was there with attorney ...Charles Blaine...from the law firm...Phillips...Lytle... Blaine...& Hitchcock... Blaine...a super lawyer...whom I knew well... and liked...was a top advisor to Marine...He also had strong connections to the Democratic Party... and was on top retainer to the Bank...

At the beginning ...of our meeting...I was startled by the quiet seriousness...on the two men's faces...Blaine handed me what he called... the draft of a legal brief ...that was to be presented to a local court...He suggested that I read it...before continuing the meeting... The draft was a proposed law suit...against Marine Midland and me personally...that alleged that I had turned down a young woman's ...business loan request... because she would not grant me a sexual relationship... She was charging me... and the bank...with sexual discrimination and seeking a large monetary settlement...from the bank... My heart dropped down to my shoes...

Blaine asked me if any of this was true...I acknowledged knowing the young...black woman...but denied her allegations vociferously... I began to sweat a little...as I told my side of the story ...As owner of a small delicatessen...she had applied for a small...commercial loan...less than $50,000...but it was a very weak request...that just could not be granted... I told them that...when I explained the turndown to her...she seemed to accept my explanation and went away without protest ...As far as I was concerned...it was as routine as the dozens of loan requests...I had also denied...routinely...

When I finished my story...I told the two men...to let the chips fall where they may...I said...I was willing to risk my reputation against hers... any day...When I finished ...John looked over the top of his glasses...and asked..."Was she good looking... Bill?...I smiled...and said...yes...Very!... We all chuckled ...and I finally felt some relief... Then Blaine said... "Don't worry...Bill...I know her attorney well...I will speak to him...I'll take care of this...Forget about it"... But I couldn't just forget about it... and I went home that night and told JoAnn about the incident... After I professed my innocence...I think...at least I hoped...she believed me...

Less than a year after that incident...the same young lady...that made the accusation against me...was arrested for a credit card scam...she and her male partner had tried to run...on a local bank... The arrests were written up in the morning newspaper...so I cut out the article ...made copies and mailed them to Hettrick...and Blaine...I attached a note that said..."As I said...I'll stack my reputation up against hers any day!"...

That incident... however...made me very...very cautious in my subsequent dealings ...with loan requests...of all kinds...My profile had been heightened in the community ...and admittedly...I was supporting some very controversial groups...For example...I was quietly ...financially supporting the BUILD organization... where all of the leadership there... felt they were being closely watched...by local authorities ...Rightly or wrongly...at that time...I felt that I had to maintain close ties to community groups...no matter how radical...to give my community development activities... and the bank's programs credibility and support...

With that in mind…there was also the afternoon I spent chauffeuring Fania Davis… sister of the highly controversial…radical prison inmate… Angela Davis… to a couple of local…"Free Angela"…community meetings …There was also… my many meetings with Minister John… head of the local… Black Muslim mosque… who sought small…business loan support for his mosque's members… I was fully aware at that time… during the 1970's …that the FBI had a very active… domestic surveillance program … called "Cointelpro"… Some…in fact a number…of the leaders of political groups…I worked with…felt they were clandestinely being watched… by some agency of the government …

For a few years after the young lady incident …I too…felt that I was being watched …and even followed by someone…It would take a few more years…a Freedom of Information request… a heavily redacted response… and some careful sleuthing…on my part…to confirm that…I was… indeed … being watched by…a law enforcement agency … Those inquiries even confirmed that a trusted…fellow employee at Marine…who lived a short distance from me… assisted that agency in their surveillance of me…

Mama's Moon

She startled me again…my Mother…
just as she'd done many times before…
She was sitting there in her favorite chair…
It was our time of truth…honesty and candor.
"I don't believe it…I don't believe it"… she said.
"These treacherous…tricky people will say or do…
damn near…anything to stay on top…be the leader…
the top dog…of humanity…king of the mountaintop!…
But they did not go to the moon!…That's a bunch of heave!…
My loins…my instincts will not for one moment let me believe…
that they conquered the heavens and got even close to my God"…

OK…Mama…OK…

"All this hype is the ultimate deception…

They filmed it all on a Hollywood contraption...
Billy!...tell me they did...Can you prove it? ...Can they?...
The rocks...the pictures...the dust...just lies and wanderlust...
Look at the men they sent...They can't face the argument...
They're troubled and evasive...ashamed...insanely living a lie...
They're trying to learn how to live...to die...with their lie of lies...
They didn't do it!...Just like always...they lied for the Country!
They sold their souls...Press them somebody!...Press them quick!...
Like grapes between fingers...they'll burst with the naked...hard truth...
I'm telling you...Billy...no man has yet to set foot on the moon!"....

OK...Mama...OK...OK...

Where We Really Are

What if we were born...but are not really here...that

here...and not here...is all the same...and that what

we think is life...living...being...is really a memory...a

recall of seconds... instants of there...but long gone by...

no longer a part of here?...If such is not so...then why do

we feel...that when summons and...remembrance ends...

we will know...finally...what...and where we really are?...

Politics Heat Up

In 1973...after spending a little more than two years...as the Manager of Marine's Main-High office...I was promoted to Vice President...and transferred to the Main Office of the bank...It was the highest rank...a non-white person had ever held at the bank...The promotion occurred ...despite the fact that some of my branch bosses...disliked ...and resented my close association... with John Hettrick...I think they also disliked...what John and I...were promoting in the bank... At the Main office...now located on the plaza level...of the brand new...Marine Midland Center... I was still an uncomfortable three management levels... below John...I was given a carefully chosen...portfolio of conventional loan customers... some of whom...barely hid their preference for someone else...to manage their banking relationship...I was also told that I was second to the office manager... in charge of back office operations...

In this new position...I visited and kept in close consultation... with my increasingly uncomfortable...successor colleagues in the old CDD... Because I had single-signature...loan authority up to $250,000...I could be and was a valuable ally for their efforts...on behalf of small minority loan requests... The CDD...however... no longer reported directly to Hettrick...As a result there was less tolerance of the Division's steady stream of delinquencies...and above average charge-offs... by the new senior managers the Division now reported to... I began to feel that someone...in the bank ....including some of the people it reported to... were taking dead aim at the CDD's fragile ...little portfolio...of about 50.. to 60 loans...that averaged less than $110,000...

The bank's appetite for risk...was also being challenged considerably... Huge losses...totaling hundreds of millions...were occurring in...a high volume... incentive-driven...off-shore lending group...based in London... That London group...for some mysterious reason...was not held to the same lending standards...as the domestic Marine Midland banks... The London group had been wildly...approving loans...to industries and individuals... that we ...in the U.S...were prohibited from accommodating... To this day... I cannot understand how such a group was able to...within a few years...do so much damage to Marine... A hundred times...I wondered where were the auditors...the examiners...the same scrutiny about losses... that my tiny... little portfolio received...That London group...clearly... without any doubt...was ultimately responsible for bringing down...a long standing...stalwart financial institution...that had been based in Western New York State...for many...many years...

At that time there was also an on-going...management strategy to consolidate the 10 Marine banks... scattered around New York State...by the beginning of 1976... Because of the London losses... Marine also now needed a huge new injection of capital...to offset those mounting loan losses... by that rogue group in London ...Senior managers began scrambling ... to position themselves for survival...As for me...despite my very busy local activities...I continued to work... and travel for the ABA... In spite of its troubles... largely because of my exposure ...the bank's national reputation ...as a savvy minority business lender...soared... As a conventional lender...I continued to push... minority lending whenever I could....

From the Main Office...I made...or recommended loans to... Attorney and former City Court Judge Wilbur Trammell...to fund a modular housing project...former State Assemblyman Arthur Hardwick ...and his wife...Congresswoman...Shirley Chisholm...to purchase property... and to the BUILD organization...to purchase business property on East Ferry Street... The latter ... among other uses... was ultimately used to start the BUILD Academy ...which exists to this day...as an eastside public school... All of my efforts continued to draw more personal praise... and recognition in the community... However...I began to worry for my future ...and as internal bank politics churned furiously... I also became concerned for my friend...John Hettrick's future prospects...

In the Spring of 1973...an ailing Buffalo Mayor...Frank Sedita... resigned from office... Deputy Mayor...Stanley Makowski...a colorless... City Hall pol...assumed the position until November...when he would have to run for a normal term... In the summer of that year...a small group of University professors...lawyers...and white businessmen invited me to an evening meeting...at a home on Tudor Place...in Buffalo...I casually knew only a couple of the attendees ...and had been told the meeting was to discuss community issues...that would be of interest to me...

As the meeting progressed...I came to realize that my bank...and community activities was the major theme of the meeting... The group wanted to know about my origins ... political philosophies ...beliefs...and ties to the eastside community... They told me that my name had come up...in academic and business gatherings a number times...and that they wondered if I was positioning myself for a public office of some kind... I told them no!...I had no interest in public office...and that my interest was focused solely...on becoming the best banker that I could be... A professor in the group...which I surmised to be mostly Democratic Party-leaning...

then explained that many people...in the white community felt that it was time for Buffalo to have a black mayor...

I agreed with them...and quickly suggested that long time politician... Assemblyman Arthur Eve...aspired to that office...and would get solid support from the eastside...I mentioned that I had raised funds for...and had a close relationship with Eve...I also explained that...in the eyes of some... because I operated outside of the normal...political patronage routes...I was considered a threat to some City Hall politicians...and supporters of the recently resigned... Mayor Sedita...The group then said...that is why they found me worthy...and that they considered Eve...a "bomb thrower"...who was more divisive than uniting....They cited his connection to the Attica Prison riots...and said that they felt I was a respected someone... who could speak to the white business community...as well as the black community...

They expressed to me...that I was the right kind of person...for that high position...at that time... I told the group...I was flattered...but really uninterested in running for political office...By the end of the meeting... I promised that I would keep the meeting confidential...and that I stood ready to help the group in any way that I could...short...of running for a political office... The meeting ended cordially... As I left...I drove past John Hettrick's home...which was also on Tudor Place ...and I couldn't help but wonder if there wasn't an empty seat...or two...at the meeting I had just left... Hettrick...later denied knowing anything about the meeting...or the group...and I believed him...

Almost exactly one year later...in July... 1974...an article profiling my family...and banking career was published by the Buffalo Evening News...A reporter...Mary Ann Lauricella ... called me and told me...the paper was planning to run a newspaper series...profiling six... Western New York families...She said she wanted to spend a few days with the families ...share their day-to-day experiences...and record their outlook on life...in the 1970's...She asked me if I would agree to let my family...be one of the families...featured in the series...I told her I would...if the bank...and JoAnn approved...since Mary Ann planned to spend a night in our home...

The bank gave me their permission...and JoAnn squeamishly agreed... The reporter ...accompanied me home from the bank one evening...had dinner...and spent the night with us...The next day she tagged along with JoAnn...on her chores...including a PTA meeting ... After the visit...the whole family…adored Mary Ann…and I gave her one of my paintings… The article…about us…was published July 15, 1974… It turned out to be a watershed moment …for my Marine Midland banking career…

The Tuesday after the article was published…my phone at work…rang constantly …Most of the calls were from friends…jokingly saying…I should immediately ask for a raise…The article…which they all had read…was mostly complimentary…describing the routine of family life for us…some of my community involvement…the usual prejudices…and sleights…we lived with…what our house was worth … (about $45,000)…and for heaven's sake… my salary… ($23,000)…While I never gave Mary Ann my exact salary… ($25,000)… she picked around and came up with her own best guess…

The published salary…apparently … embarrassed some people at the bank… One of the calls I got was from my second level report…an Executive Vice President…who asked me to come to his office… He said to me…"Bill… most of the News article…was OK…but why did you have to tell them your salary?" …I smilingly answered that I never told the reporter my salary… and that I thought she just guessed it… from the information she was able to glean…from my family… I told him… except for the salary…everything else was spot-on truthful… He didn't say it…but it seemed that there were a lot of senior people at the bank… including …I suspected… John Hettrick… who were embarrassed that one of the highest profile officers at the bank…at that time… appeared to be so underpaid … relative to others…at the same management level…

Unfortunately…there were some other minor…fall-outs from the newspaper article…that affected JoAnn and my children…JoAnn received a couple of snide remarks…about the article…from some of her fellow PTA members…and at least one neighbor…But…as was her custom… she efficiently…and without rancor…handled the incidents masterfully… Ricky …my oldest son…now an almost six…and a half foot…center for the Grand Island High School basketball team…became embroiled…in a locker room fight with three…black… fellow teammates…The fight… ostensibly over on-court… basketball occurrences…was really rooted in petty jealousies…about the newspaper article…

However… like his mother…and with just a tiny bit of rancorous physicality…(he mopped the floor up with them)…he handled the incident masterfully…A positive from the article…was an encouraging…and sympathetic letter from the famous...popular novelist...Taylor Caldwell... Given her...John Birch-like...conservative political views ... I was surprised at how she ...defended and encourage JoAnn and I...to stand tall...in spite of the sleights... mentioned in the article...I have her letter to this day...

The Wizard

What to ask the Wizard:

Oh...great Wizard...tell us what life is and what is its purpose?

What the Wizard will answer:

Human life is consciousness...and its purpose is perpetuation...If there is no consciousness...there is no meaningful...human life...

What to ask the Wizard:

Oh...great Wizard... tell us what truth is and what is its purpose?

What the Wizard will answer:

Truth is reality and reality is truth...Its purpose is to exist beyond dispute...by anyone ...or anything...absolutely...

What to ask the Wizard:

Oh... great Wizard...will we ever know the origin of life?

What the Wizard will answer:

No!...Not until we become the creators of ourselves...

What to ask the Wizard:

Oh...great Wizard...tell us what death is and what is its purpose?

What the Wizard will answer:

Death is unconsciousness...It only exists for the conscious...and that is its only purpose...

science

can only
take us to
within billionths
of an instant of
understanding creation…
therefore…we cannot
really learn the
meaning of
our existence
until we become
creators
of ourselves…

safe before I came

weeks old rabbits….
in a carefully hidden lair…
scattered when I clumsily stumbled…
upon their world…
when looking for winter damage…
on the property's west end…

I wanted to apologize…
and I hoped they would return…
for if they were safe before I came…
they most surely can be again…
even more so now…
that the worst of them has come and gone…

My Days Become Numbered

From that July...1974...newspaper article...I began to feel less...and less comfortable at the bank...For many reasons ...I had decided not to pal around with Hettrick...as much as I did when I reported to him...Also... the bank's barely tolerable...attitude toward my old department...the CDD...began to change... The people left behind in the department... grew increasingly discouraged because...in spite of government loan guarantees...in many instances... they couldn't originate...or refinance as many minority loans...as we used to...

With new requirements for bank profitability...and loss controls...the loans were becoming tougher to do...We no longer had strong advocacy for that activity...and I could sense...that powerful people...at Marine... for their own reasons ...were increasingly ...hostile to our minority lending efforts... Hettrick ...remained accessible ...and helpful occasionally... but I cautioned my CDD friends... not to put too much pressure on Hettrick for assistance ... I explained that I thought he was in his own struggle... for survival in the bank...and that if the chips fell our way...as the bank consolidated...we may have a chance to go statewide...with our efforts ... If it goes otherwise...I suggested they begin to think about their next career move... in or out...of the bank...

Out in the local community...I continued to juggle time...between my roles as principal advisor to the BBDC... the African American Cultural Center...the Gren Ki Club...the Community Mental Health Center....etc...etc...For various reasons...all of the BBDC businesses were struggling...mainly to find...and maintain decent managers...After three years of operation...the Gren Ki Club had to shut down its food operation...and membership support weakened...We had to fine...and chastise members for slow dues payments...and I felt...we waited far too long...to involve more women in the Club's activities...

Therefore ...with much similarity...to the story of the much more prestigious... Jewish Community's Montefiore Club...which closed its doors in 1978...I shut the Gren Ki Club's doors... after almost four years of operation ...After liquidation...the bank suffered only minimal loss... from the Club's loan...In the meantime...the BBDC's daycare center... and supermarket enterprises ... also struggled to find enough paying customers...

and the effort to build a strip plaza...at Jefferson and Utica streets...was abandoned...The plaza development...fell to political and community jealousies ...that were determined to blocked our way... This just added to a growing ...internal bank...lending conservatism...that ultimately...took a terrible toll...on Marine's very modest...minority loan program...

Some of our minority businesses...however...thrived...Jessie Jackson's Ascension Chemical Company...eventually made him a millionaire... His company...one of the few manufacturers in our minority portfolio... made aluminum chloride...which was used as a catalyst in the production of a number of retail products... I am told Walter Hobson's...clothes cleaning establishment...survived... and operates to this day...Some retail establishments...enabled owners to send kids to colleges...others were profitably sold... passed on to heirs....or they just shut their doors...

Very few of the businesses we helped to get started...were around after ten years... This didn't disturb me...since small businesses of all kinds...no matter who owns them... seldom stay alive for 10...or more years...In fact...most small businesses...fail within 2 or 3 years of starting up... However...the beauty of our program...was that we were giving people...who didn't feel they had a chance...a chance!... We were buying optimism...faith and hope...in American capitalism...when there was little...of either...in black America...in the 1960's...and 1970's....

I was proud of our efforts...to give blacks...in Buffalo...a chance to chase their dreams...But to me...the irony of ironies...was that it wasn't the small... high-risk...minority lending program...with its hated...higher than normal delinquencies...and losses...that caused the demise of a vaunted... 150 year old...Buffalo institution... In it's final days as Marine Midland Bank...then the nation's 13th largest commercial bank...it lost hundreds of millions...with its failed ...conventional lending efforts...mostly in London...

However ...after fully liquidating its tiny...less than five million dollar...minority loan portfolio...by the late 1970's...the bank...in total... lost less than two...and a half million dollars... That was less than it lost...financing an Arizona race track...in the 1970's...Had it paid for the positive... national publicity...the bank received... for its minority lending efforts in Buffalo ...the cost for the publicity alone... would have cost more than the bank ultimately lost... financing those fledgling... minority businesses...

As for my own career...I had luckily...exposed my abilities to executives in the industry...as I traveled around the Country for the ABA...Long-time...Charlotte...North Carolina...super banker...Hugh McColl... offered me a job...at North Carolina National Bank...after we made a presentation...on minority lending in Charlotte...A group...that included famous baseball pitcher...Bob Gibson ...invited me to come to Omaha... Nebraska...to consider running a fledgling start-up bank... for a group of minority investors...

Board members from a minority-owned bank...in Detroit ...had extended invitations...and even the bank's founding President...who had recently resigned... visited my home...in an attempt to interest me in becoming the Chief Executive...of their five year-old bank... All this interest gave me confidence in my personal worth...and the value of my training...In late 1975...I decided that I would try to stay at Marine...until July of 1976... when I would have vested in Marine's retirement plan ...I was convinced that moving on after that...would not be difficult... Sadly ...I began to quietly extract myself from most of my community activities ...and I continued to avoid too much contact with...my friend... John Hettrick...partly because I was convinced that...my telephones ...at home...and at work... were tapped...

At a Place Where What it Knew

At a place...where...what it knew...how

to do... conventionally... routinely...the Captain...
found a hostile island... in the calmest of waters...
and suffered...cruel...ugly shoals...in the least of
expected places... enough to start a leak...break
the chain...of a sturdy anchor....and leave a
nasty...fatal slick...

Forgotten will be...the 60...or so...eager eyes...
in our own backyard...peeping through knot
holes...begging... scrambling to come in...while

splashing expected...but not unusual...droplets of
mud... on shiny...well worn boots...

To let them in...would have helped to cauterize
...a long festering wound...the missing mules...
the 40 acres...a place for the second wave... to do
it better... show them...how to believe...It would
have been a gift to the lofty colors...and many
testimonials...It could have been...

a siren to find calm seas...another tie-down...of the
promise...when darker...harsher winds...swirled up
foaming waters...threatening the ship again...That brief
...over the shoulder look...in that lost vessel's journey...
was 100 times more worthy ...than the straight-away...
confident sail into danger... it took...Few knew that then...

Ode to Africa

Africa!...Oh...Africa!...cradle of humanity...first
bowl of nourishment...You have given us many things...

Human life itself...came from you...before you were...
Africa...While some stayed and remain to this day...

others of your children have thrived...as they dispersed...
and challenged the harshness of this tiny speeding globe...

Some fled and went deep into dark caves...spooked
when the wind blew...and the skies opened with cruelty...

Some swam and floated to new shores...new welcoming
places...Like competitor ants...microbes and...insects

of all kinds...they fought...struggled and stayed true...
on that universal course...that is meant for them...a

course impossible to alter…given who they are…what
they are…what they must inevitably…go to…return to…

They came together…with elaborate…fancy theories
about themselves…the moon…water…the sun…their

destiny…The clever…gifted ones…created Gods and
myths and soothing truths…to make believers…of all

who would gladly…mimic soldier ants…yielding their
labor…their bodies…for peace of mind…These elaborate…

conjured truths…unified them and made possible great
structures…clever machines…great gatherings…holy

books…and fancy rituals of mutual pleasure…The most
clever…and the curious…explored the inner world…of

themselves…and even boldly challenged the heavens…
The bloated…prideful… egos…sulked…sought struggle…

conflict…horrific…confrontation…Raw…human sacrifice
…will always be with them…for whatever reason they can

find…And in spite of it all...Africa…and the old…tiny…
blue globe…inexorably…keeps speeding to its destiny…

the dark sucking hole…hardly even annoyed…or fazed by
the goings of ants…microbes…atoms…and men… For at a

moment…maybe years and eons away…all who are conscious…
will know the only real truth…only suspected of…by some

today:…that everything…created by her…all of Africa's dear
children…will die and return to the nothing…they were before

creation...And nothing is not even imaginable...For if you can imagine it...it is something...and something...cannot

ever be nothing!...

W.R. Bailey & Co, Inc.

In the Spring of 1976...when I had decided that I would leave Marine...A sales representative for an east coast...edible oils refinery... visited me...looking for a minority individual interested in selling for the refinery...His theory was that a minority rep...with proper financing... could open doors...that perhaps would not open...for the usual white reps...given the current...affirmative action sentiments....at many companies...with minority outreach programs... He said his company was willing to finance...all the business won by the minority...and that the business could be quite profitable...for a good salesman... I told him that I didn't know of anyone that might be interested in his offer...but that I might be...if there was little risk involved...

I studied his offer...checked out the refinery...and projected the possibilities...for a successful venture... After discussing it with JoAnn... and promising her that...to be safe...I would continue to be open to other...less risky opportunities...that came along... As usual she gave me her blessing...and I proceeded to create W.R. Bailey & Co...an edible oil broker...To help finance the venture...I met with a small group of potential investors...that included Don Omel...the owner of a Main Street furniture business...Reggie McKinsey...a superb pulling guard...for the Buffalo Bills... and a physician from Buffalo General Hospital... Added to my own meager contribution...I raised $50,000 to finance the venture... and set up modest office space at 1555 Niagara Street...An introducing brochure for the company read:

> *The well known edible oil processors, now represented by W.R. Bailey & Co., Inc are among the most reliable firms in the industry. Multimillion dollar annual sales to leading food processors and drug manufacturers attest to their highly competitive pricing and thorough customer*

service. The association of these firms with W. R. Bailey & Co., Inc. provides a convenient supply source to users of soybean, palm, peanut, cottonseed and coconut oils. As a new broker, the Bailey organization is pledged to continue a high standard of customer service and to bring new and creative energy to meeting your company's requirements.

W. R. Bailey is a former Vice President and Commercial Lending Officer of the Marine Midland Bank in Buffalo, New York. In this capacity he negotiated and approved commercial loans totaling millions of dollars. He is a graduate of the State University of New York at Buffalo with a BA in Economics. An active par-ticipant in community and civic organizations, he has served on many committees and boards including the Urban Affairs Committee of the American Bankers Association, the New York State Welfare Research Corp., U.S. Small Business Advisory Board, Buffalo Urban League and the Erie County Economic Development Committee. With this background, he brings to W.R. Bailey & Co., Inc., a scrupulous regard for business integrity and reliability.

Without mentioning my plans...for W.R.Bailey & Co., to anyone in the bank...I submitted my resignation...from the bank in late July...1976... My last day at the bank...a small group of my colleagues...at the Main office ... held a going-away party for me... What was memorable about the gathering was that...not a single...senior person...other than Hettrick ...attended the party...and that the specially baked cake for the party... was in the shape of a bikini-clad...white female torso... In the midst of trivial laughter...I smiled dryly at the very... unfunny symbolism ... because I knew that the cake idea... probably came from the suggestion of...the one person...at the party...I worked with...but disliked intensely...

Everyone else there... including my few friends from the beleaguered little CDD ... I liked... and respected very much...After the small chatter ended... before I left...I shook every hand there but one... When I left the Marine Midland Center that day...no longer an employee of the bank ...I walked past the old administration building... at 241 Main Street...and tried to remember that first day...some 10 years earlier...in 1966... when

I first walked through those doors... I was full of apprehension... and uncertainty back then...This time...as I headed for the parking lot...I was taller...proud of what I had done...and a hell-of- a-lot more confident of my ability...to make my own way...in spite of it all... Without looking back...I also had no idea...that day... that I had not yet worked my last day...for Marine Midland Bank...

The day after I left Marine...I began working on my new venture... After a couple of months of calls...visits and referrals to large food processing companies...I began to doubt that...such a clubby little circle of buying and selling...between oil refineries ...and their handfuls of customers...could be interrupted by my efforts... I quickly concluded that perhaps...I had violated one of the first principles of business formation: be sure you have a real market opportunity...for your goods or services... The refinery I represented kept telling me to hang in there... that it takes time to catch on...that many companies were just beginning to establish their affirmative action programs...etc...etc... One even offered to "assign "to me one of their small accounts... However...I grew increasingly restless... and fearful of my ability to care for my home... if I kept striking out with my oil sales efforts...I also worried about the faithful group of investors... who had decided to invest in the business with me...

By mid-September...I decided to put the business venture on hold...As I considered the various options before me...partly because my mother... and other family members...now lived in Detroit...I contacted the bank group in Detroit...who had offered me a position... earlier in the year...I told them I had reconsidered ...and was now interested in pursuing the position ...they had offered...After traveling to Detroit to meet with the bank's board members ...studying the relevant financial statements...and meeting other local...mainstream bankers...I agreed to accept the position of ...President and Chief Executive Officer...of the six year old...$60 million dollar...First Independence National Bank of Detroit... Within weeks I closed down the oil brokerage...returned 90% of my fellow investor's funds ...and headed off for Detroit...Michigan...Ironically...a few days before I left...a large food processing company...I had called on... inquired about placing a $20,000...coconut oil order with us...

Endings

The real end is never…

It cannot get here…however
long it has been trying…

Always
waiting to arrest …an
ending…is a beginning…

It is
as it should be…

Just as every beginning…has
an end…
likewise
every ending…
has a beginning…

Look for it…

Is There No Love

Is there no love…no dream…that is real?…Must every desire…mock you…ask for more in return…than you can give…cravenly dismiss you…because you did not hurl yourself…upon the rocks…become a martyr for fineness… for the shadows?…Where is my leader?…Where is my teacher of danger?…Who will show me…the path beyond today…beyond the irreverent…the titillating desires and exquisite distractions?…I accept what it is…My worst weaknesses are my own…Are my strengths the same… my sky…limited to just a single vision…only one man's notions …to just me?…Why can't I speak my soul to just a single…

trusted one?...From the way I came...to the dance...seemingly no...Then I march on...fatherless...left to my own designs... my own vision of destiny...wherever...and whatever that is...

Fevers

Fevers are normally thought hot...excitable
or quick...They can also be cold...dull or slow...

Hot fevers get treated to cool down the sick...
Cold ones...you mostly leave...to go where they go...

Excitable...or quick fevers...unchecked can kill...
spread themselves wide...even take down a nation...

Dull or slow fevers...may uncover great skill...value...
and like mighty gravity...bring us all to reclamation...

The lesson:...fevers...hot or cold...usually mimic each other...
and find the same river...to the very same end...

Bailey's First Epilogue

As I crossed the Lewiston-Queenston Bridge...alone...taking the southern Ontario route...to Windsor and Detroit...I had plenty of time to remember...to think about my days at Marine Midland... In my mind...I kept trying to sort through the positives...the negatives...the lessons to be remembered... especially the mistakes...Within a matter of months... after my departure...the enemies of our fragile...little effort to reach out to Buffalo's minority business community ...descended with a vengeance... The principal champion of our effort...John Hettrick... within months after my departure... would buy a business and leave Marine...I am sure he was a casualty of the executive wars... of the bank's consolidation... and I am also sure his wounding...his departure was also partly caused...

by our efforts...to assist minority businesses ...in the city of Buffalo... But who knows... Marine's fate was sealed...in spite of what we tried to do...The bank was deeply wounded by careless lending mistakes...and the sometimes...deadly corruption that seeps into business enterprises... run by humans...

That was the deepest cut for me personally ... because I think Hettrick deserved more...far more...He was a brilliant banker...quietly...but deeply religious...and an honest observer of the lending hypocrisy...all around him...Whatever drove him...whatever he had in his soul...he wanted... through our efforts...to make a difference...However...the prejudices of some powerful people in the bank...and circumstances beyond his control... stacked the deck against us...We were laboring against... extremely heavy odds... The program we tried to run...had little chance in a deeply wounded institution...fighting...and scrambling...for its very own survival... My own inadequacies ... political immaturity...and cynicism toward the motives...of many whites surrounding me ...also kept me from seizing upon more appropriate strategies ...and directions... to help our efforts... In a city that needed so much... Marine's tiny investment in the black community... was the equivalent of tossing a small glass of water...on a creeping desert... hell-bent on swallowing up every blade of grass in it's path...

The petty community jealousies ...deep poverty...and wounded psyches...of Buffalo's black community...was also far greater than I anticipated... That community...like most black communities in this Country...did not rally its small... but significant... purchasing power ...and support for the small...mostly fragile...retail businesses we tried to help... Again...I regret that I didn't do more...to rally that support...There were some things... however...that the black community just couldn't do anything about...The City's white middle class ...was on a rapidly increasing trend of physical abandonment...and the remaining poor...working class ...ethnic neighborhoods ... were gearing up to resist any encroachments...on their political prerogatives... During this time the pathetically long...race-baiting reign...of Mayor James Griffin ...was a testament to ...what I like to call... "Little Jim Crow Light...northern style"...

Although they happened...long before Griffin...powerful... potentially city-saving symbols ...like the football stadium...and the

University ...were mistakenly... planted in faraway... characterless cornfields... This was contrary...to what was done in other great cities... like Pittsburgh... Cleveland ...St. Louis...and even Cincinnati...where those kind of popular institutions... remained in the city... In those cities...the people in charge...didn't make the development mistakes Buffalo did...While "white flight" was a reality...almost everywhere... in the Country...in many cities...whites didn't completely abandon the core city...and run...helter-skelter... from the waves...of re-locating blacks... fleeing from the cruelty...of the Jim Crow South...

In most of those cities...whites sought alliances with blacks...refused to be drawn into race-destructive divisiveness...and encouraged the election of black officials...to solidify neighborhood alliances... In Buffalo...after the race-bating... and ethnic wars subsided...and much of it's white middle class...had abandoned the City... Buffalo finally elected a black mayor...and a black dominated Common Council...to run a deeply troubled City... Today ...there are signs that investment ...and common sense is... belatedly ... returning to the City...I hope it continues... and Buffalo...a city I love...is once again... restored to the majesty it once had...

As I look back...my efforts at Marine Midland...especially my travels for the American Bankers Association ...probably did more for other cities...which had banks that...at our urging...started minority loan programs... Many did more in their own communities... than we did in my city...During that period...I traveled to 14 cities... preaching the minority-business development gospel... It's true...in large measure...it was an industry-defending ...public-relations effort ...

However...as a result of those efforts...billions of dollars were loaned to aspiring blacks... wanting to be full participants...in the Country's economic system...I am sure those programs helped to create some badly-needed optimism... in our deteriorating minority communities... at a time when we desperately needed it... In Buffalo...beyond private... personal entreaties from John Hettrick... regrettably...we never mounted a strong appeal to rival...local banks...to join Marine's small effort in Buffalo...For the city's sake ...we desperately needed allies...of all sorts... public and private...to join our efforts... ...to avoid the pitiful... hollowed-out...core city...that Buffalo...ultimately was allowed to become...

Imagination

Some things...in this brief life...
I guess you just have to go without...
what you imagine to ultimately be...
that touch...that feel...that smell...
that taste...that look...that experience...
that pure befalling of bliss and satisfaction...

It is truly a shame to be here on earth...
fight through all the offal one must...
and not have what you imagine...
to be the ultimate human affectation...
a crowning...soaring moment that makes...
it all worthwhile...Damn you...imagination..

GOD DAMN YOU!...

First Independence National Bank

As I crossed the Ambassador Bridge into Detroit...I was grateful for the training I had received at Marine...It would bode well for me...as I headed for new chapters in my banking career... Detroit...for me... became another stiff challenge...in another troubled city...where the tests for the black community were also enormous... I found Detroit's black community to be an insular...but proud aggregation of devotees to Motown legends...as those legends related to the automobile...and popular "Motown" music... Those two Detroit institutions had helped to build a relatively prosperous...and proud black middle class... something my own hometown ...Buffalo...did not really have...

Detroit was also proud of its little...stockholder-owned... "black bank"...but from the moment I arrived... I was immediately burdened with difficult... internal bank challenges... that threatened the very survival...of the small...poorly managed bank ... The bank...then almost 5 years old...had previously been headed by a black banker...a few years older than me...but with understandably...limited training and experience... compared to my own training... The same could be said for the management staff...and board of directors...They were all very proud of their little bank...but...in my opinion... almost no one...in a significant management position...really understood what it really took to manage a successful banking business...

The bank's financial history reflected modest or almost no bottom-line profits...its first 5 years of existence...It's balance sheet was very sleepy...with large balances sitting in a correspondent bank account... and a loans-to-deposit ratio of about 23%...Most of its investable funds were sitting in low-yielding treasuries...managed by a local advisory firm...It's tiny loan portfolio consisted mainly of a few mortgages...some installment loans...and a limited number of marginal risk... commercial loans...I soon learned that all commercial loans were approved by the full board ...after an arduous process...of open file examination of all of the borrowers financials... I was told...prior to my arrival...a single loan request could take up most of a single board meeting...

The bank's Board of Directors...which prior to his death... included Barry Gordy Senior ...the father of famous Motown founder...Barry Gordy Junior...The rest of the board was composed of prominent... fairly well known...local...black businessmen and women...a local college professor...a black lawyer...and a successful ...white businessman... Most of the directors... had been board members since the Bank was created in 1970...To give some sanity to the bank's new management direction... my improvement efforts... started with director seminars ...for the bank's directors...

I took them across the Detroit river to Windsor... Ontario...and taught them rudimentary analysis of financial statements... and how to read loan requests by looking at one or two loan sheet summaries...from a loan applicant's financials... Among other handouts... I gave them American Bankers Association booklets on "How to be A Bank Director"...and suggested we purchase director's liability insurance... They grumbled in the beginning... but when I pointed out the grave...and serious financial liability they faced as bank directors ...they later thanked me... Oh...and as an afterthought ...I asked each of them to open at least one...personal or business account with the Bank...

I also taught or provided similar training sessions for the bank's staff...I revised forms... procedures and systems...and purchased new equipment to make bank operations more efficient...Dozens of Marine Midland policy manuals...and procedures were scrubbed ...and made First Independence manuals and policy...To me it was the fastest...and easiest way to graft familiar policies into a company ...that had very few written policies... or coherent... recognizable procedures...To relieve the obvious stress... we all faced...I introduced...and paid for sessions on Transcendental Meditation...for my direct reports...and key supervisors ...I fired some very incompetent staff persons...and hired one of my old colleagues... Eugene Bynum... from Marine Midland...to manage the loan function at the bank...

With all of my busy days...I deeply regretted not having more time.... to spend with community leaders...and long standing organizations... that could have provided more than just token support for the bank...I did...however...spend some time meeting with some community leaders and certain highly vocal groups...to blunt criticism...and to solicit their support for the bank... I had to explain why it was necessary to have a conservative loan policy...and why we could not take certain kinds of risk... I also met with bankers from the big...local banks...to get their support for loan participations and training....I borrowed their skilled specialists... that my staff could learn from...I even ended a long-standing...but what was then...an unprofitable...correspondent bank relationship...with the National Bank of Detroit ... We became the first bank...from Detroit... in 40 years...to join the Federal Reserve Bank...for direct clearing of the bank's deposits... and receipts...

During those long days at the bank...for levity... and to relieve tension...for a few months...I created and penned a single-paneled... sports cartoon...called "Fan Cracks"...for the Detroit Free Press... The daily panel was a simply-drawn... depiction of sports situations in Detroit...as commented on by smart-alecky...sports fans...It was another form of expression for me...and it helped to relieve...some of the constant tension I faced...with daily management of the bank...Another highlight for me...was being selected as one of 40 or so... outstanding black business leaders ...in the Country...and being invited to meet President Jimmy Carter... at the White House...in June...1978... At the White House meeting...we were given briefings by the President's staff...and had our pictures taken with Mr. and Mrs. Carter... I thoroughly enjoyed the honor... and President Carter has been my all-time... favorite president... ever since...

After being at the bank a year or two... a regulatory bank examination forced a few sizeable (for us) loans to be charged-off as losses...That act strained the bank's already meager... reserve capital position... Facing difficult choices...and the tough scrutiny of skeptical...bank regulators...I set out to find new investors and new capital to save the fragile...little bank ...After a taxing...capital-seeking third year in Detroit ...with a significant assist from Henry Ford II...Chairman of the Ford Motor Company...I was able to successfully re-capitalize ...and consolidate the ownership of... the troubled bank...

My plan was to sell a combination of subordinated capital notes...and new common stock...Because of our watered-down capital...our capital raising effort resulted in selling a 51% ownership position to a single individual...with no experience in the business...Despite the fact that consolidation of ownership...in the hands of a single individual...and the resultant additional capital...kept the bank from collapse ... my actions caused a bitter riff between... some individuals on the bank's board of directors and me... My suspicious detractors felt that it was wrong to place the fate of the bank...in the hands of a single individual...with majority control... I disagreed ...and felt that new capital and firm... committed leadership...was desperately needed...if the bank was to survive...

First Independence's directors...whom I liked and respected... were all admirable ... community founding directors of the bank... However... collectively ...in my opinion...they lacked the sophistication...and business acumen ...the bank needed at that time... After many tense weeks...the ownership change was finally blessed by the bank's regulators... From then on...again...although I liked most of them...I was unable to get along with the directors... some of whom...now bitterly bad-mouthed the bank's re-structuring...and my leadership...

The new majority owner of the little bank...was bewildered by the conflicting politics...and opposition to my leadership... He had hoped to reduce the size...and composition of the board...and initially rely on my experience and direction...but his total lack of bank management experience... and regulatory scrutiny and criticism....weakened my prospects ...and desire to remain at the bank... Without regret... I left First Independence...in mid-year 1980 ... Today... the bank...about $185 million in size... is still controlled...mostly by the single individual I convinced to buy control of the bank... Although still struggling ...in a brutally competitive industry ...and a troubled city...it is now more than 42 years old...

This remarkable survivability of the bank...is a testament to...extremely conservative...and carefully controlled management ... since the bank was re-capitalized in the 1970's...In some ways I feel vindicated... by what I did...However...the bank is not...and never will be...a significant banking presence in Detroit... Like most minority-owned banks...operating in minority communities...in my opinion...First Independence is more symbolic ...than a powerhouse financial influence in its market... With its small capital base...minority community indifference...and limited... city-locked...physical locations...it is unable to take much risk...or find viable lending...and deposit opportunities ...to grow significantly...

In my opinion...unless small...so-called minority-owned banks... can find ways to grow... organically...or build through controlled mergers and acquisitions... they become vulnerable to identity-killing acquisitions or stagnation...Short of healthy growth... they become an irrelevance in a technology-driven industry... where powerful... genuine competition...has so much more to offer minority communities... Small banks... generally... have the greatest chance to survive ...if they operate in the few remaining... rural...or small protective markets...that are not attractive to the big boys...

However...one cannot overlook...and absolve the shameful lack of support... minority communities themselves...have shown in the development of minority-owned businesses ...generally... A few months... (September 9, 1980)...after I resigned from First Independence ...I penned the following Op-Ed article for the Detroit Free Press:...

> *One of the main problems facing black businesses today is the lack of support from blacks, according to an article in a recent issue of Black Enterprise magazine. The article cites two important facts:*
>
> - *Less than 10 percent of blacks' disposable income is spent with black-owned businesses.*

- *While blacks are quick to criticize others for discriminating against and excluding blacks from the mainstream, they are less quick to criticize themselves for similar behavior—and to turn self-criticism into economic channels to benefit themselves. Blacks do not demonstrate solidarity as consumers of black-produced goods and services.*

Does such an attitude prevail in Detroit? I believe it does. While blacks constitute a substantial portion of the metropolitan Detroit population, black-owned businesses, for the most part, remain anemic and fragile, and barely exist on the periphery of the real business action.

Every week, blacks in Detroit spend millions on food, clothing and other staple items, but there is not one major black-owned supermarket in the city. The 10- year-old black-owned commercial bank in Detroit grew rapidly in its early years, but really has not had as much support from blacks as was hoped for. This pattern is repeated in case after case.

Why won't black people support black-owned establishments? One response suggests that black businesses are not competitive for one reason or another. To quote one critic of black businesses, "After all, service is service and I go where I get the best service." In other words, black business owners are accused of operating less-than-first-class establishments or charging excessive prices for second-class service.

In some cases, I believe there is some truth to this accusation, but many black merchants are adamant in their disagreement. Second-rate businesses exist in every industry, they retort, whether they be black or white-owned. The merchants believe black businesses are singled out for harsher criticism by their own people. They believe it is a symptom of a deeper-rooted problem; that blacks are still bound up in subtle but thoroughly implanted psychological barriers to acceptance and support of themselves and each other.

The lack of black support or black acceptance of black businesses, I believe, is mainly rooted in the historical personal relationships that blacks have shared in this country. I have heard psychologists and black intellectuals say that these "mental barriers" to solidarity stem from the subconscious self-hatred that blacks had deeply implanted in their psyche during years of slavery and exclusion from the mainstream of American society.

It was suggested to me that blacks came to despise their physical and emotional characteristics and generally rejected themselves and each other in ways more critical than white rejection. To overcome this, blacks have boosted deflated egos by consuming in very conspicuous fashion and by buying from business establishments patronized predominately by whites, the notion being that if whites go there, it must be the best; and "since I want the best, I'll go there too."

Such attitudes severely penalize black-owned businesses and ultimately penalize all black Americans by depriving them of economic clout, and therefore political strength.

Although blacks have become the majority population in Detroit and are basically running the governmental apparatus, they have yet to develop a strong commercial base with strong, black-owned and operated enterprises. In my opinion, it is full black participation in all aspects of American life that will truly strengthen and mature the black community. To achieve this, a sense of self-responsibility for black commercial development is needed.

There are, of course, black-owned businesses that blacks support. They provide mainly the close personal services such as barbering, medical treatment, funeral arrangements and fast-food bodegas. These businesses have fared well in the black community.

But even that is changing. Very able, competitive, white businesses are making advances in the lucrative personal care market, which blacks have traditionally had all to themselves.

The black-oriented cosmetic industry is a case in point. White companies, with tremendous resources and competitive advantages, are seriously challenging black-owned cosmetic companies. The vast majority of black consumers, however, are unaware of these inroads and of the enormous competitive barriers to entry when blacks try to expand from ethnic markets into the general economy.

Black professionals—lawyers, doctors and dentists—have also noted patterns of non-support by blacks. However, many black professionals believe this is slowly changing because of the demonstrated competence of blacks, and, in the case of physicians, a great shortage in urban or rural areas where blacks are concentrated.

Even black civil rights and social betterment organizations have suffered from a lack of widespread black support. Organizations such as the Urban League, the NAACP, and the United Negro College Fund would be in severe trouble if white corporations and white individuals withdrew financial support.

If blacks were to galvanize their spending patterns into support for black-owned institutions and black businesses, the estimated $120-billion income that blacks control every year could become a formidable force for change in the overall political and economic status of blacks in the United States.

As a businessman, I believe in the free enterprise system. All people, whatever color, have the right to buy from whomever they choose.

However, as black people look for ways to improve their lot in American society, they should hold the mirror up to themselves and ask, "What am I doing for myself, and what are we doing together?"

When black people spend their dollars they are voting; and if they vote for themselves, they are giving themselves just that much more power to control their own destiny.

Another Bailey

Glad to meet you...
legend...
Glad to hear we may...
be cousins...
Love your energy....
Love your effervescent
reach to all...who come
within your presence...

Thank you for the gift...
to bestow confidence...
friendship...
While I distrust some of
your friends...I love what
you remind me of...Pearls...
and the best of all the women
that have been in my life...

The Renewal

They once saw only sunny days…drenching…cool
nourishing rains…tantalizing moments…when

life itself…every awakening…had great beauty…
and exciting promise…all for a struggling seedling…

reaching for the heavens…defying the wind…and
challenging all heart storms…Every instant was a

lift…perhaps a rare gift…to show appreciation for
presence…for just being here…There were no dream

destroying threats…only bright hope…hope without
end…desire that only gladdened a soul…hope…that

so eagerly screamed…"follow me…I will set you free!"…
But lo…the days slowed…stopped tilting downward for

speed…stopped giving a steady stream of promise…
and instead…shifted the path to incline…where the

journey…was no longer joyous…where legs tightened…
grew stiff…stopped running… The belly delights…which

used to visit…with welcome…every dry day…no
longer danced…with flirting expectation…Then it all

seemed lost… without assurance… Bereft of ambition…it
stopped visiting at all… That dark speck…called doom…

never seen before…now blinked…grew by the hour…then
by the instant… But in the illusion…called time…spiritual

immolation… was stayed…made wet…soaked for a new

coming... a new onset...with fresh promise... The lesson is...

every wilted rose...or broken branch...need not die...The blood of existence dwells serenely...until beckoned again...

by the authentic...who believe in the prize...Breath can surely come again...to the almost lifeless...yes...to even the nearly dead...

A Banking Career is Revived

After resigning from First Independence...I spent a few years...as a financial consultant... to a few local businesses in Detroit...and the Bank of the Commonwealth... One of the businesses I worked for was Pinkard Plumbing...whose owner...Bill Pinkard...was a former customer at First Independence... I also worked as a financial consultant to a business promoting food products under a label called "Pearl's Kitchen"...In that capacity I had the opportunity to work... and travel with Pearl Bailey...the noted singer...actress and stage performer ...Pearl and I traded stories... and convinced ourselves that we may have been distant cousins...We often joked about me being her little brother "Bill 2"...since she already had another brother named Bill Bailey... Even though I disapproved of...and was not a supporter of most of Pearl's political friends... I adored her for her warmth ... and loving friendship... that I cherished right up to her death in 1990....

However...those were also lean...financial years for me...and I struggled to support my family...and stay afloat...After contacting old friends...and with some reluctance...I decided to return to Marine Midland's New York City offices ...in 1983... I owe that return to ...Art Ziegler...a senior corporate...Marine executive...Nelson Civello...whom I had worked with in Buffalo...and others whom I knew and respected... from my earlier days...at Marine...I am certain that I received the support of those former colleagues... because they felt that... perhaps I was unfairly ushered out of Marine...when I left Marine in 1976... Now commuting into New York City... from River Vale... New Jersey...my second career... as a public finance banker with Marine...would prove to be a good deal more successful…and satisfying…than my first Marine Midland banking career in Buffalo …

As manager of the Public Banking Sector of Marine's Municipal Securities Division…we performed a wide range of commercial banking services…for both public…and private business entities… We did direct loans…credit enhancements for bond issues…liquidity facilities…and other short term investments for dozens of municipalities… private business…and industrial development projects…My group financed "bond banks" in Hudson…Monmouth…and Essex Counties…New Jersey… Bond banks…were fund raising methods to raise large amounts of public funds to fund smaller municipalities…and public authorities…

We did the same with facilities for Delaware…Montgomery…and Chester Counties in Pennsylvania … We financed school districts in Cleveland…and Toledo…Ohio …The same was done in Newark…New Jersey…and we provided liquidity and short term… equipment financing for the Port Authority of New York and New Jersey…A couple of high profile…fun projects for me…was financing the Joe Robbie Stadium… in south Florida…and the Harold Washington Library …and supporting O'Hare Airport development bonds in Chicago… llinois …. All-in-all… in New York City…I had an opportunity to help successfully build and manage…a more than two billion dollar portfolio…of public finance risk for the bank… Once again…I personally… received bank awards and thankful commendations … both in…and out of the bank…for that success…

During this time in New York…regrettably…in some ways…I was almost totally focused on my traveling career…and job at Marine… My travels prevented me from being at home…as much as I would have liked… I missed too much of BJ's Little League baseball and too many young daughter moments…left to JoAnn…I did…however…yearn for the old days of struggle …and advocacy for black community betterment…and advancement …which stayed embedded in my blood… Once in a while… the fire in my belly flared again…and I would fire off a letter… or pen a poem…to vent my continued frustration… at black people suppression around the World…Besides the racial conflicts around the U. S.…the struggle of blacks in Apartheid South Africa…was another major vex in my brain…One morning…I penned the following letter to the New York Times that…to my knowledge…was never published…

April 5, 1985

The Editor
New York Times Company
229 West 43rd Street
New York, NY 10036

Sir:

I read, with sadness, the musings of Alan Paton, white citizen of South Africa, (Op-Ed, April 3, 1985) as he spoke to his friends in the United States about the sorry state of affairs his beloved South Africa finds itself in these days. His lamentations about black violence and black hatred of Apartheid laws, just as the Afrikaner Conqueror begins his first, "tottering step toward the undoing," of Apartheid, is the argument of an apologist who would deny black human beings the right to be passionate, today, about their right to life, liberty and the pursuit of happiness.

His plea, that as a Christian he will have nothing to do with the disinvestment movement in the United States, which of course everyone knows will hurt only black people, is again a sad, weakly disguised argument that misses the point. The issue is not that tiny fraction of black South Africans who might get hurt by disinvestment, nor is it the sly reference to the United States' greed or need for a few "strategic minerals." The issue is, and always will be, the economic and political support, whether significant or symbolic, of the only nation on earth that officially defines the rights of its citizens by the color of their skin.

South Africa, and all that it is today, depends economically, morally and spiritually on white dominated Western nations for its continued survival. There is nowhere else for it to go. The blacks of South Africa have not only been vanquished by the proud Afrikaner Conqueror, they are also the victims and the captives of the whole family of nations in the West, who can somehow make room and excuses for the rogue white tribe of South Africa.

In the United States the current Regan administration not only undermines the boycott efforts for change in South Africa, but some believe it has, using Israel, secretly transferred strategic nuclear weapons to the South African government, in its support of the vicious system of Apartheid being spread to other parts of southern Africa. This is a dangerous game of nuclear proliferation that can backfire on all of us.

It is the height of hypocrisy when Western nations feign embarrassment, and tacitly succumb to the White South African government's argument that they are a Christian, civilized people in the midst of so many uncivilized blacks; who will surely starve to death if they do not accept their fate and realize that their ultimate salvation lies in the benevolence of white dominance, however long it takes whites to finally accept them as human beings.

William R. Bailey
River Vale, New Jersey

Earlier… in that same year…I had sent a letter off to my past friends at the Detroit Free Press…after I read Lee Iacocca's biographical best seller… "Iacocca"… I felt compelled to defend my old friend Henry Ford II…who had been so helpful to my efforts in Detroit…That letter was published and it solicited a letter of response from Mr. Ford…My letter to the Free Press read:

February 19, 1985

Sir:

After reading Lee Iacocca's runaway best seller, "Iacocca," I was somewhat disturbed by the depth of his bitterness toward Henry Ford II.

Iacocca's recall of the episode when Ford, at a management meeting, encouraged his subordinates to hire and promote minorities, only to complain later, in a more private setting, about the "coons" driving up and down Lakeshore Drive, was especially biting.

I have never met Iacocca, but I have met Ford. The first meeting happened in 1979 when I was part of a three-man delegation of black Detroiters who— like so many others before us---went to ask for Ford's help. We were members of the board of directors of First Independence National Bank, Detroit's black-owned commercial bank. We faced the task of selling a new issue of bank stock and debt securities to shore up a badly depleted equity situation. Our goal was $2 million in additional funds, and we felt we had to start with Ford.

There was a precedent for Ford family involvement in First Independence. When the bank was created in 1970, many Ford family members—including Henry and his mother—had been among the many founding stockholders. Our delegation felt that if the Fords had invested in the bank once, perhaps they would do so again.

We were hopeful as we drove to Ford headquarters. We had been told that Ford would allow us 30 minutes to tell our story. An hour and a half later, we walked away with Ford's commitment for at least 10 percent of our goal. We left buoyed by our initial success and confident that if we had Ford, we had a good chance to reach our goal, in spite of an increasingly tough Detroit economy.

We were right. Others stepped up and invested. Cushioned by the first commitment from Ford, the bank was successfully recapitalized and, with expanded ownership and new management, it has grown to new heights of success.

I don't feel qualified to comment on the bitterness between these two giants. Lee Iacocca is clearly in a special class as a manager and as a salesman. No less so is Henry Ford, who saved the Ford Motor Co. for the Iacocca who came later, many years ago. If the "coon" story is a true one, in my heart and I suspect in the hearts of many black Detroiters, Ford can be forgiven. His actions on behalf of black Americans through the years have been more magnanimous. History will show that he has more than paid his dues.

BILL BAILEY
Former President
First Independence National Bank
River Vale, N. J.

After my letter to the Free Press...Mr. Ford sent me the following letter... It joined an earlier letter I had received from Mr. Ford...when we successfully re-capitalized First Independence..

Henry Ford II

March 7, 1985

Mr. William R. Bailey,
550 Wayne Drive,
River Vale, New Jersey 07675.

Dear Bill:

I just returned to the office this morning, and I want to thank you for writing the letter the Detroit Free Press published on February 19. It was most thoughtful of you to take the time to write this letter, and I appreciate very much the statements of support you made on my behalf.

Hope our paths cross in the not-too-distant future.

All the Best.
Henry

Goodbye Marine Midland

I left Marine Midland a final time…in 1988…a little more than one year… before the bank was… sadly… swallowed up 100%…by the British banking company…Hong Kong and Shanghai Banking Corporation… Most of those of us at the bank… knew it was just a matter of time….as we watched the bank's senior management…knowing the inevitable… shamelessly jockey for retirement bonuses…and profitable landing parachutes… With what I had learned … from my years on Wall Street… almost 33 years after I met her…I took JoAnn and my family… and moved to Minneapolis …Minnesota …to work for First Bank System… I did so when my Marine Midland colleague…Nelson Civello… was recruited to Minnesota …and very soon thereafter invited me to join him…Our stated goal…in Minnesota was to try to…duplicate what we had… successfully done in New York City…

In Minnesota…I helped to successfully manage First Bank's Public Finance Division…and a $300 million dollar…Credit Enhancement business...Along with many small...municipal projects... and small private industrial undertakings...we financed airport bonds in Denver... industrial and housing development projects in Boulder and Beaver Creek... Colorado... We financed liquidity facilities for the Target Center...in Minneapolis ...and an auto parking facility for the city of Madison... Wisconsin... We also accommodated short-term... excise tax-secured...financing for bond issues in the U. S. Virgin Islands...The latter...of course required annual...spring-time... due diligence trips... (wink...wink) to the Islands...to discuss the financial health... and well-being of the Islands...(And...of course get a short...welcome break from the long Minnesota winters...)

Unfortunately...in the early 1990's...after a failed bond portfolio strategy...First Bank fell into financial difficulty...and lost its valuable credit ratings... This severely hampered my department's ability to bid on certain bond issue solicitations... My colleague Nelson Civello ...whom I reported to at the time...was abruptly let go in a management re-structuring... The bank then began to de-emphasize the business I managed ...and my staff began to dwindle away...I was basically put in a holding status... with no real prospects for departmental growth... At the request of senior managers ...I agreed to stay with the bank... another five or six years... efficaciously down-sizing my department's credit exposure... I am proud to say...we did this without a single dollar of loss to the bank...

One of the main...personal reasons I agreed to stay at the bank... was something that happened to our family...A year after moving to Minnesota...in 1989...my youngest son... William (BJ)... was diagnosed with a bi-polar disorder...which would disable him...and disrupt the family for years... His illness was...and continues to plague a son that I had so much hope for... To me...Minnesota seemed...better than any other place I had ever lived in... to offer the kind of medical ... and social support for BJ...that I thought he needed...

Also while living in Minnesota...in July 1996...my beloved mother... Dimple ...died...and later in July 2004...my younger brother James died... Both deaths...and BJ's illness were tremendous blows for me... but the family weathered the dark days and disruptions... and we... JoAnn...Stuart ...Carmen...Donna ....and Angela... just as we had always done…rallied together for collective support…After all these years… I am deeply grateful for this unity of support…from a family that I am very proud of…

Summer Snow in Minnesota

Summer snow in Minnesota…is really a Spring snow…

May is still Spring…and it is in May…in Minnesota…

when the Cottonwoods yield their furry…floating pitch

for new life…a new beginning… If granted its every wish…

for life…every year…Minnesota would become a land of

lakes…and Cottonwood trees…soaring…shimmering leaves…

and mostly calm and docile waters…challenging the sprawl

of people and macadam… Some are annoyed by Summer snow

when it gathers…and coats the awakening lawns…and lifeless

carpets… Others welcome the gentle fluff…that floats as the

winds allow…but never with more purpose…than just to land…

on a friendly bed…that will let it sleep peacefully…until its loins

beckon…and that new beginning…a contribution…furthering life…

becomes a time-worn…glorious possibility…once again…

Cold Winds Sing Songs In Minnesota

A song can be any sound…an ear can hear…
melodic…harsh…rhythmic…slow…cutting…

sweet as sugar…or as bitter as Epsom…
Everything sings its own song…most unheard…

but nevertheless there…Lucky is the ear…
that can hear the song…of leaves air floating…

a waterfall before it falls… a squirrel before
it chirps…or a season…before it arrives…

Envy me…the hearer of the most delicate…
the softest touch…upon an ear…when I

heard…the cold…still winds…of Minnesota…
sing their song…long before they came…yes

…even before…they arrived…in full perfection…
to remind us that…yes…we do live…in Minnesota…

Goodbye Banking

Ten years or so…after arriving in Minnesota …I retired from U.S. Bank…the successor bank to First Bank System… I elected to retire when the bank declined to remain in the public… credit enhancement business… and my efforts to move to other areas of the bank failed... I was deeply disappointed with this failure…and reluctantly concluded that the narrow mindedness …and prejudice…of some white males in the business… unfortunately …continued to dog some of us…even into the 21st Century… While I was a highly respected department head…and the highest ranked minority in the local bank...after a number of inquiries and appeals...I was unable to transfer into other departments in the bank...I also have to admit that...by the time of my retirement...I had become somewhat disillusioned... and disappointed at what the banking industry had become...

From my earlier days in banking... the industry had moved away from a primary focus on providing fairly-priced...consumer products...and financing businesses and individuals... to profitably spur local and national economic growth... Back then...banks were properly regulated... and they provided many beneficial... and essential services...to the public... Also... back then...the banks seemed satisfied with a decent level of profits... and the controlled... risk management of plain vanilla banking...

In 1999...with passage of the Gramm-Leach-Bliley Act...the 1933 Glass-Steagall Act...which prohibited bank affiliation with securities firms...was essentially repealed... Banks immediately began affiliating with insurance and securities firms...and again...similar to the early Twentieth Century in this Country...they shifted to risky...securities and derivative trading... Because of government-backed deposit insurance... this...of course... puts U.S. taxpayers at a much higher risk for disastrous industry bailouts....than they were previously ...

With their proprietary trading...in every physical commodity...or synthetic derivative imaginable ...banks have...once again...become major players in the same ....dangerous financial speculation... that helped to cause the Great Depression of the 1930's...Given major banks enormous size these days...a big bank failure could do untold damage to the Nation's... and perhaps even...the World's economy...I also have a problem with the present-day attitude...banks have toward consumers... Their retail credit card rates...and 500% plus... payday loan businesses...(I call it loan sharking)... would make my early neighborhood's Mafia lenders... blush... I recently read a Federal Reserve Report that concluded.....that current-day speculation in physical commodities trading...by banks and others... unnecessarily... cost American consumers more than $300 billion annually ...

This kind of massive...consumer gouging...interest rate rigging... and skimming... by some banks...certainly offsets the many positive contributions many other... respectable financial institutions.... bring to the American financial marketplace... It's too bad our current political environment appears to be unable to correct...or properly regulate an industry that grows more essential... for consumers every year...Quite frankly...to insulate the public from current day...financial excesses by large banks...I would be in favor of a "public option" in banking... similar to the publically-owned...Bank of North Dakota...I would reserve subsidies...such as "no cost" borrowing from the Federal Reserve...and deposit insurance for publically owned...non-speculating bank models... It would be the best way to keep the Nation's financial system...from what I believe is an inevitable...catastrophic...financial failure...

In Minnesota...during my early years at First Bank...unlike other locations in my banking career...I had focused almost exclusively on my job... I had only modest interaction with minority community groups... That came briefly...later in my activities...in Minneapolis ...after my banking career ...when I briefly managed a very modest...minority loan program for the Metropolitan Economic Development Association (MEDA)... The objective of the program...like my early banking career... was to find ways to finance minority-owned businesses...The program was a very modest 8-bank... participation consortium...that doubled in size ($11 million) while I managed it...Despite my chance to once again return to an activity that I loved...my two and a half year tenure at MEDA... ended when I left...of my own accord in 2001... I left because I lost faith in the sincerity...and productivity of MEDA's minority-business programs... and the direction the staff and organization wanted to pursue ....After leaving...I drifted into mostly small business consulting ...writing...and painting for my own pleasure and satisfaction...

As I finish this Memoir...nearly 56 years after JoAnn and I were married...I harbor no regrets ... about the ups and downs...of a fascinating career and life... All through the many storms ...mistakes and triumphs...in my business career and personal life...I was always able to seek refuge ... as much as I could...in writing... painting ...and enjoying what I considered to be the very essence of human life: "personal expression"... In whatever way you choose... I would encourage everyone to express themselves...in some lasting way...To me...there is no greater joy in life than finding ways to express your inner feelings...and creating... a view... an image...or a thought for someone else to ponder...benefit from...or enjoy... I believe that is the only way to make a lasting mark... or truly leave a legacy of your presence here on Earth...In my opinion... there is no other...more noble reason...for having been here...

She's Gone

Not perfect….no life ever is….but I got the best…
of whatever she had… It was her gift to me…as it
should have been…when you are a mother…a
birther of people…a giver of life…giver of my life…
Thank you… Thank you for showing me how…I
too…must love…must give…must be…no matter
what… I will never forget…and I will always try to
be …at least half…of the best that you were to me…
It will be my gift…my giving back to you…Thank you…

James Leon

(My Brother)

This is a dark and gloomy day… and writing this is hard to do…
When I first saw him he was days old…dark…silky…smooth…
and I thought he was beautiful…He even had hair…and tiny
fingers…and tiny toes…His mouth was always moving…
sucking…My mother…pronounced that he was my little
brother…and his name was James Leon…Gwen…my only
sister…who followed me everywhere…was there too…that
day…I 'm told…She was just wide-eyed…not awed…but
suspicious…wondering…like any other two-year old…in
Charlotte…North Carolina…in 1940…
In time…I delighted in James Leon… because he was so easy
to tickle…I even learned to change his diaper…I hated the smell
and the bucket where the diapers went…before they got shook
out in the toilet…but I loved the smell… of oil and baby powder…
and how smooth he was…when you rubbed him…By then…
Gwen had learned to use the little brown potty…most of the
time…but not at night…Me?…I could use the big toilet…like
Richard…my Daddy…like Dimple…my Mother…like all the
big people…I was later told…

I watched him learn to say things…then crawl…walk…and pull things down…I learned to take care of him…and Gwen… especially after Richard left…I learned early that I could make him laugh… and I did all the time…At first Gwen did not like him… as much as I did…Sometimes she would hit him… or pinch him…when I took them for rides in the wagon…and if they were really good…they could ride in my fire truck… with the bell…and the ladders…James Leon loved to ride… in anything…just ride and ride…and laugh and laugh…

Soon he got a kick out of trying me…He grew to know… that it was my job to watch out for him…like Dimple said I should…And sometimes he told on me… when the fire went out…or when I took him and Gwen… to Wilbert's house… He was cleverly mischievous… in a fun kind of way …like the time in Buffalo… when we ran…and jumped the snow mounds…on the sidewalks…Sometimes he would roll…or slide down a mound…into a parked car… or some other danger…that scared all hell out of me…I would race to get him and when I did…he just laughed…and laughed…and made me sick…Dozens of times I wanted to slug that kid…

He grew up a husky…tough kid…who would fight someone… at the drop of a hat…There were not too many kids…his size …he couldn't whip…He was a natural athlete...football… swimming and later boxing… He learned to swagger when he knew he could win…He also learned to back off …and even run … when the heat became fire…We played a lot with each other …cowboys and sword fighting…that kind of stuff…All the years we slept together… and that was most of my childhood…I could make him laugh…imitating some TV clown…or just being clever…I don't think…he ever knew…I got more fun out of making him laugh…than he got out of laughing…at my silliness…

Once on Adams Street…he confronted me…for what…I can't remember…He was determined to prove…that he was a better man... (at age 14)... than me..."I can kick your ass too," he said ...about something long forgotten...The quick sting of his first blow...was surprising and hurtful...and I retaliated...subdued him... and found my hands... dangerously...choking his breath away...He struggled and his eyes bulged...I wanted him to think that he was going to die...He begged for his life...then suddenly I remembered what Dimple said...take care of him...not kill him fool!...For years...and years after...we would laugh about Adams Street...and he never challenged me again...thank God...

As we grew older...I knew he admired his older brother...He wanted to do everything I did...play ball...craps...poker...have tons of girlfriends...join the Air Force...Most times he did what I did...Sometimes he could not...He was never very spiritual or religious... (Neither was I)...It never mattered to me...I only wanted to take care of him...if he needed me...And there were times he needed my help...with jobs...with women...or two fists ...to help get us out of a dangerous... bar brawl...I was there if he needed me...He paid me back by being bolder...introducing me to the O'Jays...color TV...delightful little neighborhood urchins... and beloved old drunks...who loved him...

There was a time...when he came to resent me totally...and for what I'll never know...On quiet days...Dimple and I...talked about it...and there was speculation...and rumors...For a few years... I sensed a constrained sort of anger...I stayed in touch... but mostly I left him alone...I let him work it out... and mature...let the red become orange...then purple...then cool blue...Looking back...I was right to let whatever it was...run its course...grow old and be wiped away ...by a lifetime of love... and comradeship...Love... friendship... hugs ...laughs...and memories won out...Deep in our lives... we grew close again... more understanding...and even mellow and supportive...especially after Dimple died...He was the only brother I ever had... and I only wanted to take care of him ...I hope he knew...before he left...forever...that I loved him every single day of his life...here on this earth...

Final

Eye….closed….swirling….dropping….
looking….trying….hard….seeing…tear…
darkness…feeling……there….nothing….
something….here….anything….no…what….
yes….where….falling…please….again…
desperate….stop….fear….sweat….speak….
blood….cling….straw….scream……fight….
scratch….rope….spit….reach….now….
chains….will….strength….hand……kick…
bone……..breathe….threat….cry….try….
hate….green…rain….hot…heat….red….cold
…moon…low….float…flutter….heart….beat
…..mother….shiver….feet…..shake….grab….
tumble….blue…..fly….stand….father…hope…
wet….dry….night…throat…water…cool…love
…sun….warm....sinking…day…over…hope…
yell…air…silence...calm....high…light…finished
…final….

Miss Vaughn

She is truly an angel…
a beautiful black angel…
with a voice to stop the moon…
Her gift challenges trumpets…
saxes…flutes…and the dead
of every silent moment…Sassy…
bold…self-effacing…emitting…
she translates all pleas…or pain
from every woman who ever lived…
With a breath for every soul…she
is the best…the eminent…unchallenged…
a superb queen…for my very own soul…

Keeper of Memories

Here is to every soul...
devoured by...the
beast of hunger...
by the chance of...
lightning...by the
cannibalism...of
fellow human beings...
even they who said
they loved you...May
your soul rest...in the
innocence of peace...
and may you and it...be
rewarded...by the keeper
of...memories...and by
the eternal...warm winds...
that travel forever...losing
absolutely nothing...while
bearing the memory of you...
and all that you ever were...

Leader in The Boat

Here I am in this great boat...riding the heaving waves...
like Odysseus' weary sailors...unable to do more...than

ride out the exhausting journey...How I got in this boat...
is a long bloody story...filled with fascinating tales...some

good...some bad...You see...I am led by wicked...relative
children...who know no more than I...but they are more

aggressive...more abrasive and much more clever...
They know how to dazzle and bedazzle...challenge

the elements…and like Thor…brutalize their enemies…
From their early harsh environment…they learned how

to be the most brutal…the most loving…the most caring…
the most stupid…the most intelligent…the most vain…the

most religious…the most uncaring…the most creative…
the most duplicitous… the most dangerous…the epitome

…of all that is possible…in the high one…the creature…
some call…with all due respect to apes…the naked ape…

They insisted on taking the helm of the ship…but I
shutter at the thought of our ultimate…final destiny…

I cringe for their victims along the way…I reject their
rationales…their freedom theories…their cock-sureness…

Bereft of long memories… they are steering the boat and
leading us again…onto the shoals of death and disgrace…

Like the arrogant black ones…eons ago…they too will
repeat the steps…the history and the same missteps again…

Are we always to be drawn…inexorably…to a fate we
cannot change?…Are we always to be self-destructive

creatures…who disdainfully reject patience….evolution…
maturity?…I think so…It seems to be in our being…like

the third corpuscle of our blood… Are we too…marching
like microbes and ants…stars and galaxies…into that black

nothing…that waits for us all?…Yes!…Then I ache for
the helm of the boat…Give it to me!…In the few short…

human moments remaining…I think I can make a difference…
I say think…because who knows…if there is a difference

in me…if my soul is purer…my vision surer…my worth
any more…than these prideful…blind…and bumbling fools…

Nevertheless…I would try…and I have a plan…First…I
would reject brutality…nourish the loving…temper pride…

destroy race…religion…and cannibalism…I would teach
the origin of our sameness…the ultimate cosmic destiny

of all of us…and show that we still have a chance…to
find real comfort …in truly understanding what…and who

we are…The lessons will have nothing to do with crosses…
stars…crescents…Buddha's…miracle births…900-year old

men…stoning of infidels…eternal hells…perfect books…
and cannons….handed down by man-made gods…carrying

weapons to punish… the hapless…the ignorant…the innocent…
I would put down…and render to their place…the dazzling

systems…technology miracles and…the seductive opium…
of our supposed intelligence…The lesson would be that all

of us…each and every one …is God…The atoms we are
composed of…are older than God…We all share the chemical

and spiritual elements…the imperfections…the greatness…
the mystery…of the beginning…and the inevitable story…

of final truths…For we cannot escape…or alter our end…
just as we cannot know…or change our beginning…Our

challenge...our salvation...will come from how we learn to cherish...nurture and care for each other...in the briefness

of this...all too human...all too fleeting...consciousness... There is nothing else...*THERE IS NOTHING ELSE!...*

Lament for America

America...America...you aggressive...muscular... young giant... You were created out of a rebellion...out of a new ...enlightenment religion... about individual fitness...self worth...free range...human competition...and survival... The dynamics were there...to give you momentum... Like all new human aggregations...your rise was timely ...fortuitous...and inevitable...as the old...un-apologetically pure... imperialist empires...sputtered...coughed...and slowly died... Violent events flowed sporadically...unevenly...at your birth... A great ocean and imperial exhaustion...helped your tooth-cutting... Yet you never dreamed...that your lofty pronouncements...about the worth of men... received from God...you said...would impale you...upon laws...and commandments...not really meant for others in the beginning...Your freedom theories...as defined by a timeserving few...were intoxicating... but mainly for you...the homogeneous few...who knew...who believed... But fortune also smiled upon you...as collective bloodletting...through the years...helped you to become the new sovereign...of a continent...

of freedom…of liberty…you said… All of your people drank the wine… from your cup…and came to mistakenly believe…that they too…were blessed by God…your God… This became your benediction…your chance to act like all religions…old and new…to march forward…to proselytize… to convert…to stratify…to be the new imperialist…to be the new bearer of glad tidings…to the Philistines… Your converts' own certain…inclusive assumptions…about your spoken brand of freedom…your stated theories of …but not real democracy…your flawed concepts of prosperity…liberty was faith personified… But converts didn't know…that what you said…was said for you…not necessarily for them…least not until they become like you…

Your character became distinctive…assertive…inventive…American… Treacherously militaristic…at times brilliantly mimicking old empires … culturally…imperiously…you became a fusion of new…warm rhythms of ease… and color…and sweet sounds…from a different experience… along with the cold fire and hot ice…of the continent's amalgamated human engine… It is unwritten…if it ever has occurred before… Could you truly be new to history?… No…but maybe so…as a point in the line of time…but certainly not new…in the cycle of most human experience… Humans have been this way before… Their aggregations just have not held…so long…to the solemn principals of so few…and allowed…or was forced to allow…such rapid inclusion... It was...and is so unintended... Could it be that within...those very same tenants of universality...unknowingly lie...the seeds...of your very own demise... the end of your very definition of freedom?...

Then what will become of you...America?...You...the nation-force... loved...and feared...respected and hated... Will you too...fall... stumble...from the intoxicant called power...slip from the certain... sureness of your theories...bend to the inevitable destruction...that too much freedom...too much capitalism...too much false religion brings?... Can you find it...in your soul...or even in the soul...of your converts... some saving grace...some humbling experience....to temper the negatives...to atone for the sins......and find a positive way...for all who would...just simply believe?... The odds are not with you...if the past is remembered... The young and bold...eventually become...withered and old...and where does...an aging giant go...when the world is converted... when old victims become aggressors...when markets mature...when converts laugh...and become unbelievers again...when swords become dull and useless...because everyone...will have swords... when doubt enwraps even you...America...the blossomed religion... Will you go with the rest...who flickered...became flaccid...and left only a faint hint...of their light?... My guess...is yes!...But only time will tell!...Only time will tell!...

Deception

It was a powerful deception…a misdirection worthy of Blackstone… Yes… the plan was foreign…willfully meant to destroy…to be painful…to get even… The hapless soldiers…given the task…over estimated their deep cover…Their steps were seen…watched…enhanced… Few knew…but that was too many… since greed always becomes a partaker…To this day…the scheme has worked… blood…treasure…and sorrow is spent…Pockets were filled…But the desirable was not born…The sordid tale continues…The truth struggles to find the day…The people continue to be deceived… What will they do… when the left hand is seen?…when the deception is finally exposed…when the desperate scoundrels…are shown to be what they really are…That day will come…Trust me!….

Flawed Children of the Enlightenment

Their gift…to humankind…was to be a monumental stance for individual freedom…liberty…from the ugly

imprisonment…and holy despotism of kings…priests… definers…emissaries…even god herself…Yet many of

the inheritors…harbor an arrogance…a much too narrow definition of "us"…a far too constricting…contradictory

belief in a special-ness…that they…alone…presume to claim…Regrettably…these are…the flawed children of

the Enlightenment…heirs…who are only half made… who cannot yet give of themselves…trust the principles…

give up the terrible fear…They are the new kings… the newly self-anointed…who dare not be whole…who fail to

be the believers...the defenders they were supposed to be...
who still labor to return...to old false opium...to cleverly

deceive...and soak up the innocence... of our children...
They are the new devils...in our midst...the returners of

mankind to a mindless servitude...the clever subversives
who would undermine...the people's will...It is they

whom we must guard against...surround... bathe...and
purify...least it all be for naught...The struggle for the true

disciples is clear...They will have to stay on guard... defend
the creed...resist the retreat...of Enlightenment betrayers...

stamp down the eternal tendency...to restore old myths...and
religions...that promise salvation...equity...and freedom...

but in reality...bring nothing but division...and a return to
the long misery...of unenlightened...evil...human slavery...

Jim-in-nee, Jim-in-nee
(A Rap)

Every day the best ball playin' hoopsters in town,
Gathered at the playground when the sun went down.

They chose up sides and divided up the troops,
To find out who was bad; the king of the hoops.

Everybody hoped they'd get one chance to see,
A young ballin' phe-nom, called bad Jim-in-nee.

The boy had a rep that flew before him.
When he showed up, the fish forgot to swim.

But listen up! Listen up Dogs! Listen to me!
All y'all ballers just gotta wanna see,
A real thoroughbred run the hall,
And Jim-in-nee get down with a ball! With a ball!

But Jim-in-nee wasn't born in no ghetto.
His mama was a fox and his daddy had dough.

He hung out in a bad pad cleaned by a maid,
And rode to the playground in a black Escalade.

People came out from all over the wide land,
To see if they could catch Jim-in-nee's next plan.

Would it be to lay down a few funky, funks,
Or do one of them nasty, flip around dunks.

But listen up! Listen up Dogs! Listen to me!
All y'all ballers just gotta wanna see,
A real thoroughbred run the hall,
And Jim-in-nee get down with a ball! With a ball!

The Dude could leap so high, up in the sky,
Before he came down you could bake a cherry pie.

Quick as lightning, he was like a long greasy snake,
He could take your shorts down, with a little shake n' bake.

Everybody who played, wanted him on their team,
To just pass him the ball and hear the girls scream.

One of the playground girls swore he made her come,
From just jookin' 'n jiving and giving baby some.

But listen up! Listen up Dogs! Listen to me!
All y'all ballers just gotta wanna see,

A real thoroughbred run the hall,
And Jim-in-nee get down with a ball! With a ball!

Jim-in-nee could run the base line like Jesus Christ.
Then take all your money like you been had twice.

He had the playground record for makin' hard three's.
Even made a walk-off winner that bounced off the trees.

The Dude was so bad, he let his mama take a shot,
When people started shouting, "let's see what she got."

I saw him make a play that sent chills down my spine,
When he made a high flying dunk from the mid-court line.

But listen up! Listen up Dogs! Listen to me!
All y'all ballers just gotta wanna see,
A real thoroughbred run the hall,
And Jim-in-nee get down with a ball! With a ball!

One night Jim-in-nee played nine on one.
Determined to prove that he couldn't be outgunned.

The boy faked to his left then drove to his right.
People stopped and stared at the spinning, whirling sight.

He did a cool Marcus Haynes and dribbled past six.
Then leaped over three more, as he waved to the chicks.

Some of his moves were too tough to conceive.
The Mother was so bad, I found it hard to believe.

But listen up! Listen up Dogs! Listen to me!
All y'all ballers just gotta wanna see,
A real thoroughbred run the hall,
And Jim-in-nee get down with a ball! With a ball!

That boy could fake you outta your *new* Nike shoes,
And whip you so bad, he gave you Muddy Waters' blues.

The NBA had sent scouts when he was just ten.
Even then they thought he could be a man among men.

One night Michael Jordan happened to be in town.
He tried to challenge Jimmy on his own playground.

Mike played well and made a real strong bid,
But even he couldn't handle the bad ballin' kid.

> *But listen up! Listen up Dogs! Listen to me!*
> *All y'all ballers just gotta wanna see,*
> *A real thoroughbred run the hall,*
> *And Jim-in-nee get down with a ball! With a ball!*

While most people thought he could go all the way,
Jim-in-nee never made it to the mighty NBA.

He lost his last game to a punk with a gun,
Looking for pennies where there really was none.

Jim-in-nee! Jim-in-nee! Don't hurt 'um up so.
Have a little mercy, don't Pimp-take their dough.

Give 'um a chance to have a little dignity,
But don't let 'um ever forget, ballin' Jim-in-nee.

> *But listen up! Listen up Dogs! Listen to me!*
> *All y'all ballers just gotta wanna see,*
> *A real thoroughbred run the hall,*
> *And Jim-in-nee get down with a ball! With a ball!*

Super Daddy High

(A Rap)

Hey! somebody said…what's in your head…
You showing a new pep…in a cool new step…
Now you got hip…in your long legged dip…
And a quick slick smile…in your new rags style…

So what's up! What's up! This brand new you!
Tell us all brother…how to get there too!

For weeks you been floating…up here…up there…
Swimming on air…with a new found flare…
It's like you've run down…a new base sound…
Or a dynamite high…nobody else can try…

So what's up! What's up! This brand new you!
Tell us all brother…how to get there too!

Back up! Back up y'all…there's a reason I'm tall…
It's not the same old high…pull down from the sky…
My new chilly float…is an old…ancient boat…
Like a new body glove…I found a bona fide love…

So what's up! What's up! This brand new you!
Tell us all brother…how to get there too!

After juking and jiving…stealing kisses and feelings…
Me and my main girl…took a trip round the world…
We never stopped to think…just where we might sink..
We just did it real good… like you do in the hood…

So what's up! What's up! This brand new you!
Tell us all brother…how to get there too!

The first time lead to two…then more than just a few…
The girl looked so good…I forgot to do what I should…
She gave me so much stuff…I just couldn't get enough…
We took so many trips…we got hooked at the hips…

So what's up! What's up! This brand new you!
Tell us all brother…how to get there too!

But wait up y'all…hear me say…there's a real hard price to pay…
Those trips we took were serious…far beyond lust and curious…
After nine months walking…we had new people talking…
Stuff we could never see… and a ton of responsibility…

So what's up! What's up! This brand new you!
Tell us all brother…how to get there too!

Listen up and hear this…it's more than just a peck and a kiss..
When you bring new life… make the mama your wife…
I never ducked and hid…and you can do like I did…
You too can man up…and try…my new super daddy high…

It's called spilling nothing…every drop is something…
And that's what's up! What's up! This new me you see…you see…
is what a tall…new…super Daddy…like me…can be!…

katrina lamentation

from a real conservative

how dare you embarrass us…

you poor excuse for the american

dream…you lazy…wait-for-the-

government good-for-nothings…you

received ample…more than ample

warning…you were told a cat 4 was

coming…you were told to clear out…

now look at you…embarrassing us like

this…scrambling for…food…water…a

place to sleep…dropping babies on the

street…defecating in our beautiful…foot-

ball palace…dying and contaminating our

drinking water…our streets…shooting and

stabbing each other…before saturday night…

raping and begging…why didn't you drive

out of that hell-hole…like most sensible…

americans…with just an ounce of brains…

would do…age and infirmary are no excuse…

all it takes is a high school education…and

cutting down on illegitimate babies…you

had jobs…at walmart and burger king…and

the marriott…why didn't you save…prepare

…get credit cards…for emergencies…like

most americans do…don't blame the president…

we…the citizens of america voted for…blame

that mayor…and that governor…you voted for…

they're sitting on all kinds of "assets"…they

could have saved you…if they were competent

…like our president…like our congressional

politicians…like our wonderful mayor up in new

york city…like our powerful business companies

…now look at what you've done…now you have…

of all kinds of people…castro…and chavez…offering

help…and people from iraq and afganistan…are

sending some of our own war…and aid money… back

to you…now we've got to…mount up…an all out…

outpouring…of aid and good american stuff…and send

developers…down there…to clean up…to rebuild…

to correct our image…around the world…all because

of you…it's a damn shame…you can't stay in the

kitchen…out of sight…like you always used to…

The Water Bowl

Mama…where we going?…

Hush now…and eat your apple…

Are we coming back soon?…

Boy…you button that shirt up right…

Will I ever see…Nippy…again?…

I'm not thinking 'bout…no Nippy now…

I hope he can find something to eat…

Not with all that water…he won't…

You think Aunt Hattie…got away too?…

God…only knows…I hope so…I hope so…

What gonna happen to my school now?…

Will you stop…asking me all that foolishness!…

I hope we come back to…New Orleans…pretty soon…

Yeah…Maybe we will…But…maybe we won't…

Barfield's

(For Carmen)

She delights in it so…
From out of her own creative urges…

and a mind numbing boredom…
that computers and stupid people bring…

and I am sure…with a soft pull from ghosts
out of the past…who worshiped the medley of

rich green… shoots of life…from fertile soil…
and sweet fruits from sun-warmed blossoms…

Out of this came Barfield's…without life-giving
dirt…but still the hint…without salty wet sweat…

but still the toil...It is called pure satisfaction...
quieting the agitating genes...welcoming the first...

and last rays of the day's sun...summoning the first...
and last day's sigh of pleasure...searching for love again...

Saving Haiti

You wretched inheritors of half a lowly land.....
How dare you try to join God's chosen children...

Your sins...your religion...your regal beauty...
cannot overcome the resentment...the uppity

arrogance...many children of the Conquistadors..
bear against you... Yet still they love you...

are drawn to you...want to save you...and your
precious children... It is like the laconic jail guard...

who falls in love with his charge...but cannot
safely set him free... Haiti...you should curse...

the Olmecs...for such a meager...skimpy dowry...
You should curse again...the Great Liberator...

L'Overture...for setting such a high...tall bar...
most of your pathetic leaders...have not met since...

Sing at...and continue to curse...the sibling bully..
living above you...meddling and feigning love...

not once...showing the gratitude...the kinship...
For without you...half of them would not be...

We…the conflicted children of the Conquistadors…
must do all we can to save Haiti…and then mercifully..

gratefully…let Haiti…save us…again!…

Where Did It Go

Relativity…the universally…
unchallenged…… discriminates…

Einstein aside…or especially
between…fifty and seventy

circumferences…of the fragment we ride…
around the energy…

It seems as if there is no difference…but maybe so…
Perhaps it is…

…..the smaller things…we never noticed…
that began losing

the race… long before we realized…
that light was slowing…

darkness was harkening…and there just might be…
an end to this journey…..soon…

Phoebe Snow

Sometimes we are born for just one thing…
There is nothing wrong with that…Who says…

we have to be all things…do all things…this
and that…Who says we have to eternally…

say the acceptable ...look right ...even defer to
company...we don't like...all for the crowd...

They told Phoebe...you loosened your loins...
lost your head...now take your medicine...

from our God...who knows it all...after all...
Phoebe looked straight ahead...then she

answered...get out of my face...I am a
woman...who feels...who loves...who keeps...

the promise...and the word...from the God
I know... if it is the only...and last thing I do...

sandy rock

that early morning...they were asked to lead we
...who are blind...even though...they had barely
opened their own eyes...

at first...led by six brave souls...
who stood just a bit taller...they...bright eyed...&
able...raised their hands...& volunteered to be the
next shepherds...next beacons of light...to show a
nation...their nation...where it must go...where to
find...the luscious...green meadow...of sanity...&
redemption...for the ever faithless...the cowards...
the lost souls...who must be fed ...who direly
need to also be saved...from their hades worship...

as we struggle to understand...this sacrifice...
this unevolved relic...in so much of america...
could it just be a simple repeat of..."and the little
children shall lead them"...i think so!...i think so!...

Old Gogg

The usual friendly...warm sun time...unhindered
by earth covers...floating high above...that partners
with the dead...white...hard water that comes to us...

every cold time...was back again...Gone was the
loud crack of the unhappy one...who reminds us to
obey the omens of the sacred keepers...and the ugly...

black and gray veils...that hurl their wetness...shivers
and shafts of fire...just as fast bent spears... every harsh
time...Once again...thankfully...warm...steady light...

yielded the expected nourishment...the hopeful...
green and yellow...sweet and sour berries...that
fall on eager palates...tired of rodent bones...and

old...dried up grains... Hard lakes...and cold still
rivers...now rippled and welcomed drink again...
Our clan...everyone...was on the move once more...

Time again...it was good to stretch legs...and arms...
weakened by many months in cool...dark cavities...
and long squats...smoking twigs...sleeping...and

taking the females... In preparation for an early hunt...
we sharpened spears...and refined the accuracy of our
throws...with new skin strips...soaked in a mysterious

resin stolen from the Anadaki clan... Young male
legs...were now eager to outrun the best hunters...
to be the first...to bring down a large...four-legged

elusive one... The females strutted...threatened to milk
from us the white magic again...and roughly pulled
along the young ones...who wanted to wander...and

be awed by the brightness of this warm time…perhaps
their first…since standing… We needed to leave our
sleeping place…climb the high…cold rocks…and

descend…into the warm greening land…where
furry herds…our quest…dwells… Once again we
passed the place…of the burning meat…passed the

great opening…where two males fell…and were
swallowed up by the hard water… The march went…
almost well…except for old Gogg…who…once

again…was slowing us…holding us back…from
the swiftest days…the surest hunt… Even with help…
she still slipped…slid…and fell…whether on rocks

or in easy sand… Old Gogg had grown old with us…
even though she came…from another clan… She
had no off-spring…and her loins were not very

welcoming any more… With age she could not
help with the hunt…and more and more had to
be assisted…to bring her load of wood…Two

warm times ago…she was nearly taken by a
large…long-tooth cat…looking for food… Rocks
and sharp sticks…from the young males…saved

her from a painful end… Most of the females were
glad she was saved… some were not…The chosen
elders…this past long sleep…debated her presence…

her meager importance to the clan…her fate… There
was talk of the time…not long ago…when the clan
just walked away…and left the old…and wounded…

like old Gogg … to their final destiny… There was
also talk…mostly from the youngest…of the elders…
who spoke of the bad spirits…the ill times…that

befell us…when we left the old behind… Some
told of the time…when old Gogg was the best of
the females…at setting snares and traps…to catch

small creatures…how she could spin and jump
at celebrations…and how the young males…favored
her…and competed for her embrace… But the keeper

of our history…the one who heals…the one who
is rigid…to move to your side…the one who always
holds the sacred bones…and shiny stones…insisted

that we keep the old ways…that we cannot continue
to care for more…and more old…and must still drive
the old…the carriers of demons…and evilness…from

our presence…lest we be punished for our neglect…
by the great one who watches… He said we must
focus our best on the young…who will grow our clan…

and keep it strong… He insisted that if we change
our old ways…the clan's burden will grow…our
rivals will best us…maybe even enslave us…to

do their bidding… Surely he argued…it is best
to save the clan…than to worry of…and be held
back…by the old or possessed… After fasting…and

long talks with the sacred bones…and shiny stones..
his story carried the elders… With a concession…
to cut the wailing of the near old…and sympathies of

the immature…it was agreed that our clan…would
not attack those who stayed behind…to help the
old…the ailing…but they could not rejoin the clan…

unless they brought great tribute…or advantage
with them… This would be the order of our clan…
until new inspiration…or guidance from the wise one …

who speaks to us…through the sacred bones…and
shiny stones… Within a few suns and sleeps…old
Gogg was banished…and driven from the clan…

The judgement…brought great wailing…moaning
and deep caring… Two younger females protested…
and chose to go…with old Gogg… It was a sad time…

Some in the clan…committed heresy…befoulment…
They cursed the keeper of our history…and challenged
the words…of the sacred bones and shiny stones…

They were akin to all of those…not wise enough to
know…the ends of their means…nor old enough to
recall…the wisdom of our ancient rules and laws…

Their words mocked…and challenged us…put
distance between the meanings…the purpose
of our presence…our very loyalty to each one…

The sentiments…the values of the old…near old…
the strong and able…flew before our fires…They
became…both whisper and shout…before our clan..

Alertly…the near old…became wary…and pushed
their effort…for the clan… They sang alone…and
many screamed out…wide eyed…from their sleep…

In passing we would hear stories of old Gogg...and
the two who went with her... They had tried to stay
in our trails...where we hunted and slept...It was

not good for them... Without male legs...they ate
little meat... They were driven away...by other clans...
and old Gogg grew older...weaker...and weaker...

A sun soon...when we had traveled long...past
the fire belching...high rock...beyond the hiding
grass...and way over the high trees...one of the two...

who went with old Gogg...asked to return to our
clan... She said she bemoaned going with the old one...
and told us...the story of old Gogg's final end... She

said...one sun...as old Gogg tried to bring wood...
a large winged bird...lit upon her...and lifted
her frailness into the air... The evil bird tried to

swoop her away...to its nest...but dropped old
Gogg...before the roost...upon a pile of hard rocks...
They used the black mud...and wide smooth leaves...

from the chief tree of healing...to soothe and give
care...to old Gogg... But even with the long sweats...
old Gogg lasted just two sleeps...and finally expired...

They found smooth stones...circled the fire...and
dusted their faces...with the white ground...No
spirit came to them...nor did old Gogg stir again...

As is our custom...they found a hole...in the soft
rocks...to lay old Gogg...and with care...covered
her with stones...and a stinging...prickly bush ...

One other…who went with old Gogg…was soon
stolen…by a strange clan…of hairy…beast-men…
from the far away…dark place…behind…the

high…night star… When asked what her offered
tribute would be…to return to the clan they left…
the last one…said sadly…she only brings herself…

After much …open ponder…and long talks…
with the sacred bones…and shiny stones…by
the keeper of our history…she was accepted

back into the clan… It was good that she was
still young…that she could still gather berries
and wood…and welcome others to her loins…

Beyond many warm times…and long sleeps
our clan upheld to the rules…and did not
let the group grow too old… Our young ones

hardened to the notion of old…even though…
they crept to that time…every sun… It was
a quick thought…that blinded the reality…

of their own fate… It was as if…none thought
they would ever be old…slow…or unwanted…
that our moment…was all that there would

ever be… It brought minds to a pitilessly…slow
wander…Is human purpose to be only young…
or is there a time to be old…to still belong...

when old eyes may yet see…old thoughts and
words…may still remember the early steps…the
ancient paths…that saved sun times…darkness too?…

They…who are nearly old…still grow among us…
Their pillar grows…when they speak before the fires…
discarding the ancient rules…thus fading our clan…

We know the last lot of the old…the wounded…
Should we also know…the nearly last fate…that
prepares us all…for the change…the long journey?…

One sun…maybe our clan will know that way…
as it will be shown to us…in the sacred bones…
and shiny stones…from the keeper of our history…

Until then…should we keep the old ways…temper
the young…help them to learn…that current or past
newness…is not always the best way to save us?…

Or will they show us that…all who are here…imperfect
or old…weeded out…before their end time…slowly shape…
a kin of fewer…lesser…perhaps down…to just a single one…

God Is Gravity Gravity Is God

The sheaves bent…when it made little sense…river currents
spun in ovals…bears stayed awake…What magic was afoot?…
Am I possessed?…demented?…being tormented by spirits…

I should know…but don't?…Is it Lucifer…who plays with our reason…
or is it just a molecule…an atom…that lost its way…when the
impulse was late?… Who rules us…the sun?…the heavens?…the

myths in our heads?…God?…Or is it Gravity…which holds us all…but
has no time for us?…Is it the true God…that rules all of existence…that
bends everything…binds all the places…yet no mortal can define it?…

We…all of the elements…everything…may come from the stars…
telling us…the source of every perception…all there ever will be…
Still even the mighty stars…bow to…and are captured by gravity…

But even gravity…our God…may have a superior…unseen…
but surely felt… when mighty light bends to its command…Yes…
even God…has a superior…an upper…demanding supplication…

Feed my brain…or fuel my soul…Is there really a difference?…
I may have no choice…For surely…I can never be the first doubter…
So put me in the long line…to be the latest…but hopefully not the last…

the sky rock

it is hard to see...yet we need it so
...one life of consciousness...
is just not enough...it takes faith...old
prayer...those deceptive salves...
used for comfort...let us hope that...
evolution...arrives...before a simple...
obtuse...sky rock...obviates...it all...

CPSIA information can be obtained
at www.ICGtesting.com
Printed in the USA
BVHW071931070819
555340BV00005B/20/P